LIFE SENTENCE

LIFE SENTENCE

MY LAST EIGHTEEN MONTHS

CARL WILLIAMS

ALLEN&UNWIN
SYDNEY • MELBOURNE • AUCKLAND • LONDON

First published in 2019

Allen & Unwin
83 Alexander Street
Crows Nest NSW 2065
Australia
Phone: (61 2) 8425 0100
Email: info@allenandunwin.com
Web: www.allenandunwin.com

NATIONAL LIBRARY OF AUSTRALIA

A catalogue record for this book is available from the National Library of Australia

ISBN 978 1 76087 515 2

Internal design by Romina Panetta Edwards
Set in 12/20 pt Sabon by Midland Typesetters, Australia
Printed and bound in Australia by Griffin Press, part of Ovato

FSC www.fsc.org MIX Paper from responsible sources FSC® C009448

The paper in this book is FSC® certified. FSC® promotes environmentally responsible, socially beneficial and economically viable management of the world's forests.

CONTENTS

CAST OF CHARACTERS

Andrew *see* Andrew Veniamin

'Ange' or 'Ang' *see* Evangelos Goussis

Rocco 'Rocky' Arico, a violent drug trafficker whose only record of employment was a short stint making pizzas in his family's restaurant. He is currently serving a sentence for drug trafficking and extortion and his earliest release date is 2024, at which time he will be deported from Australia to his native home of Italy. Rocco was the first person Tommy Ivanovic called from his cell after Matty had bashed Carl to death. The police suspected Rocky's involvement in this hit.

'Benji' *see* Andrew Veniamin

'Betty' *see* Betty June King

Christopher 'Badness' Binse, a former stick-up man and a despised figure among inmates, Binse became a snitch in juvenile detention and was frequently counselled on his sexually predatory nature as a youth. Senior staff at the Ararat prison where Binse was housed say he was known as 'the Cat from Ararat', a reference to him selling his body for cigarettes and other canteen provisions.

Kath Bourke, partner of George Williams, Carl's dad, and sister of Carl's mother, Barbara.

Greg 'Bluey' Brazel, a convicted serial killer, arsonist and armed robber currently serving three consecutive life sentences for the murder of two prostitutes. On 1 October 1998 he was set upon in the Acacia Unit by Matty Johnson, Sean Sonnet and one other prisoner, who were armed with a sandwich maker, an exercise bike seat and a vacuum cleaner extension pole. He almost died from this assault.

'Brea' *see* Breanane Stephens

Penny Brown, a friend and correspondent of Carl's.

Karina Cacopardo, one of Carl's correspondents and possible family friend.

Rob Carpenter, Roberta Williams' partner.

Ali 'Chooky' Chaouk, a Hells Angels bikie who lost his patch while in Barwon. In 2018 he was found guilty of a June 2009 murder while awaiting parole.

'Chinaman' *see* Bill Ho

'Chooky' *see* Ali Chaouk

'Chopper' *see* Mark Read

Rodney 'The Duke' Collins, also known as 'Rod', a notorious hitman serving jail time for the 1987 murders of Ray and Dorothy Abbey at their Heidelberg West home in Melbourne. He was suspected of having killed at least seven other people, including Mario Condello, and Terry and Christine Hodson. He died of cancer in Barwon Prison in 2018, at the age of 72.

Mario Condello, Italian–Australian former lawyer and acting head of the Carlton Crew while Mick Gatto was serving time. In 2005 he was charged with conspiring to murder Carl Williams. He was shot dead by Rodney Collins in 2006, a day before his trial for conspiracy to murder Carl commenced. Mick Gatto was a pallbearer at his funeral.

Paul Dale, former drug squad detective charged with the murders of Terry and Christine Hodson. After the death of Carl, a Crown witness in the case, this charge was dropped. Dale has always denied any involvement with the Hodson murders.

'Dan' *see* Danielle McGuire

Danielle *see* Danielle Stephens

Travis Day, a school friend of Carl's, a housepainter and non-criminal.

Kerry Denman, Nikki Denman's sister and Carl's cousin.

Nikki Denman, Carl's cousin and daughter of Carol Denman, who is the wife of Barbara Williams' brother Bill.

Dino Dibra, a western suburbs underworld figure murdered in October 2000. The case is unsolved.

'The Don' *see* Mick Gatto

'The Duke' *see* Rodney Collins

'Fab' *see* Fabian Quaid

Peter Faris, QC, a Victorian barrister.

Kevin Farrugia, customarily described as a violent kidnapper and drug trafficker. On 11 March 2009 his jail sentence was extended by a further sixteen months for the illegal possession of firearms.

'Fat Tony' *see* Tony Mokbel

Aaron 'Goldie' Fenton, former leader of the prison gang, POW (Prisoners of War), who died of a drug overdose soon after being released from prison.

'Gangland Milly' *see* Milad Mokbel

Zarah Garde-Wilson, a solicitor who represented many Melbourne gang members. She was the girlfriend of organised crime figure Lewis Caine, who was killed by Ange Goussis.

Mick 'The Don' Gatto, an Italian–Australian businessman named as a standover man in the 2001 Royal Commission into the Building and Construction Industry. In 2004 he was charged with murder over the killing of Andrew Veniamin but was acquitted on grounds of self-defence. He featured heavily in the *Underbelly* series and in 2009 he released his biography, *I, Mick Gatto*.

Nicola Gobbo, a former Melbourne barrister who represented criminals but also informed on them for Victoria Police until 2010. She represented Tony Mokbel and Carl Williams in the early 2000s, and received a death threat in 2003 after representing Lewis Moran, one of Carl's rivals.

Beau Goddard, the half-brother of St Kilda star Brendon Goddard, was jailed for at least nine years in 2007 for heroin supply. In her memoir, *Roberta Williams: My life*, Roberta describes Beau as a 'great friend', who had previously spent time in jail with Tommy Ivanovic.

'Goldie' *see* Aaron Fenton

Evangelos 'Ange' Goussis, a former boxer and associate of career criminal and enforcer Nik Radev, convicted of murdering Lewis Moran and Lewis Caine in 2004 and sentenced to life imprisonment. He was also charged with the 2003 murder of Shane Chartres-Abbott in August 2012 but acquitted.

Daniel 'Danny' Heaney, a friend of Carl's, was sentenced in 1984 to thirteen years' jail for nine armed robberies; in 2004 he was sentenced for nine years with a minimum of six years for stabbing a woman.

Con Heliotis, QC, a Victorian barrister.

'Highchair' *see* Mick Gatto. Carl's nickname for Mick Gatto, based on Carl's perception that Gatto should come down from his 'highchair'; Carl believed that Gatto was always 'putting him down' in a derogatory fashion.

Bill 'Chinaman' Ho was convicted of shooting two men, one of whom was killed, while collecting a 'drug debt' and was sentenced to 22 years in prison with a non-parole period of nineteen years. He spent a considerable number of years in management units.

Paul Holdenson, QC, part of Carl's appeal team in 2009.

Horty *see* Horty Mokbel

Shaune Howlett, brother of Wayne, and sometime owner of Hobart gym Xtreme Physique.

Wayne Howlett, a Tasmanian powerlifter who was sentenced to two years in Risdon Prison in 2010 for drug trafficking. In December 2008, Howlett attempted to exchange 27 grams of methylamphetamine and $4000 for five pistols. The counterparty was a police informant and Howlett was arrested straight after the exchange took place. He was introduced to powerlifting while in Risdon Prison, and in 2013 became the first Australian powerlifter to heft a total of 1000 kilograms. He was found guilty of shooting up Pablo's nightclub in Hobart in June 2018.

Tommy 'Two Guns'/'Little Tommy' Ivanovic, a pastry chef and drug dealer, and a trusted member of the Williams gang. He was serving a fifteen-year sentence for a 2002 murder and was a fellow member of the Acacia Unit. After watching Carl die, the first person Ivanovic called was Rocco Arico. In 2017 Ivanovic was stabbed in the exercise yard of Barwon Prison.

Matthew 'Matty' Johnson, a career criminal, was jointly charged with the shooting murder of eighteen-year-old Bryan Conyers in 2007 over a drug deal gone wrong. Police alleged that Johnson shot Conyers, then cut open his stomach and poured in petrol before setting it alight, because Conyers had failed to deliver $50 worth of marijuana.

Johnson was found not guilty after the jury deliberated for 27 hours. However, he was given a thirteen-year minimum term for a series of violent armed robberies using the same gun that had been used to kill Conyers. Johnson amassed 158 convictions between 1991 and 2006. In 2010 he clubbed Carl to death in the prison gym.

Kabalan *see* Kabalan Mokbel

Paul 'PK' Kallipolitis was a drug dealer and the leader of the Sunshine Crew until he was shot in the head in October 2002. Benji Veniamin then became the leader of the Sunshine Crew, and was the person who stood to gain most from the murder.

Kerry *see* Kerry Denman

Betty June King, former judge of the Supreme Court of Victoria until August 2015. She presided over several of the Melbourne gangland trials, and handed down Carl's life sentence in 2007.

Graham 'Munster' Kinniburgh, one of Australia's foremost safecrackers and an elder statesman of the Australian criminal underworld, respected later for his negotiating skills and ability to step in and calm tensions between underworld factions in dispute. Senior police acknowledge that without the Munster's calming influence more gangland murders may have occurred.

Kinniburgh got his nickname from a TV series called *The Munsters*, in which Herman Munster, an amiable, Frankenstein-style monster, was the patriarch of the household.

Such was the Munster's status, he had a table permanently reserved at Melbourne's world-renowned Chinese restaurant Flower Drum. Kinniburgh would dine there with a who's who of Australian crime and would also host visiting crims from around the world.

'Kiwi Joe' *see* Richard Moran

Julian Knight, a former Duntroon cadet, shot dead seven people and injured nineteen during a shooting spree in August 1987 at Clifton Hill, in what is known as the Hoddle Street Massacre. As Victoria's worst mass murderer, he was originally serving seven concurrent life sentences with a non-parole period of 27 years; he was due for parole in 2014 but the Victorian government at that time passed legislation that will keep him in jail for life. At the time of the massacre he was nineteen years of age.

'Kota' *see* Dhakota Williams

Jenny Laureano, correspondent, and sister of Pauline and Renata Laureano.

Pauline Laureano, correspondent, and sister of Renata and Jenny Laureano.

Renata Laureano, Carl's girlfriend at the time of his 2007 trial. Sister of Jenny and Pauline Laureano.

'Little Tommy' *see* Tommy Ivanovic

Colin Lovitt, QC, a Victorian barrister.

David 'Scottish Dave' McCulloch, convicted of drug trafficking in 2005. McCulloch had been pushing for a royal commission into Victoria Police's drug squad. His appeal failed and he did thirteen years' jail during which time he dedicated himself to helping other inmates to fight against unjust sentences.

Danielle McGuire, Tony Mokbel's de facto wife and mother of Renate.

Theo Magazis, Carl's solicitor.

Maila *see* Maila Reardon

Mark Mallia, a drug trafficker and friend of career criminal and enforcer Nik Radev. He was interrogated and tortured by four men in 2003 before being killed. It was alleged that Carl had instructed Andrew Veniamin and four other men to interrogate Mallia about missing drug money. Carl was charged with conspiracy to murder him and was convicted of his murder.

Joe Mansour, along with Bart Rizzo, ran 'The Company' for Tony Mokbel during Mokbel's Greek sojourn, according to police.

Michael Marshall, a hotdog stand owner and ecstasy runner who was killed in 2003 by two of Carl's hired hands.

'Matty' *see* Matthew Johnson

Troy Mercanti, a friend of both Fabian Quaid and Ben Cousins, and former head of the Coffin Cheaters bikie gang, was sentenced to seven years' jail for a long reign of physical and psychological abuse against his former partner.

Michelle Mercieca, one of Roberta Williams' sisters.

Mick *see* Mick Gatto

Horty Mokbel, brother of Tony and Milad.

Kabalan Mokbel, older brother of Tony Mokbel, the quiet member of the Mokbel clan.

Milad 'Gangland Milly' Mokbel, younger brother of Tony Mokbel, husband of Renate Mokbel. In 2006 Milad was sentenced to five years' jail on drug trafficking offences.

Renate Mokbel, housewife, wife of Milad Mokbel. She was jailed for two years after failing to pay Tony Mokbel's $1 million surety when he fled the country in 2006.

Tony 'Fat Tony' Mokbel, Carl's partner in drug manufacture since the nineties and head of 'The Company', skipped bail on cocaine importation charges in 2006 and fled to Greece where he was joined by his girlfriend, Danielle McGuire. He was recaptured in June 2007, and extradited to Australia in May 2008. In 2012 he was sentenced to 30 years' jail for running a drug cartel. He was stabbed in Barwon Prison in February 2019 but survived.

Desmond 'Tuppence' Moran, brother of Lewis Moran. Survived a shooting outside his home in March 2009 but was killed on 15 June 2009 at an Ascot Vale café. The hit was orchestrated by Judy Moran.

Jason Moran, son of Lewis Moran and half-brother of Mark Moran. Suspected of the killing of Alphonse Gangitano, head of the Carlton Crew, that kicked off Melbourne's Gangland War in 1998. He also shot Carl in a park in 1999, starting a chain of retaliatory murders. Jason was murdered in June 2003, along with Pasquale Barbaro, in front of five children.

Judy Moran, partner of Lewis Moran and matriarch of the Moran family. The mother of Mark Moran by Leslie 'Johnny' Cole. After divorcing Cole she had a child, Jason, with Lewis Moran, whose surname she adopted. She was sentenced in 2011 to 26 years' jail for ordering the death of Des Moran in 2009.

Lewis Moran, father of Jason and stepfather of Mark, husband of Judy Moran. Crime lord and associate of Graham Kinniburgh, murdered in March 2004 in a club in Brunswick while on bail facing drug trafficking charges. Carl had commissioned three of his henchmen to carry out the hit.

Mark Moran, stepson of Lewis Moran and son of Judy Moran by Leslie 'Johnny' Cole, was killed in June 2000.

Richard 'Kiwi Joe' Moran, local drug dealer (no relation to Lewis, Mark or Jason Moran) and Carl's early employer.

Natasha 'Tash' Morgan, correspondent of Carl's and former girlfriend of Tommy Ivanovic.

Peter Morrissey, SC, a prominent Melbourne barrister.

Nicole Mottram, one of Carl's former girlfriends.

'Munster' *see* Graham Kinniburgh

Nicola *see* Nicola Gobbo

Nikki *see* Nikki Denman

Jason 'Plugger' Paisley, a notorious criminal also known as the 'Trial from Hell' crook because, when he was before the County Court in 2000 (together with Matty Johnson) for the prison bashing of a triple-murderer, he flung excrement at the jury and bared his bum at the judge.

Penny *see* Penny Brown

Pizza Maker *see* Rocco Arico

PK *see* Paul 'PK' Kallipolitis

'Plugger' *see* Jason Paisley

Roy Anthony 'Red Rat' Pollitt, armed robber, jail escapee and contract killer who after his release became a renowned artist. He was jailed at the age of eighteen in 1972 and spent less than eight months on the outside (six of those as an escapee) over the next 36 years. In 1990 he was sentenced to a further eighteen years for murder, but he ultimately became famous for the paintings he produced in prison and when he was released in January 2008, he had a bank balance of $100,000 from the sale of his art. In 2017 Home Affairs Minister Peter Dutton ordered him to leave Australia and to return to Britain, where he was born.

David Prideaux, the former general manager of Barwon Prison while Carl was in the jail. He disappeared in June 2011 while on a hunting trip in Victoria's high alpine country near Mount Buller. No trace of him has been found. In 2014 the coroner ruled that his death was not suspicious and unrelated to Carl Williams' death.

Fabian Quaid, represented Australia in taekwondo at the Sydney Olympics in 2000. A close friend of footballer Ben Cousins, he was arrested in May 2008 on the charge of conspiring to traffic 45 kilograms of ecstasy with a value of around $24 million. In March 2010 he was finally sentenced to seventeen years' jail with a minimum of ten and a half years.

'Ray' *see* Radoslav Spadina

Mark 'Chopper' Read, an underworld figure who once told *The New York Times*: 'Look, honestly, I haven't killed that many people, probably about four or seven, depending on how you look at it.' Beginning in 1991, he wrote fifteen books, which in total sold more than half a million copies. His first book, *Chopper: From the inside* was a collection of letters he wrote while in Pentridge jail. He was paid a reported fee of $250,000 by the Nine Network to make detailed confessions to four murders. Even the most cursory research revealed that Read had made up the confessions in three out of the four cases. He died in 2013 of liver cancer.

Dennis Reardon, husband of Maila Reardon, had been a family friend since Carl's childhood, and Carl's soccer coach. In 2004 he was described as George Williams' right-hand man.

Maila Reardon, wife of Dennis Reardon, family friend of Carl's.

'Red Rat' *see* Roy Anthony Pollitt

Renata *see* Renata Laureano

Robert Richter, QC, a Victorian barrister who has represented numerous defendants in high-profile cases.

Bart Rizzo, along with Joe Mansour, ran 'The Company' for Tony Mokbel during Mokbel's Greek sojourn, according to the police. In November 2008 Rizzo pleaded guilty to three drug charges and a charge of dealing with the proceeds of crime.

'Rob' *see* Robert Carpenter

Jason Roberts, who was convicted of the murder of two police officers, Gary Silk and Rod Miller, in August 1998.

'Rocky' *see* Rocco Arico

'Rod' *see* Rodney Collins

'Roy Boy' *see* Roy Anthony Pollitt

Dimitrios Samsonidis, Australian underworld figure arrested in Greece in 2006 and jailed for life over a $4 billion plot to manufacture ice and speed in Melbourne.

'Scottish Dave' *see* David McCulloch

Sean *see* Sean Sonnet

Mick Selim and Dennis Basic were acquitted in July 2009 of being gunmen hired by Swedish model Charlotte Lindstrom in a conspiracy to kill two witnesses due to testify against her boyfriend who was on drug charges.

Shaune *see* Shaune Howlett

Sean Sonnet, sentenced to twenty years' jail by Justice Betty King in May 2008. She said that he had gone to Brighton Cemetery on 9 June 2004 with co-offender Gregg Hildebrandt, on the orders of Carl Williams, to shoot Mario Condello in broad daylight as he walked his dogs. Victoria Police said that their arrest of Sonnet and Hildebrandt at this time saved Condello from becoming the 28th Gangland War victim; Condello was later murdered by Rodney Collins.

Radoslav 'Ray' Spadina, a close friend and associate of John Kizon and Fabian Quaid, both West Australian crime figures. Spadina was also an associate of former corrupt policeman Roger Rogerson, who is now serving a life sentence for murder. Spadina was snared in a coordinated covert operation in Europe, Japan, Britain and the United Arab Emirates and was charged with conspiring to import 210 kilograms of pseudoephedrine from the Congo in September 2008 and convicted in 2015.

Stacey *see* Stacey Vella

Breanane Stephens, the youngest of Roberta's daughters by Dean Stephens, and Carl's stepdaughter.

Danielle Stephens, the eldest of Roberta's daughters by Dean Stephens, and Carl's stepdaughter.

Tye Stephens, Carl's stepson, eldest son of Roberta by Dean Stephens. He was arrested for being the getaway driver during a series of raids in Melbourne that netted stolen safes and $60,000 cash. He later pleaded guilty and was sentenced to two years' jail in 2009.

Tash *see* Natasha Morgan

Theo *see* Theo Magazis

Michael Thorneycroft, Carl's cousin, one of three accused of planning to kill Mario Condello, who was acting head of the Carlton Crew while Mick Gatto was serving time.

Tommy *see* Tommy Ivanovic

Trav *see* Travis Day

Troy *see* Troy Mercanti

'Two Guns' *see* Tommy Ivanovic

Tye *see* Tye Stephens

Shane Tyrrell, a Melbourne barrister. Carl regarded Tyrrell as the most trustworthy of his barristers.

Stacey Vella, a hairdresser from Kurunjang on Melbourne's western fringe and Carl's girlfriend while in jail until she moved on in 2009.

Andrew 'Benji' Veniamin, allegedly killed seven people on orders from Carl. He was eventually shot dead at La Porcella restaurant in Carlton in March 2004 by Mick Gatto, who was found to have acted in self-defence by a jury.

Barbara Williams, née Denman, Carl's mother. She married George Williams in 1966 and had two sons by him, Shane and Carl. She committed suicide in 2008.

Dhakota 'Kota' Williams, Carl's only daughter, born to Roberta in March 2001.

George Williams, Carl's father. In 1999 he and Carl were charged with drug offences after George's Broadmeadows property was raided by police and drugs were found. The charges were later dropped. However, he was jailed in 2007 for four and a half years after pleading guilty to smuggling 5 kilograms of amphetamines for Carl. He was released in June 2009 for good behaviour, and died in 2016 after a heart attack.

Roberta Williams (née Mercieca) was one of seven children. Her first marriage was to Dean Stephens, an associate of the Morans, with whom she had two daughters, Danielle and Breanane, and a son, Tye. She married Carl on 14 January 2001 and they had a daughter, Dhakota, in 2001.

Shane Williams, Carl's older brother, who died of a drug overdose in 1997.

Rod Wise, acting commissioner, Corrections Victoria, during the time Carl was incarcerated at Barwon.

Herbert 'Bertie' Wrout, long-time driver and friend of Lewis Moran. He was wounded in the attack that killed Lewis Moran in 2004 and died in his sleep in 2015.

A note on the text

When Carl Williams died in 2010, police seized all his possessions, including his laptop computer. In early 2016 Roberta Williams made a court application to regain possession of the computer and its contents. Originally the police refused Roberta's request, because of the 'sensitive nature' of some of the documents it contained, but in the end they acquiesced without her having to go to court.

What Roberta then obtained was access to more than 500,000 words in intimate and revealing communications, some of them hidden behind a password that needed to be professionally cracked. The laptop contained personal letters Carl had written during the last eighteen months of his life to underworld figures and family members. He had later printed these letters out and sent them by mail to his correspondents.

What is published here is a selection. Some deletions have been made in the letters chosen, for legal reasons and to avoid repetition; in some cases, changes have been made to protect the privacy of individuals or because of court suppression orders that prevent the naming of some criminals. However, apart from that, Carl's letters have been reproduced without any of the editing that professional publishers normally impose. This has been done in order to give readers an unmediated experience of a man who, for all his many sins, loved his family and was a keen observer of human behaviour.

Richard Walsh, May 2019

CHAPTER 1

Dancing in the rain

For thirteen extraordinary years, the big story in Melbourne gangland was The Rise & Rise of Carl Williams.

Carl's twenty-first birthday, on 13 October 1991, was typical of the Williams madhouse. His mother, Barbara, was caught in flagrante with a minor criminal. Carl had a huge punch-up with his brother, Shane, who would be dead within a few years from an overdose. The birthday boy himself was working as a drug courier for local drug dealer Richard 'Kiwi Joe' Moran. Later, when Carl served a term in jail after a deal fell over (his conviction was later overturned), he temporarily parked his customer base with Mark Moran (no relation to Kiwi Joe) on the understanding that he would get a commission on those sales on his release from custody.

When he left jail, Carl believed Mark owed him $1 million.

Mark Moran's failure to pay that debt was like the assassination of Archduke Ferdinand in Sarajevo in June 1914—a seemingly minor event that triggered a major cataclysm. Carl's 1999 birthday saw him being shot in the stomach by Jason Moran, and so began a vendetta that lasted for another decade. By the end of the so-called Gangland War at least 36 people had been killed.

....

On 9 June 2004 Carl Williams was riding high. Among the road kill were his three sworn enemies—the half-brothers, Mark and Jason Moran, and their father, Lewis Moran, were all now dead. Sure, Carl was out on bail on three serious offences at this time, but he could afford the best defence lawyers money could buy and they seemed to be running rings around the hapless Purana Taskforce, which Victoria Police had established to bring an end to the public slaughter. Nothing really for Carl to fear. And if he did, he could usually quell the feeling with cocaine, which he was habitually taking in his last years on the outside.

At 7.30 a.m. the police arrived at Carl's mum's place. Barb hadn't seen her son yet that morning, but she was planning to spoil him with his favourite breakfast: eggs, baked beans and chips. She hoped the smell might waft into his bedroom and rouse him. Instead, the police hauled him from his bed.

Carl was arrested and subsequently charged with ordering the murder of Michael Marshall, a hotdog stand owner and ecstasy runner who had been killed by two of Carl's hired hands. Unfortunately for them, their van had been bugged and the police had in their possession some pretty incriminating tapes of discussions between the killers and their paymaster, Carl. Not to mention audio of the killing as it took place.

Carl spent his time awaiting trial in the Melaleuca and Acacia units of HM Prison Barwon, which is situated just outside the town of Lara, near Geelong. At first, he was blithely confident of a good result, freedom even. In a note he sent to journalist Adam Shand in July 2004, he wrote cheerily:

Hello Adam
Well it was good to hear from you as it always is. As for me, I'm back here at HOTEL ACACIA, just taking a break for a while, everything's good no problems.

But Carl was on 23-hour lockdown in a cell that measured 4 by 3 metres and the Hotel Acacia knew very well how to play with the minds of its guests. As a small example, prisoners were allowed access to both newspapers and TV, but experience had shown that this only increased their sense of isolation. 'It's Hannibal Lecter stuff, mate,' was crime lord Mick Gatto's considered verdict after his release. 'A jail inside a jail.'

The hotel had on its guest list a Who's Who of the Gangland War. Apart from Gatto—a sworn enemy of

Carl, who always referred to him as 'The Don'—there was Evangelos 'Ange' Goussis, who had killed Lewis Moran among others, and Carl's cousin Michael Thorneycroft, one of three accused of planning to kill Mario Condello (acting head of the Carlton Crew while Mick Gatto was serving time) and the first to crack under police pressure, testifying to the cops that Carl had confided to him he'd killed seven of his rivals. Flushed with this success, Purana Taskforce collaborated with jail authorities to make life as difficult as possible for these gangland inmates. This included carefully vetting placements inside Barwon, limiting visits and even human contact. They were fed disinformation about what their mates were saying about them, and what their wives and girlfriends were doing on the outside. At the same time, they were offered a way out by informing on their former associates, including Carl. It would prove the most successful tactic in achieving convictions from the Gangland War—probably the only one that actually worked.

The modus operandi of the Purana Taskforce, in collaboration with Corrections Victoria, was to move already-turned informers out of the mainstream prison population and into the various management units, such as Acacia. This was done by removing informers who may have initially been placed in Barwon's mainstream population by way of subterfuge.

The process would begin with a code aqua siren sounding, signifying a return of all inmates to their cells, then the Special Emergency Security Group would conduct a search of a tier of the particular unit that housed the informer.

A rumour would be planted that contraband had been located in his cell and the inmate would be moved to a management unit. This operation would provide suitable cover for the informer to be moved into the unit targeted by the taskforce without arousing questions from other prisoners.

Sometimes official paperwork such as a police statement signed by the inmate, was received surreptitiously in the prison, revealing an inmate to be an informer. In the prison, this is called a professional bail, referring to 'bailing out' meaning—in prison terms—running away and escaping.

Under immense pressure, some of Carl's closest mates were bailing on him in order to lighten their sentences. Even Carl himself was beginning to ponder the wisdom of cooperation.

In July 2006 he was sentenced to 25 years' jail after a jury found him guilty of the murder of Michael Marshall. The following May he pleaded guilty to the murder of Jason and Lewis Moran, to the murder of drug trafficker Mark Mallia and to conspiracy to murder Mario Condello.

On 7 May 2007 Carl faced Justice Betty King and was sentenced to life imprisonment with a minimum of 35 years, commencing immediately. With almost three years already served, it was effectively a 38-year sentence.

Carl later wrote a letter to the media, claiming he was not guilty of the murder of Lewis Moran, but had only cut a deal to keep his father, George, and his wife, Roberta, out of jail. He said Justice King had prevented him from using his barrister of choice, Peter Faris, QC, by scheduling his trial when Faris was unavailable.

Addressing King, he said: 'I knew that you were placed here for a purpose, and that purpose is to convict anyone who comes before [you] in this so-called Gangland stuff despite what the evidence is. [How] can you come from the County Court with not very much experience and be given the biggest, highest profile case this state has seen in a long time?

'Last but certainly not least, you might have taken my freedom, but one thing I can assure you, you haven't and you will never be able to break me. I can look in the mirror and I'm proud of the person who I see, my family can always hold their head up high as I stood up for what I believed in, and I never sold my soul to the devil and I never will. Life isn't about waiting for the storm to pass, it's about learning to dance in the rain.' At this stage, Carl's customary bravado was in evidence, but over time he would come to understand that life inside Barwon was hardly like life at all, at least as he had known it.

....

After the trial, Carl returned to Hotel Acacia and watched events continue to unfold.

Tony Mokbel had been Carl's partner in drug manufacture since the nineties. In 2002 'Fat Tony', as the media mob unkindly called him, had almost been beaten to death by bikies from Perth's Coffin Cheaters at a meeting Mick Gatto had convened at La Porcella restaurant in Carlton.

The Kuwaiti-born Mokbel was accused of paying Ange

Goussis and another man $150,000 to kill Lewis Moran; having got wind that he would be charged with this crime, he skipped bail in March 2006 but was recaptured in Greece in June 2007.

Mokbel felt vulnerable in the Greek prison where he was placed but was taken under the wing of one of Australia's most respected underworld figures, Dimitrios Samsonidis, who in 2006 had been jailed for life in Greece over a $4 billion plot to manufacture ice and speed in Melbourne. Samsonidis had been arrested while trying to smuggle a tonne of ephedrine into Australia.

After unsuccessfully appealing against his extradition in the Greek courts, Mokbel finally arrived back in Melbourne on 17 May 2008 and checked into the Hotel Acacia.

Meanwhile the wife of his brother Milad, mother-of-three Renate Mokbel, was sentenced to two years' jail in 2006 for failing to provide the $1 million surety she had pledged for Fat Tony's bail. Described by those who knew her as an ordinary suburban housewife, Renate was allowed to take her two-year-old into the Dame Phyllis Frost women's prison.

In October 2008 Carl was residing in the Melaleuca Unit of Barwon Prison and had just been provided with a personal computer. This was a special privilege afforded very few inmates. Typically, a request would be granted only if the inmate was involved in preparing legal briefs or some other vital paperwork. And Carl was not doing that. In fact, he used the computer almost exclusively to write personal correspondence and to play games.

What emerges from his letters is a picture of Carl's circle of friends and associates. At one time, he had been a normal kid growing up in Broadmeadows, a working-class suburb in Melbourne's north. His friends had been the kids from the local area, schools and sports clubs. The Williams' family home had been full of these kids every weekend, and only a handful had ever got into trouble. But as Carl's criminal career blossomed, he began to drop these old mates. Some were afraid to be near him. A few stayed loyal, but Carl was living a different life in the underworld. He learnt that friendship was impermanent and alliances could shift swiftly and dramatically. After he was shot in 1999 by Jason Moran, Carl's personality began to change. The happy-go-lucky disposition of his youth gave way to a more serious and calculating one. He began to consume more of his own product and paranoia started to affect his personality. He wasn't alone. During this period, the gangland mindset didn't allow for any uncertainty: it was a case of where there was any doubt, there was no doubt. Killing someone whose loyalties were questioned was easier than taking a risk on trusting them. Discerning friends from phonies through a haze of drugs became a daily challenge in this twisted subculture.

After his incarceration, Carl withdrew even more into this criminal fraternity and the scope of his correspondence reflects this. Inmates understand the importance of letters—'kites' as they call them—from inside jail, even if they know that every word is scrutinised. Hearing someone else's news—even from another jail—is a welcome relief from the crushing monotony of their lives. Even if Carl hadn't been close to his pen pals on the outside, a feeling of unity was created if they could maintain a steady correspondence. But there were restrictions on what he could write about. Barwon's postmaster Charlene would collect the written letters and read through them for key words and phrases. If she found anything relating to violence, crime or war they would not be sent. Likewise, if they contained any sexually explicit material or images, they would be marked return to sender. Any attempt to send coded messages in letters between inmates in the jail could result in the correspondents being moved to a management unit or losing their privileges. For prisoners like Carl the only exception to this control was when inmates left management units for placements in the mainstream jail. Those inmates could often manage to carry mail hidden in their papers for delivery to select recipients. Otherwise, Barwon had a vice-like grip on body and mind. If an inmate agreed to become an informer, that grip could be relaxed. All they had to do was tell a few tales and a vista of opportunity could open up: sentence reductions, special placements with friends, lifting of restrictions on correspondence, even secret furloughs out of prison.

And so began Carl's written account of the last eighteen months of his life. He began to compose an avalanche of letters on his new toy—to his fellow inmates, to his out mates, to his family and to the occasional female fan. Naturally Tony Mokbel needed his advice on lawyers; Renate's husband, Milad Mokbel, needed cheering up. But his first letter was to his Tasmanian mate, Wayne Howlett.

17 October 2008 to Wayne Howlett

Wayne Howlett was a Tasmanian powerlifter who was sentenced to two years in Risdon Prison in December 2008 for drug trafficking. He was introduced to powerlifting as a young inmate at Risdon Prison by a prison guard.

Dear Wayne,
I trust this letter finds you in the very best of both health and spirits, as it leaves me fine.

I received your letter last night, and it was good to hear from you again as it always is.

I also received the paper clipping you sent me with your letter. That Ange is big for 74 kilo – all muscle, he looks a lot heavier than that, you yourself look pretty big in that photo – big shoulders.

You asked when will my appeal most likely be heard – sometime early next year – I'm tipping about February.

Also you asked who I think is the best Barrister in Victoria – in my opinion Robert Richter is the best. Others may say Con Heliotis, those two have a reputation as being the best in this state, people say Heliotis is the best cross-examiner in the Country, he is the one who represented me *(but I could have had Merlin the magician representing me, and it would've made no difference – my case was too political – they just wanted me off the streets at all costs)*. I also like Colin Lovitt, and Peter Farris. Farris used to represent me for years.

Well I finally got my computer – and I'm rapt with it, its got everything I need, it helps pass the time like you wouldn't believe.

Roberta came out to see me earlier this week, it was good to see her, we had a good laugh – which you need to have in these places, especially when you're housed in this environment I am, and have been for years (around the corner – ha ha).

Well buddy I don't really have much more to say, therefore I'll leave it there for now, and I hope to hear from you again soon

Keep in touch.

Best wishes & respect – ______________________

Ps) Please give my best to your brother – thanks

26 October 2008 to Danny Heaney

Danny Heaney was sentenced in 1984 to thirteen years' jail for nine armed robberies; in 2004 he was sentenced for nine years with a minimum of six years for stabbing a woman.

Dear Danny,

I trust this letter finds you in the best of health and spirits, as it leaves me fine.

I received a letter from you late last week, and it was good to hear from you again as it always is.

Cox-Plate, what I would've given to be there with you. I love that day, in my opinion that's the best day of the carnival. I had a quaddie, and I went out in the 1st leg, and I got the other 3 legs, I liked [name deleted for legal reasons], the bloke who trains it gets the best juice.[1]

I see that Roberta is now making T-shirts, fuck you've got to hand it to her, she's a tryer. Although I would much prefer it

---

1 Etorphine or elephant juice is a synthetic cousin to morphine and 1000 times more effective. Racing's most notorious 'go-fast' drug, it is actually used as a tranquilliser for large animals. At the time of this letter, etorphine had not been detected in horses by racing officials for nearly 30 years.

if my name was kept out of everything all together, but let's be realistic that's not going to happen anytime soon, so in saying that if it's going to be mentioned, I'd much rather her making money off my name, then the likes of the scum who have been, with lies and untruths.

Well buddy that's all for now, and I hope to hear from you again soon.

Best wishes & respect,
Your friend always – Carl

27 October 2008 to Danny Heaney

Dear Danny,
Well hello there my true and trusted, how's life treating you all good I hope as for me I'm fine.

I just received your letter in which you wrote yesterday, and it was my pleasure to hear from you again, as it always is.

We were locked down today from 11.30, some staff training or some bullshit. So it was a lazy day for me, I just messed around on the computer, leaning more and more things about it everyday, by the time I get out I should/will be a genius.

I have a different pin on my last 4 digits of my CRN. But you're some scum would be working overtime trying to crack the code, but let's be honest with one another, if they did crack it, what would they do, worst case scenario – call someone names, and if they got Roberta she'd call them worse names (ha ha). Mate they're all full of shit, weak loud mouths, who wouldn't do anything if you killed their loved ones in front of their faces – true!

Today I seen MOU,[2] and as usual they didn't really have

2 Major Offenders Unit, a Corrections Victoria head office committee that makes all decisions in relation to high-profile inmates in management units.

any news for me. If you were to believe them, they reckon the fortnightly contact visits will come into place soon, most likely December, or January at the latest, but I say – when it happens, it happens. I don't take too much notice of what they say, because at times they say anything, and they tell you things that you want to hear just to keep or make you happy.

They also said that I won't be getting cleared into the mainstream for about another 5 years. And they said with Roberta making the T-shirts like she is, isn't helping my cause – what a load of shit that is. First they said it's because I'm high profile, then Underbelly, then it's because the media are always writing about me, now it's the T-shirts Roberta is making – give me a break, what's next???? So if Roberta weren't making those T-shirts, would I be getting cleared into mainstream anytime soon? The answer is NO – They can do as they please, and I'll be taking my lawyers advice, and taking Legal action through the Courts about my placement and treatment like I'm current doing, and whatever happens happens.

I just received a letter from Rod,[3] and he was telling me that his got a statement Mr. Fantasma made against him, he seem pretty happy about it too, he says I always said he was another Brad A.[4] and he did.

I hope to hear from you again soon.
Best wishes & respect,
Your friend always – Carl

3 Rodney 'The Duke' Collins.
4 Name changed for legal reasons.

31 October 2008 to Tony Mokbel

Tony Mokbel was Carl's partner in drug manufacture and head of 'The Company'. He skipped bail on cocaine importation charges in 2006 and fled to Greece but was recaptured in June 2007 and extradited to Australia in May 2008. At the time of this letter he was awaiting sentencing.

Mr. Carl Williams
C/- Melaleuca Unit
Locked Bag No. 7. Lara. Vic. 3212

Dear Tony,
I trust this letter finds you in the best of health and spirits, as it leaves me fine.

I just received your letter, and it was my pleasure to hear from you again, as it always is.

When you write, if you remember can you please put the date on the top of your letters – thanks.

So Horty's[5] off to PPP,[6] he'll enjoy himself there, plus Gangland Milly[7] will have anything sorted for him. Fuck he's funny, Gangland Milly, I really enjoy his company, he's good for a laugh.

Now Allan T.,[8] what's happened, is he also a witness against you, if so in what case?? I know everything about him, as he was the witness against me in the Marshall, Mark Moran and Moran/Barbaro[9] cases. What I suggest you do is talk to

5 Horty Mokbel.
6 Port Phillip Prison.
7 Milad Mokbel.
8 Name changed for legal reasons.
9 Jason Moran was murdered in June 2003, along with Pasquale Barbaro, in front of five children.

Rob,[10] and tell him what you want or need, and get him to tell me, and I'll do it all ASAP – no problems.

Nothing much has been happening over here, I've just been using my computer, and the more I use it, the more I'm learning, it makes the time fly.

I seen MOU, and surprise, surprise, I aren't going anywhere soon. They tell me that I'll be in these sorts of unit for another 5 years, that'll mean I'll have to serve 10 years in the slot[11] before being cleared to mainstream – what a joke. I talked to Rob, and a few others to help me, Shane TYRELL (whom I get along well with), and Julian BURNSIDE (QC). And I think, or I know, that they're preparing to take Corrections to Court about my placement, and treatment, as they believe it's inhuman – and I agree, especially for long periods of time, and considering that I've done nothing at all wrong to warrant it. It's a punishment regime, whatever way you look at it, and it not fair on us, or our loved ones – true.

I hope to hear from you again soon.

Best wishes & respect,
Your friend always –

Ps) Please give my best wishes to your mum, kids, and Dan – thanks

10 Rob Stary.

11 'Slots' at Barwon Prison are management units Banksia, Acacia and Melaleuca. Traditionally 'the slot' means solitary confinement and Carl sometimes uses it in that sense. But he also uses the term to describe the special high-security unit in which he is currently imprisoned.

4 November 2008 to Fabian Quaid

Fabian Quaid was arrested in May 2008 on the charge of conspiring to traffic 45 kilograms of ecstasy with a value of around $24 million. In March 2010 he was finally sentenced to seventeen years' jail with a minimum of ten and a half years.

Dear Fab,
I trust this letter finds you in the best of health and spirits, as it leaves me fine.

I just received your letter, and it was my pleasure to hear from you again, as it always is.

When you write, if you remember can you please put the date on the top of your letters – thanks.

So you're now at the High Security Unit, Ange actually passed the message onto me to let me know. Where you are sounds better than where I am, 2-contact visit per-weeks, that's pretty good, we only get one contact visit per-month.

So you haven't read or heard about Allan T., hmmmm – well he was the first one to roll – with Mick's blessing of course. John. W.,[12] you have heard of, I'll tell you a funny story about him. When he first rolled and certain people thought that he'd only roll on me, and not others, they thought it was ok. Then when he talked about everyone, all of a sudden they were all calling him a lying dog. It's a funny world we live in that's for sure, some people think that it's ok to lag – as long as it's not them you're lagging. I could tell you some stories that would make you hair curly.

As you know Andrew (Benji)[13] was my mate, he was a close friend of mine. When he was killed, he never went there to kill

---

12 Name changed for legal reasons.

13 Andrew 'Benji' Veniamin.

Mick, that's the truth, despite what happened at Mick's trial, and good luck to Mick – I don't want to see anyone locked up. But Andrew trusted and thought certain people were his true friends, but they turned out to be anything but, and I for one, aren't into false people, as I believe they can't be trusted, and they're snakes, that's just my opinion.

I didn't know that Ray[14] had been pinched, as I have previous told you – I haven't heard from him for years. Is he currently locked up, or did he get bail, and what is it exactly that he is pinched on?

Yeh I read all about Ben COUSINS and the police commissioner virtually putting a stop on him going to Collingwood. I like the loyalty that he show to you, when others might not think it's in his best interest, he seems like a really good person, with rare qualities. Can you tell that I said "when he comes to Melbourne, he can come to visit me if he wants too". In addition, Roberta and the kids want to meet him, and take him out for dinner when he comes to Melb, she asked me the other day, to tell you to give him her phone number, or visa–versa.

I haven't really got much else to add, therefore I'll leave it there for now, and hope to hear from you again soon.

Best wishes & respect,
Your friend always –

14 Radoslav 'Ray' Spadina.

5 November 2008 to Wayne Howlett

Mr. Carl Williams
C/- Melaleuca Unit
Locked Bag No. 7. Lara. Vic. 3212

Dear Wayne,
I trust this letter finds you in the best of health and spirits, as it leaves me fine.

I just received your letter, dated 2–11, and it was my pleasure to hear from you again, as it always is.

It's good to hear that you were granted parole, even though your conditions are strict, one thing is for sure though, you are much better off at home, then you are stuck in prison.

I dare say if the Parole board are concerned about you being in contact with Roberta, they wouldn't be at all impressed with you being in contact with me. How long parole do you have?

I don't mind if you put that poem that I sent your newsletter over there. In this letter, I have attached a brainteaser for you to read, let me know how you go at it when you write back to me.

I hope you like the pictures that I've done for you, as I put a lot of work into them (ha ha).

Thanks for offering to Buy and send me those DVD programs that you did for my computer. However, I cannot have things like that sent to me, everything I get I need to purchase through the prison (special buy), so I am ok, but your offer in itself does mean alot to me.

Nothing much has been happening here worth telling you about, same shit, day in day out, you know what it's like.

Well buddy I have really got much else to say, therefore I'll leave it there for now, and I hope to hear from you again soon.

Best wishes & respect,
Your friend –
Ps) Please give my best to your brother – thanks

7 November 2008 to Milad Mokbel

Milad Mokbel was the younger brother of Tony Mokbel, husband of Renate Mokbel, and father of Robbie and Jade. In 2006 Milad was sentenced to five years' jail on drug trafficking offences. Renate, his wife, received a two-year jail term after failing to pay Tony Mokbel's $1 million surety when he skipped the country in 2006.

Dear Milad,
I trust this letter finds you in the best of health and spirits, as it leaves me fine.

I just received your letter, and once again, it was my pleasure to hear from you again.

In your letter, which I just received, you asked me for my opinion, if you should or should not let Claire visit you. With what Renate has been forced to endure over the past 2, or more years, through no fault of her own, (simply just for being your wife), this is, and has to be the only answer I can give you. If you tell Renate and she thinks it'd be ok for Claire to visit you, then I'm all for it. If you were to do it without her knowing, I'd say you were the wrong thing, ***especially*** if Clair has feeling for you, or visa-versa.

I sincerely hope that Renate gets home detention. If she does – she'll be home with the kids just after Christmas, where she should be, so fingers crossed for her.

You forgot to tell me if Melanie still lives in Dubai or not? As I send her a card thanking her for my belated Birthday card, and it cost me 3 stamps. ☺ Why didn't Mel's sister also send me a card for my birthday – snob she is, I always told you Mel was the best out of them, she alright Mel, that's my opinion anyway.

I do not really have much else to say, therefore I will leave it there for now, and hopefully I hear from you again soon.

Best wishes, your friend always –

Ps) Please give my best to your Mum, Renate and the kids – thanks

Pss) You should have told me it was MJ's birthday, as I would've sent him a card, and a little gift. When are Robbie and Jade's B/Days?????

11 November 2008 to Mick Selim

Mick Selim, together with Dennis Basic, was accused of being a gunman hired by Swedish model Charlotte Lindstrom to kill two witnesses due to testify against her boyfriend. Both were acquitted in July 2009.

Dear Mick,

Last night I received your letter, and naturally, it was my pleasure to hear from you again, as it always is.

My family are all holding up ok, and thanks for asking how they are. Please give my best wishes to your brother.

I see you were saying that Purana have been giving you a hard time – they're relentless if they have it in for you, they not only turn your life upside down, but they also do the same to everyone you know.

Nothing much else is or has been happening down here to tell you about, I've been doing my daily exercising – light jogging, and riding the exercise bike. Apart from that I've been spending alot of time on my computer, writing letters and playing a Tennis game (Virtua Tennis 3), which is pretty good – it's actually quite fun once you get into it.

I don't really have anything else to say, so I suppose I'll leave it there for now, and I hope to hear from you again soon.

Best wishes,
Your friend always –

11 November 2008 to Danny Heaney

Dear Danny,
I received a letter from you late last week, and naturally, it was my pleasure to hear from you again, as it always is.

Nothing much has been happening down here to tell you about, it's the same thing different day – you know what it's like.

On the Sunday just past, I had a really good visit with my mum, Dhakota,[15] and Stacey,[16] it was a Contact Visit, in the main visit centre. Dhakota and I played chasey, and she was showing me her new dance moves, she's so cute, it was fun – and we all really enjoyed it so much, but when it was time for them to leave, it was hard watching and let them leave.

GT[17] hey, his off his head – his lost the plot, what can you say..................

I wonder if the Crown intends on calling him as a witness, and whether or not he'll jump up, he was always declaring people here and there – unreal. Nothing ceases to amaze me these days, a large majority of the people in this world are selfish people, and it's only getting worse, imagine what it's going to be like in 20 years time.

The police recently came out here to see me again, I seen them because if I didn't, and they really wanted to see me they'd

---

15 Carl's daughter, Dhakota 'Kota' Williams.
16 Carl's then girlfriend, Stacey Vella.
17 Identity unknown.

just 464[18] me, plus I have no problems listening to what they have to say. Anyway, they said if I would be prepared to jump on board with them, they'd give me virtually anything I asked for – anything within reason – unbelievable isn't it.[19]

I haven't really got anything else to say, so I suppose I'll leave it there for now, and I hope to hear from you again soon.

Best wishes,
Your friend always –

14 November 2008 to Beau Goddard

Beau Goddard, the half-brother of St Kilda star Brendon Goddard, was jailed for at least nine years in 2007 for heroin supply. He had previously spent time in jail with Tommy Ivanovic.

Dear Huddo,
I trust this letter finds you in the best of health and spirits, as it leaves me fine. I just received your letter, and it was good to hear from you again, as it always is.

I like that one – Milad's moto, if someone gives him respect – he'll give them 10% more back – that's sounds fantastic. Come to think of it I might give it a try myself – I wonder if everyone's including – after all it's prison we're in – that's if he hasn't noticed. Does it matter if they're low life junkies,

---

18 To be 464-ed is to be taken into police custody for the purpose of interrogation or for taking a forensic sample. This is authorised under section 464 of the *Victorian Crimes Act 1958*.

19 Within weeks of writing this letter, Carl and his father George would spend a week out of jail at the Special Air Service Regiment base on Swan Island off Geelong, assisting police with investigations into the 2004 murder of police informers Terry and Christine Hodson. From this moment, Carl knew that his days were numbered. Eventually, someone would learn that he and George had assisted police with their enquiries.

who'd sell their mother for a hit, or they hit up someone else spit on a daily basis – give me a break, he just wants to be friends with everyone – my motto is a friend to all is a friend to none. I wouldn't talk to a large majority of the people – never mind show them respect, Fuck his completely off his head. I told you he would talk to anyone.

You're 100% right if I was there we'd be laughing our heads off – nonstop – Milad would be cursing me – as I'd tell all these fuck head who he talks too – to fuck off and keep away from me, and he'd be spewing big time (ha ha) .

I hope you get yourself up to Loddon,[20] its bullshit how these cunts who you don't even know, put flags up and stop you from going where they are. I can only imagine how many cowards will flag me over my sentence, I wouldn't mind a dollar for everyone who does, or has.

My training's still going good, I don't go to hard – I only plod along, and I'm really enjoy it. Unfortunately, I don't have a lolly jar here full of M&M's, as they don't sell them here, but if they did I'd have a jar full – I love them. Hey, I just thought of something funny regarding M&M. I was charged with 6 murders, 3 of them are MM – Mick Marshall, Mark Mallia, Mark Moran. ☺

I haven't really got anything else to say, so I suppose I'll leave it there for now, and I hope to hear from you again soon.

Best wishes & respect,
Your friend –

20 Loddon Prison, a medium-security prison in Central Victoria.

14 November 2008 to Stacey Vella

Stacey Vella, a hairdresser from Kurunjang on Melbourne's western fringe and Carl's girlfriend while in jail until she moved on in 2009.

Mr. Carl Williams
C/- Melaleuca Unit
Locked Bag No. 7.
LARA VIC. 3212

Dear Stacey,
I trust this letter finds you in the best of health and spirits, as it leaves me fine.

I just received a letter from you, and it was a good one at that, it hit the spot as your letters always do. ☺

So you're hoping you get the shop so you can keep yourself busy, and your mind occupied from ME, and you mean that in a good way (he he). Do you honestly think that when/if you get this shop – you'll be able to keep your mind off me, when I'll be ringing you more often, chatting you up – and talking dirty to you –

I think NOT! ☺ After all it wouldn't be fair if you could do that, look what I have to go through – try locking yourself in your toilet for at least 18 hours per-day, with photos of me all over the place – gee, funny isn't it – yeh stop laughing – it's not that funny .... I'm addicted to you – and the more I get of you – the more I want (he he).

It was good to talk to you this morning for 3 calls – although I wish I was there with you, talking face to face – what a thought. Another day you had off work today – you bludger you – I can't wait to tell Kota, she's going to give you heaps.

17 November 2008 to Danny Heaney

Dear Danny,
I trust this letter finds you in the best of health and spirits, as it leaves me fine.

I just received your letter, and it was good to hear from you again, as it always is.

I hear you loud and clear re: the Police's latest offers. I do consider you a very close friend of mine, and my families, so I do tell you things that I wouldn't tell others, about the offers that are, or have been made to me, to me offer are just that offers. Yeh I am only human – and I would be lying if I said I wouldn't like a big slice taken off my sentence. Naturally I'd rather get out when I am in my late 50's or early 60's instead of 71 years-old, ect, ect, ect, but as you said that's not me, so that's dead and buried, and we'll just have to take the good with the bad – I'm alive, and that by far is the main thing.

I know what you mean about going to the hospital shackled, and everyone looking at you – a couple of years ago the same thing happened to me, when they took me there for an X-Ray, but lucky for me my heads not known, so I flew under the radar a little bit (ha ha).

The other day I got a date for my Appeal – the 5th of February, so I'm up just after Christmas. I have Lachlan Carter as the junior to Paul Holdenson (QC), so I have a good team on my side, but in saying that I'm not at all confident of getting a reduction, although you and I both know I should. I should at least get the 3 years off I did before I was finally sentenced. On top of that surely in anyone's eyes these condition that I'm house under, and I will continue to be housed under for god only knows how long, must be viewed as harsh. Much harsher than the normal prisoners has to endure anyway – this is punishment, on top of punishment, and blind Freddy could see that, and so will these Judges if they're at all fair dinkum. I could go on and on, but I won't as to you I guess I'm just stating the obvious.

I haven't really got anything else to say, so I suppose I'll leave it there for now, and I hope to hear from you again soon.

Best wishes,
Your friend always –

19 November 2008 to Breanane Stephens

Breanane Stephens, one of Roberta's daughters by Dean Stephens, and Carl's stepdaughter.

Hello Brea,
How you are going? As good as can be expected I hope, as for me here I'm fine – hot.

I thought I'd write you a letter – with the hope that you might will reply – as my other 2 girls never seem too – Dhakota and Roberta.

Brea – do I have some gossip for you – Hhmmmmm – take a seat – sit down, otherwise after hearing what I have to tell you, you're likely to fall down. Before I start, you have to promise me that you'll keep it to yourself though – pinky promise, ok then – oh one more thing before I forget – no paying me back for me accidently lagging you to Danielle.[21] Are you sitting down now – Ok, I'll tell you then – believe me, the chemistry was amazing, and I loved it. ☺ The "L" word was being thrown around a fair bit too, and I don't mean "LIKE". The whole time they couldn't keep their hands off one another, hands were going everywhere

---

21 Brea's older sister.

(*that might be a bit of an exaggeration* ☺), honestly, you had to see it to believe it – staring into one another eyes – I thought they looked as though they needed a room, I bet they both would've loved it if that were to happen. (lol). I will fill you more about it when I see you face to face. ☺

I hope you get into this new school EKFC that you're trying too, as you don't seem to like the one you're at.

What about Dhakota, she reckons that she's now on a diet, and when I asked her why? She said, well you keep going on about my weight dad. She reckons that she's already lost weight – I'd like to see where. (ha ha) Let's see how far this diet goes we we're on our next visit – and you and I start hogging into all the chips, chocolate, and soft drinks (*there'll be hell to pay*). You should get a bottle of water, and when I come out, I'll give it to her, I think the dummy will be going straight in the mouth – she so cute isn't she, and funny too.

I don't really have much more to add, therefore I guess I'll leave it there for now, and I hope to hear from you again soon.

I hope you enjoyed my letter, and it gave you a laugh – remember you picky promised – ok, you can tell Roberta, but only her, & when no one else is on ears shot, don't go telling anyone else though – otherwise you might bomb things out, and we don't want that happening. (lmao[22])

Love you heaps
Always and forever – Carl –xoxox–

22 Laughing my ass off.

20 November 2008 to Dhakota Williams

Dhakota Williams, whom he often calls 'Kota', is Carl's only daughter, born to Roberta in March 2001.

Carl Williams

C/- Melaleuca Unit
Locked Bag No. 7.
LARA VIC. 3212

Dear Dhakota,

Well hello there my little Princess, how are you? Good I hope. I hope you have been behaving yourself, and you have been looking after your teeth, by brushing then twice a day – you better be.[23]

Hey Dhakota, I think I have found a picture of your teacher at little kitchen, the hat his wearing looks very similar to the one you wear. Speaking about your hat, I got the photos of you wearing your chef's hat, and with all you cooking stuff – I love it, I put it straight up on my wall, you look so cute.

I also got a photo of Milo[24] wearing sunglasses, he looked cute as, he thinks his pretty cool too, his a cheeky little fella. Do you think his as cool as this little puppy in the picture? In the photo were Milo was wearing sunglasses, I couldn't believe that someone had her dummy in her mouth, I hope she gets rid of it before her 8th birthday.

23 Carl was obsessed with brushing his teeth. Growing up, he might brush them at least three times a day. He was also fastidious about his general hygiene and wearing clean clothes.

24 Roberta and Carl's Maltese/Shih Tzu dog.

I bet you love this letter, with all the pictures that I have done for you. I found a picture of a butterfly and as you can see, I put it up in the top corner, as I know how much you love butterflies.

What about these cute little teddy bears, they're so cute. I love the Teddy that you have, the one that has a photo of me on there.

I can't wait to see you this coming Sunday, and we'll see if you have the guts to say to my face that I'm not the best tickler, and if you do I'm going to hold you down and tickle you, the we'll see then who you say is the best. ☺

Lots & lots of love,
Always & forever,
Your loving father
-xoxoxoxoxoxoxox

20 November 2008 to George Williams

George Williams was Carl's father. In 1999 he and Carl were charged with drug offences after George's Broadmeadows property was raided by police and drugs were found. The charges were later dropped. However, he was jailed in 2007 for four and a half years after pleading guilty to smuggling 5 kilograms of amphetamines for Carl. This letter had a decorative border to accompany the illustration of a prisoner's hands behind bars.

Mr. Carl Williams
C/- Melaleuca Unit
Locked Bag No. 7
Lara. Vic. 3212

Dear Dad,
I trust this letter finds you in the best of health and spirits, as it leaves me fine.

It was good to hear your voice today, I know that I was running short of calls, but I really do enjoy talking to you for 2 calls, instead of one – one call's just not enough.

Rob Stary was supposed to get out here to see me today, this afternoon, but he couldn't make it, so he said he'll get up here for sure on Monday afternoon. It'll be good to see him on Monday, and just nut everything out, so we're ready for my appeal – which isn't far away, it's on couple of months – February the 5th, just after Christmas, not far is it.

Dad I spoke to Rob Stary today about your TAX issue, and I asked him about Graeme Steart, and he said as far as he knows he'd be a good choice to look after you with your TAX,[25] as he's a criminal Solicitor as well as Civil, and I for one think you need someone who works in both departments. I'll talk to you more about it when I see you on the video link, and I'll be talking to Rob more about it when I see him.

I seen Roberta and Rob[26] today, on a box visit, it wasn't a bad visit, they're funny, fuck she bosses him around.

Dhakota's coming up here to see me on Monday, Stacey's bringing her and mum up here, and I'm looking forward to

25 George Williams owed the ATO $700,000 as at October 2011. Williams agreed to pay $576,000 to the ATO, a figure he had earlier argued was to be paid by Victoria Police as part of negotiations for his son's cooperation.

26 Rob Carpenter, Roberta's partner.

seeing them. It's always a good visit with them, we're in the big room, we'll have to play stack on – what do you reckon?

Christmas isn't far away now – only 5 weeks away, that's another year gone.

Ange still hasn't been sentenced as yet, he was found guilty in June (5 months ago), had a Plea hearing in October, and now he gets sentenced when ever suits Betty,[27] that's fucking bullshit – that's not how it suppose to work, surely the accused has a right to know where he stands.

I haven't really got much else to add, therefore I'll leave it there for now, and I hope to hear from you again soon.

Best wishes & respect, ____________________________

21 November 2008 to Danny Heaney

Dear Danny,
I trust this letter finds you in the best of health and spirits, as it leaves me fine.

I just received your letter that you wrote to me this morning, and it was good to hear from you again, as it always is. I must thank-you for the kind words you wrote in your letter, they meant alot to me, and touched my heart, they really did – so thank-you again. I know what not only me, but also my family have been through over let's say the last 10 years, and it hasn't been easy to say the least. And to be honest with you – I'm not pumping

27 Justice Betty King.

my own tyres up, but I don't know too many people, if any, who could've done what I did, and continue to do. Yeh I'm sure lots of people will say that they could've and would've done the same, but as we both know most people are full of shit, and delusional, it's hard for them to turn anything into reality, when they're dreaming all the time, firstly to accomplish anything they must wake up.

Hey, before I forget to tell you, I would never take offence to anything you said to me, I've always respected you, I know you speak your mind, that's why from time to time I do ask you for your advice, you're a true friend, and one I'm very proud to have.

Yesterday I spoke to my dad about all these offers of late, and he said to me if they want you to talk about coppers, and you know anything at all about them, go for it, and do whatever you can to help yourself. He seems to be going along Ok, his hip is playing up a little bit, he needs a hip replacement, maybe he'll get one when he gets out. On top of that, the TAX Department are trying there upmost to take his house off him, which his owned for the last 30 years – they are fucking kidding aren't they, they want him to get out homeless, with nothing at all, it fucking wrong isn't it.

So Dave's[28] up for his Appeal, his case is full of Corruption – just ask him, read the brief and you judge for yourself, because I've read it. ☺

I haven't really got much else to add, therefore I'll leave it there for now, and I hope to hear from you again soon.

Best wishes & respect,

---

28 David McCulloch.

21 November 2008 to Tony Mokbel

Dear Tony,

I hope everything is going as good as it can be for you over there. I'm guessing that you must be pretty busy. I bet you're probably thinking to yourself right now what makes him say that. Well it has been about 3 weeks, and you still haven't responded to my last letter. ☺

I hear that you finally got your computer. Good, it will help you kill heaps of time, and now I should get a letter more regularly, as you've lost your handbrake. I'm a bad writer, I'm not the best speller – give me a spell – now you have no excuses.

It's already Christmas time again, it's here in about another 5 weeks. Another year's gone – gee time flies when you're having fun, before I know it I'll be fronting the Parole board.

Since you're now here – locked up, that is – if you can, and I'm not pushing the friendship. I'd be very grateful, and in debt to you, if you could get a $2000 gift voucher from Emido for me, for Stacey for Christmas. Sorry to ask, but there's not a lot of people I'd ask to do anything for me, as I wouldn't let them have it over me – thanks.

With best wishes and respect,
Your friend always, ______________________________

CHAPTER 2

'The sudden passing away of my mother'

When Barbara Denman married George Williams in 1966, he was a small-time crim; she was from a dirt-poor family of eleven and was already pregnant with the couple's first child, Shane. It was not exactly a fairytale marriage and there was much for Barb to forgive over the years that followed, particularly when her sister Kathleen Bourke fell pregnant with George's child. This boy was ultimately raised by Kath and her husband; another son of Kathleen's was John Bourke, the notorious Collingwood footballer who was banned from the game for ten years.

Barb had two sons with George: Shane, who died from a drug overdose in 1997, and Carl, who she adored, even though she never approved of his marriage to Roberta.

Everyone said Carl was a 'mother's boy' and, even after his marriage, he spent as much time with his mother as he did with Roberta. Barb once offered this doting description of him: 'He was just so gentle. I've only ever seen him get angry two or three times in his lifetime. He used to just wake up every morning just smiling, happy.'

But by late November 2008 Barbara Williams was in a state of despair. She had been in court when Carl was sentenced to life imprisonment; in fact she had been ejected from the courtroom that day when she had shouted at Justice Betty King: 'You are a puppet for corruption. You are a puppet of Purana; you don't deserve your wig and your gown.'

The previous year her estranged husband, George, had been sentenced to four and a half years' jail for trafficking a commercial quantity of methylamphetamine.

She had been depressed before but this was something different altogether. Seeing Carl in prison was the hardest thing she had ever had to endure. It was confirmation of the utter failure of her family. It had begun with her first son, Shane, and his descent into heroin addiction and crime. Barb and George had done everything they could to save him, paying for expensive rehab and counselling. By the end, Shane had wanted to die, he had given up. His eventual death was something of a release for the family. Carl had stepped up and supported the family, organising Shane's funeral down to the last detail. She had known Carl was trafficking drugs by that time too but she could console herself that he was doing it for his family, to give her the life that she and George deserved. When Carl began killing his rivals, she persuaded herself that he was in the right and would somehow come out on top. She had lived in a fantasy world that came crashing down with the 35-year sentence Carl was handed. It felt like anything she had ever valued was sliding into a sinkhole, taking her with it.

On the evening of 21 November 2008, Barb phoned her only granddaughter, Dhakota, and asked her, as she often did, to sing her favourite song, the old lullaby made famous by Jimmy Boyd and Frankie Laine in 1953: 'Tell me a story, tell me a story . . . Tell me a story, then I'll go to bed.' When Dhakota finished singing, Barb told her she loved her.

Barb then filled a glass with champagne and, using a black eyeliner pencil, she scrawled on the mirror of her en suite bathroom the words 'I'm sorry'. Washing down a generous handful of sleeping pills with her champagne, she lay back on her bed and slowly allowed her life to drift away.

Barbara's body was discovered by relatives and a local shopkeeper after they forced their way into the house in Primrose Street, Essendon, where she had lived alone under tight security. Roberta was photographed by the media weeping in a car outside the home.

Barb's funeral, on 30 November, was held at the Melbourne underworld's favourite church, St Therese's Catholic Church in Essendon (the funeral of rival underworld boss Lewis Moran, one of Carl's many victims, had also been held there). Fifteen minutes before the service, George Williams arrived on day release. Carl remained in jail, deemed too great a security risk to attend the funeral; Roberta hired a cameraman to film the service and he viewed it later.

Carl watched Roberta deliver a moving eulogy she had prepared for the occasion. She told the gathering: 'Barb stood up to our enemies, the police and even Supreme Court judges because she believed loyalty was a lifetime thing, not just a luxury for when things were going well. She knew loyalty was a sacrifice and she was prepared to pay the cost. She loved us unconditionally.'

Carl had written a death notice for Barbara in the newspaper: 'There's nothing in the world I would not have done for you. Losing you is the hardest thing I have ever had to deal with.'

No doubt saddened by this unexpected loss, Carl nonetheless recovered quickly enough to perceive that here was an opportunity for him to petition the authorities to allow his father to come and share his cell with him. Other than his girlfriend, Stacey Vella, he felt deserted by his friends and needed his dad's company.

He was hoping that he and George would be joined by Tommy Ivanovic, a pastry chef and drug dealer who was a trusted member of the Williams gang and had been sentenced to eighteen years' jail for a murder in 2002. Tommy was Dhakota Williams' godfather.

Carl's mind was also occupied with more significant issues that would have a bearing on his future. With his mother gone, police knew that Carl was vulnerable and open to offers that might result in him passing on information about unsolved murders, especially the 2004 slaying of police informer Terry Hodson and his wife, Christine. The Purana investigators believed that the assassin was Rodney Collins, who had been a hitman for Carl.

The saga had begun in 2003 when Hodson, in the company of drug squad officer David Miechel, attempted to burgle a drug house in suburban Oakleigh in Melbourne connected to Carl's ally Tony Mokbel. The pair were caught and Hodson agreed to give evidence against Miechel and other drug squad officers.

Before Hodson could give evidence he and his wife were murdered in their Kew home. The killing of Christine Hodson appalled Carl. Killing an informer was one thing, but the cold-blooded execution of a wife and mother was another.

While Barb was alive, Carl would never confess to being connected to the Hodson murders but now she was gone he was no longer bound by that shame. The Purana Taskforce was determined to charge Paul Dale with the murders but they needed Carl's assistance (Dale has always denied any involvement with the Hodson murders). This was the last cheque he could cash, a final piece of leverage to improve his conditions in Barwon, or maybe even to get home early. However, he knew such a course of action was fraught with danger if his cellmates ever got wind of it, which was almost inevitable.

Behind the scenes, his father George was in favour of Carl assisting police and that would prove decisive in Carl's thinking. As he weighed the risks and rewards, Carl gave away no inkling of these matters in his correspondence.

27 November 2008 to Danny Heaney

Dear Danny
I trust this letter find you in the best of health and spirits, as it leaves me as good as can be under the current circumstances.

Last night I just received your letter, and yes, it was my pleasure to hear from you again, as it always is. You're 100 % right I don't really feel like writing of talking to anyone, however you aren't just anyone.

Late yesterday afternoon I was refused permission to attend my mother's funeral, surprise, surprise, I seen that coming from a mile away. I will say though the GM,[29] the stand in Governor Mr Martin, and Mr Heffernan have been fantastic to me during these tough times, I couldn't be more happier with the way they have been treating me – the decision not to let me attend came from the city. Over the recent years I've realized its always best to hope for the best, but always expect and prepare yourself for the worst – that way you don't drive yourself mad, nor will you be disappointed. With all these cocksucking media outlets, running poles to vote whether I should, or shouldn't be allowed to go to my mum funeral obviously doesn't do me any favour, but what can you do my name sell papers.

Thankfully, they will be allowing my dad to attend my mum's funeral, well at least that's a good thing for him. I just hope they find it in their hearts to allow him to be moved down here with me after the funeral, to finish off his sentence with me. As that would make life easier for the both of us, and ease both our pain by up to 90%, one can only hope they show compassion in that department, surely I'm well overdue for a change of luck.

29 David Prideaux was general manager of Barwon at this time; he disappeared on a hunting trip in Victoria's high country in June 2011.

I don't really have much more to add, so I guess I'll leave it there for now, and I hope to hear from you again soon.

Best wishes & respect,
Your friend always – Carl

28 November 2008 to Sean Sonnet

Sean Sonnet was sentenced to twenty years' gaol by Justice Betty King in May 2008. He was accused of going to Brighton Cemetery on 9 June 2004, with co-offender Gregg Hildebrandt, to shoot Mario Condello on Carl's orders.

Dear Sean,
I trust this letter find you in the best of health and spirits, as it leaves me getting better and stronger day by day, however let me tell you this is by far the hardest thing that I've ever had to deal with. I really feel so sorry for Dhakota, as her and my mum were so close, she seems to be accepting things and coping really well at the moment, I only hope it stays that way, she's such a strong little girl, who has been through a lot in her 7 years of life.

I just received your letter, and it was good to hear from you again.

Roberta told me that you've been keeping in contact with her, and you've been asking how I'm holding up – thanks for being concerned.

I'm trying my best to get my dad down here with me, I feel if his here with me I'll be 1 million percent better. I only hope Corrections show compassion and let him finish off the remaining of his sentence here with me.

Sean my mum really did like you, and she had a lot of time for you, she would always tell me off for shit stirring you, as she said that you are a true friend.

With best wishes and respect,
Your friend always – Carl

Ps) Please give my best to Rod and Jason[30] – thanks

28 November 2008 to Rod Wise

Rod Wise was acting commissioner, Corrections Victoria, during the time Carl was incarcerated at Barwon.

Dear Mr Wise,
I am writing to you to request for my father, Mr. George Williams, to be moved down here with me to finish off the remaining of his sentence, on compassionate grounds, after the sudden passing away of my mother. If he were here with me, I am sure it would help improve my mental wellbeing, as well as his. I have spoken to him about this, and I know this is what he would like too, he is keen to be moved down here with me – even though the condition here are more restricted.

If for some reason you do not want to move him down here to be with me for the remaining of his sentence, could you please find it in your heart to move him down here for at least one or two months

Thank-you very much for your time.

30 Jason Roberts.

I look forward to your response in writing, in regards to the above-mentioned matter, at your earliest convenient time.

Yours Sincerely,
CARL WILLIAMS.

28 November 2008 to Milad Mokbel

Dear Milad,
I trust this letter finds you in the best of health and spirits, as it leaves me fine.

I just received your letter, and it was good to hear from you again, as it always is.

I see they gave Renate more time, another 6 months. I honestly thought she'd get more time for that, only because they can do it to her. It's fucking wrong, unfortunately she's been fucked over the poor woman. She should never have served one days jail, now by the time she gets out she would've done 2 ½ years, and for what ***– for nothing***. I don't think she did anything wrong – intentionally anyway. Mate I'm going to be honest with you, I'm really concerned about her, there's only so much she can take.

As you know I was waiting for my computer to arrive, and thank-god it arrived last week, it is the best thing that I could have brought, I am so happy with it. It has Bose speakers, Sony headphones, a Logitech wave keyboard – which is ideal for me to learn how to touch type, which is what I want to do. Everyday I'm slowing learning more and more things on it. I've been playing the car racing games on it (Grid & V8 Supercars 3), as well as poker, and at first in the car racing all I was doing was smashing into everything, but within a few minutes I improved, and it's fun – it helps beat the boredom that exists in this place anyway.

On Monday I had another video link up with my dad, I get one every month for 1 hour, which is good, it's better than phone calls, because at least I get to see him, even if it's only over a TV. In addition, it saves me $1o (ha ha). He seems to be going along ok; he only has 8 months to go now, not long is it.

Last night I received a belated B/Day card from Melanie, which was nice of her. I wrote straight back to her, and sent my letter to the address you gave me in Dubai, is she still there? Let her know that the card was nice BUT I have one complaint, she never enclosed any photos with her card ☺. However, she can make up for that, and send them to me ASAP – True?

I do not really have much else to say, therefore I will leave it there for now, and hopefully I hear from you again soon.

Best wishes, your friend always – Carl

Ps) Please give my best to your Mum, Renate and the kids – thanks

1 December 2008 to Danny Heaney

Dear Danny,

I trust this letter finds you in the best of health and spirits, as it leaves holding up ok, Danny this is by far the hardest thing that I have ever had to deal with, I feel so empty.

I just received your letter and it was good to hear from you again, as it always is.

As you know they refused my request to attend my mum funeral, and then today after we were locked up for the day, the General Manger and Governor came and wanted to talk to me, they had no good news for me – what's new? They said my request to view my mum's body has also been reused – just what I expected to hear.

However, I do believe the GM and Governor tried there hardest to push my request though, I firmly believe they are both pretty decent people – they have been so supportive – but it's the powers above that like to play God, and thump there chest who denied my request. Carl Williams give him nothing – he stood up for himself, and whilst doing so killed the states informers – what a fucken joke. You know I would've liked to go view her, but on the same token I want to remember her from the last time I seen her, smiling, laughing, and playing chasing with Dakota and I in the visit centre. So I'm not to fussed about that request being refused after all what can I do, what's the point in me doing head miles over things that I have absolutely no control over.

They said that they'd be back here tomorrow, to see me and let me know if there's any further news on my dad, and him being moved down here with me. I'm hoping for the best, but expecting the worst – that way I can't be disappointed. I know 100% for sure if I were to tell the Police what they wanted to hear, my dad would be here with me in the blink of an eye, I could have anything I wanted – its fucken wrong.

I'll leave it there for now, and I hope to hear from you again soon.

Best wishes, your friend always – Car

Ps, Danny believe it or not tonight I actually received a card from Roy boy[31] – the red rat, giving me his condolences, I for one thought that was nice of him – especially when people I've known and spoon fed for year can't even send one. Out of sight out of mind, however if were to take that deal offered, they would be a few back here – who'd I'd actually beat home. ☺

31 Roy Anthony 'Red Rat' Pollitt.

5 December 2008 to Danny Heaney

Dear Danny,
I trust this letter finds you in the best of health and spirits, as it leaves holding up ok.

Last night I received your card and it was good to hear from you again as it always is.

I am glad my mum's funeral is now over, hopefully they'll now leave her to rest. Roberta did a terrific job in organizing it all, I can't praise her enough for what she did, I am so proud of her, and how she stepped up in a time of need and did what she did for my mum, my dad, Dhakota and I. I know at times her and my mum never seen eye to eye, but for her to step up like she did, will never go unforgotten from me.

On Wednesday a barrister came up here to visit me. I never knew him prior to me coming to jail. He offered to help out with any expenses for the funeral if needed. He also offered to help me, and my dad out with our monthly money if we needed it, and believe it not his the only person who had made an offer like that, and there are scumbags outside at the moment who owe me money, and have been spoon fed from me all their lives. It really makes my stomach turn how the majority of the population are.

As you're aware I had a visit with my dad the other day, it was so good to see him, and just give him a hug. I'm still battling to get him down here with me, who knows it might happen, one can only try.

As I have told you before, I could not agree with you more the GM is a decent bloke, and I firmly believe that he has done everything in his power to try to make this difficult time for me, as easy as he possible can.

I'll leave it there for now, and I hope to hear from you again soon.

Best wishes, your friend always – Carl

5 December 2008 to Dhakota Williams

Dear Dhakota,
Well hello there my beautiful daughter, who I love with all my heart, I'm so proud of you, you are the best daughter – there's no-one better than you.

I'm going ok, just missing you like crazy, I'm trying to keep myself busy by learning things in the computer, and playing games, which I'm enjoying its fun.

I am looking so forward to seeing you on Sunday.

I've been loving talking to you on the phone. I could talk to you all day, and all night, and still not have enough of you.

Hey I was going through my photos, and I found an old picture of your mum – don't let her know I said that, otherwise she'll bash the both of us up. ☺ Ok tell her if you want – but if she hits me, you had better help me – or else!

I hope I get a letter from you soon, as I love it when I get letters from you.

Well my gorgeous girl, I'll leave it there for now, and I hope you get off you bum and write back to me, as you know how happy that would make me – so do it don't just talk about it.

Lots & lots of love,
Always & forever, you loving Dad
-xxoxoxoxoxoxoxox-

7 December 2008 to Danny Heaney

Dear Danny,

I hope this letter finds you fit and well, as it leaves me fine.

I just thought I would drop you a quick few lines to say hello, keep you updated on what's going on regarding my dad placement, and see if you can check with Barb[32] from the canteen, to see if she has any new cards, love feelings, and blank. If she has them, can you please get her to put anything up to 10 away for me, say 5 love feeling cards for Stacey – a couple of good blank cards, and a few others for Dhakota, let me know when you write back how many to order and I'll order them next canteen.

In addition, can you let me know what T/Bag they have, and anything else new that they now have on the canteen?

Last Friday I received a letter from Brendan Money, who is the Assistant Commissioner, Offender Management Services, in response to a letter I wrote to him, requesting that my dad be placed down here with me on compassionate grounds at the very least. I will quote you a couple of paragraphs he wrote to me, word for word.

I understand the difficult time you are experiencing giving the recent passing of your mother and I acknowledge there is likely to be a number of emotional and practical family issues that you need to deal with.

As you are aware, there has been a range of previous correspondence explaining that your father is a minimum security prisoner and therefore his placement in high Security is not appropriate.

32 The Barwon Prison civilian employee who ran the prison canteen. She was well-known for being a compassionate person.

I accept your circumstances have altered in recent weeks however; I am still reluctant to place your father in a high security environment.

You father has a range of issues and individual needs that are best facilitated in his current location, and I am hesitant to disrupt what is a relative stable situation at the moment.

What a load of shit that is, who is he supposed to talk at the moment, about how he feeling, the wall, or some junkie who hits up someone else's spit, its bullshits, and it really does frustrate the shit out of me. We both need to be with each other especially at this current stage, and I will keep battling to get him down here with me. They aren't looking after his best interest, and they know it – it's wrong Danny, it really is.

Let's say I never plead guilty when I did to the murders – and they charged my dad as they were going to do with murder, would they have placed him here with me, or somewhere else to look after his health – need I say anymore.

On a brighter note, today I had a really good visit with Stacey, Dhakota and Brea. We had a laugh, and whilst I was with them, it helped keep my mind off my mum for that short period. I still can't believe she gone, and I'll never see her or talk to her again, I miss her so much, I just can't seem to accept she did what she did, I have to many unanswered questions. Dhakota is coping well with it, she such a strong little girl, Stacey keeps an eye on her, and tries to spend as much time with her as she can, my mum was such a positive influence on Dhakota, I just hope Dhakota remains strong like she currently is.

I've been told that I will soon be moving back to Acacia Unit 3, with Tony, I think that'll do me the world of good, the sooner I move the better, in this unit I'm confined to a little unit all day, with virtually nothing do, no sunlight, just a treadmill and bike, I've done 14 months here – that's enough.

Well buddy I haven't really got much else to add, therefore I'll leave it there for now, and I hope to hear from you again soon.

Best wishes and respect,

Your friend always – Carl

10 December 2008 to Danny Heaney

Dear Danny,

I trust this letter finds you in the very best of health, and spirits, as for me travelling along the best I can be.

I received your letter last night, and it was good to hear from you again, as it always is.

You're 100% correct, cream always rises to the top, its living proof isn't it? It really makes my stomach turn how some so-called friends have turned out. Over the past few weeks, I've really thought long and hard about a lot things, and mate at the end of the day, the only think I keep coming back to is, that 99.9 % of the population, or unfortunately the people we know, believe that when times get tough it is every man for themselves – sad but true.

I am still finding it extremely difficult to accept that my mum has gone, and I will never see her, or hear her voice again – I use to look so forward to talking to her every morning on the phone – she gave me so much strength, and she never even knew it. I honestly feel like 75% of me is now missing, fuck it's hard, I really hope in time it gets easier. In my life, I have endured a lot, but nothing compares to this, whatever I have gone through in the past is not even 10% of what I'm currently going through – after losing my mum.

I agree with you the sooner they move me back to Acacia Unit 3, where Tony is the better, this Unit I'm currently in is to confined, there's nothing at all to do, and I have at least another 5–10 years of these environments to look forward too – Woohoo.

I don't really have much more to add, therefore I will leave it there for now.

Keep in touch – and I hope to hear from you again soon.

Best wishes & respect,
Your friend always – Carl

10 December 2008 to Beau Goddard

Dear Beau,
I trust this letter find you in the best of health and spirits, as it leaves me fine.

Over the past week or so I have received a few letters/Cards from you – sorry I haven't replied until now, I just haven't been in the mood to write – I'm sure you understand – thanks for your support Beau, it really does means a lot to me – as I know you genuinely mean it.

You know when my mum passed away – a lot of people who are currently on the outside, and who I have helped out over the years, never even had the decency to make contact with Roberta, or anyone, simply to ask if any help was need with anything. I guess when you're in here for years and years like I'm going to be, people forget you, people have short memories.

So Milad's had an argument with a screw, and has found himself in the slot – did Milad overcook the screws bacon, or put too much sugar in his coffee. I couldn't imagine him arguing with a screw – oh well maybe now he might now realise there not his friends.

Can you please let Brendan[33] know that I received the poster he sent me, and tell him I said thanks heaps.

---

33 Brendon Goddard, AFL footballer and Beau's half-brother.

Well buddy I don't really have much more to add, therefore I'll leave it there for now, and hopefully I hear from you again soon.

With best wishes and respect,
Your friend always – Carl

11 December 2008 to Dhakota Williams

Carl Williams

C/- Melaleuca Unit
Locked Bag No. 7.
LARA VIC. 3212

Dear Dhakota,

Hello my beautiful, gorgeous, daughter, how are you going? Good I hope, as for me I'm good.

As you can see, in this letter, I have put 4 pictures of monkeys. One is of you (the cutest one up the top holding the balloon) – one is your mum – one is Stacey and the other is Nan, Nan is the one with her hands in the air like she use to do when you and her played chasy up here, when you were seeing me.

Who do you this this one is ????? Ok you do not know, so I will give you a hint – I am stressed, depressed, I have a headache, and have no money, you guessed it in one, need I say any more. I never said that is whom it is you did.

So that means this one of here is who? – Don't tell me you need another hint – ok I will give you one. How would you like your hair cut love? – Like mine (ha ha)

I hope you lied this letter and it gave you a laugh, I love you Dhakota so, so, much.

Lots & lots of love,
Always & forever,
Your Dad –XOXOXO–

14 December 2008 to Tommy Ivanovic

Tommy Ivanovic was a pastry chef by trade, and a trusted member of the Williams gang. He was serving a fifteen-year sentence for a 2002 murder in Barwon Prison and was later to become Carl's cellmate in Acacia Unit.

Dear Tommy,
On Friday the Police who are investigating my mother's death (Paul Rowe[34]), came and seen me at my request – I had a few unanswered questions which I wanted to ask them, about my mother, as they were really troubling me. Without going into any detail, the answers I got have were the ones I was looking for – which did put my mind at rest a little bit.

I know my mum was fighting a battle – although I honestly thought both Dhakota and I would get her through. Just the thought of losing your house, car ect ect, at 60 years old, without any of the other stress would be more than enough to trouble anyone, it was a combination of factors.

However when Paul Rowe was here I asked him what's going on with Milad. I asked him how long does he think Milad will get. He said 5 years minimum, although the Crown reckon 10, and the other charges he has he's also trying to do a deal to plea with some part concurrent & the rest on top.

Tony: the murders – who cares? The drug ones, especially the company[35] from overseas, is the strongest case against him according to all the smarties. He can't possibly beat that one, however if he goes to trial and loses on that one (which he'll do) they will give him the maximum – life – without a minimum term. Interesting days lay ahead.

I haven't really got that much else to add, therefore I will leave it there for now, and I hope to hear from you again soon.

Best wishes & respect,
Your friend always – Carl

---

34 Detective Sergeant Paul Rowe is a prominent police investigator who was later responsible for convicting Adrian Bayley for the notorious rape and murder of Jill Meagher.

35 This is a reference to Mokbel's operation of his drug business while in Greece. There were extensive telephone intercepts and witness statements attesting to its operation.

15 December 2008 to Tony Mokbel

Dear Tony,

I just received your letter, and it was my pleasure to hear from you again, as it always is.

You're doing well on the treadmill. 12 kms in a hour is good, keep it up, it's good for you mentally. I haven't been on it that much lately, but when I do I only do 10–10½ km in one hour. I jumped on there the other day, and I did 30 minutes speed 10, and I was fucked. I've been riding the bike a fair bit – as whilst I'm on there, I read, and it takes my mind off things.

You asked me my thoughts on Julian McMahon. From all the good judges I've ever spoke to, he's the best Junior barrister around – very thorough, good reader, and preparer. How is he on his feet? I have no idea. As for Terry Forrest (QC), I do not know him, nor have ever met him.

Mate I'm going to be completely honest with you, and tell you something that you probably don't want to hear. I don't think it matters if you have 10 Robert Richters, the way the media have portrayed you – like they did me – unfortunately the chances of you winning are minimal. The chances of you getting 8–9 acquittals are zero to none. Is it fair? No – but it is the truth, unfortunately.

Believe me, I know it's extremely hard to accept, but once you accept that, you must accept on top of that, that you will be doing a large portion of your sentence in these environments – which isn't healthy for anyone. Limited contact visits, limited phone calls, ect, ect, – it's very political. I hate telling you this; however, after going through it all myself, I firmly believe this is the truth. I hope that they move me over there with you soon, then I can talk to you face to face.[36]

36 Once it became known that Carl was cooperating, people in the system began to doubt his motives in seeking to have former associates placed with him

I will get Stacey to ring your mate, and then go there wherever best suits him – again, can you please thank him very much for his generosity.

Keep in touch, and I hope to hear from you again soon.

With best wishes and respect,
Your friend always – Carl

30 December 2008 to Danny Heaney

Dear Danny,
I just received a card from you, and it was good to hear from you again, as it always is.

Now for some good news my dad is here with me, his my next door neighbour, at the moment there's only the two of us are in this unit. Yesterday they moved Ocka,[37] Dale and Matty over to unit 2 of Acacia, and moved my dad in here with me. From what I've been told, I'm led to believe that they will be moving my dad, me and Matty[38] into Unit 3 of Acacia really soon – for that well overdue rotation with Tony, Ange and Barry Q.[39] – the boys over there won't at all be impressed about that move. Unit 3 is better than here for dad's health, and with only 3 of us in there the door will remain open at all times, and we'll have the unit to ourselves, all day access to cells, dayroom, gym, and yard – which will be good.

---

or to have face-to-face contact in management units. It was well known that listening devices were constantly deployed in Barwon during this period, not only indoors, but out in the small attached yards of the management units housing the so-called 'gangland inmates'.

37 Ocka Scholes.

38 Matthew Johnson, who had become Carl's cellmate at the beginning of 2009.

39 Name changed for legal reasons.

It's been good to see him, he looks ok, but I can tell everything is or has taking its toll on him.

Thank-God Christmas has been and gone, all I need now is for the next couple of days to hurry up and and pass – and then we'll be into a new year.

Would you believe this one, not one single person from the outer, made contact with me, or Roberta, to ask if I need any money to buy a Christmas present for Dhakota – not one!

I don't really have much up to add, therefore I guess I will leave it there for now, and I hope to hear from you again soon.

With best wishes & respect,
Your friend always – Carl

ALL THE BEST FOR THE NEW YEAR

CHAPTER 3

A well-overdue rotation

Carl took a short top-secret break from Barwon Prison a few days before Christmas 2008. Faced with an eternity of jail time ahead of him and the slow desertion of so many of his accomplices, he had finally decided to assist police.

On 22 December Carl secretly left Barwon in the hands of officers from Petra Taskforce, which had been established to investigate the murder of Terry and Christine Hodson. They believed Carl had been instrumental in hiring the hitman who killed the Hodsons, and that he could tell them who had ordered the double execution. By quietly removing Carl from prison and interviewing him over the course of a week, they intended to get Carl's version of the events surrounding this unsolved mystery.

Also present during that week was Carl's father, George, who had been brought from Dhurringile Prison, near

Shepparton. George had first been taken to Barwon for the night and then, blindfolded, placed in a prison van that seemed to go round and round for about an hour, possibly to disorient him. When it arrived at its final destination he caught the unmistakable smell of the sea.

George and Carl reunited in a lounge room, where they were left to their own devices. They had no idea where they were until George flipped over a *Foxtel* magazine that had been carelessly left on a table. It bore the address of their location: Swan Island, a top-secret military base off the coast of Victoria, which is joined to nearby Queenscliff by a causeway and has become a training ground for Australia's special forces and counterterrorism teams.

There was to be no record of the interrogation that took place there. Not even Barwon's governor knew where Carl was going. There would be no records beyond the taped interviews; the police involved simply wrote in their diaries that they were at an 'undisclosed location'. If the media heard of it, Carl's life might be in danger.

Within a fortnight the Melbourne *Sunday Herald Sun*'s Peter Rolfe got wind of the fact that Carl and George had taken a 'coastal holiday' and splashed news of it in their issue of 11 January 2009 under the intriguing headline 'Carl Williams coastal mystery'.

Fortunately, the *Herald Sun* either did not know or chose not to publish where they had been holidaying. Surf Coast Mayor Libby Meares said authorities would have been lucky to find a vacant house then, at the peak of the holiday season: 'There is a high occupancy at that time of year, so they must have good resources,' she said. 'I can say for certain Carl hasn't been sighted in the main street of Aireys Inlet or Torquay.' In fact Carl and his dad had been housed in a military brig on Swan Island, talking interminably to Petra detectives.

As police interrogators pushed Carl for more and more details on the Hodson murders and other criminal activities, they even arranged for Carl's girlfriend, Stacey Vella, to visit him on the island. There was a later claim that the police even laid on a couple of prostitutes, but George denied this and said there was no sex. Just plenty of food.

George told Shand that the cops had wanted the pair of them to extend their stay for another week, but Carl was anxious that his absence would be noticed at Barwon and that dangerous conclusions might be drawn from it by interested parties. He said that so long as the police were as good as their word on what had been agreed, he would sign statements drawn up from his taped interviews.

It had been agreed that the police would pay Dhakota's school fees at Penleigh and Essendon Grammar School, and also $750,000 that George owed the tax office. There would be a reduction in Carl's sentence of up to seventeen years, but there also needed to be discussion about who his future cellmates would be. Carl needed people around him he could trust, particularly if anyone suspected him of turning dog. It was agreed that George would do the rest of his time at Acacia with Carl, but George was also about to get a reduction in his sentence as part of the deal with Petra. There was one spot to fill while George was there, and then, after that, there would be two vacancies.

Carl desperately wanted Tony Mokbel and Ange Goussis to join him, but this was refused. Carl's next choice was Matthew Charles Johnson. The screws knew that Carl and Matty seemed to get on well and, given that Johnson had no links to the Gangland War, that seemed acceptable. But clearly Carl's safety depended on confidentiality being maintained around the circumstances of his pre-Christmas break.

He returned to Barwon on 29 December and George joined him there. Ominously, soon after the pair's return a senior screw came up to them and asked, 'So, how was the holiday on Swan Island?' Remarkably it took another sixteen months before the news hit the press. Adam Shand had been told about Carl's deal with police but declined to publish it for fear of the consequences from police and repercussions for Carl.

His time at Swan Island was only mentioned in passing in his extensive correspondence.

7 January 2009 to Kevin Farrugia

Kevin Farrugia was a violent kidnapper and drug trafficker. On 11 March 2009 his jail sentence was extended by a further sixteen months for the illegal possession of firearms.

Dear Kev,
I trust this letter finds you in the best of health and spirits, as it leaves me fine.

I just received your letter dated 29/12, and it was my pleasure to hear from you again, as it always is.

It's been good to catch up with my dad, and spend time with him, he looks ok, but I can tell everything is, or has, taken its toll on him.

I actually tried getting you up her with my dad and I – but I think I have more chance of winning Tattslotto than that happening, and I don't even have a ticket.

Out of sight, out of mind – Kev I have 35 years to do, on top of the 3 years I already did, and I've been told that I will be kept here for another 10 years. People whom I spoon fed when I was outside, and I thought were my friends have dropped off – hardly anyone except for you and Mish, and obviously, Stacey brought Dhakota in for Xmas. When my mum passed away, no one asked if we needed any help to pay for her funeral. No one even asks if my dad and I are ok for our monthly money. Mate, times have changed, and so have people.

Thank God Christmas has been and gone, and we're into a new year.

Gangland Milly – hey, mate, the bloke's not all there thinking he'd get 6/4 years. He got 11/8 years, and he's still got another matter to front (*which he's trying to do a Plea to).* Oh yeah, he might not be very smart, but he can lift heavy things. If his brain were made out of dynamite, there would be insufficient material to blow his nose.

Stacey sees Mish a fair bit, Stacey really like her a lot, Mish is welcome at Stacey's place anytime. At least you know Stacey is genuine, and a sincere friend to her.

With best wishes & respect,
Your friend always – Carl

Ps) Please please give my best to your Mish, Ros and the rest of your family

7 January 2009 to Fabian Quaid

Dear Fab,
I received your letter the other day, and it was my pleasure to hear from you again, as it always is.

Thank-God Christmas has been and gone, and we're now into a new year.

That bloke you asked me, I personally don't know him, although I know he gave evidence against his co-accused.

Hey before I forget, I received a condolence card from Ray after my mum passed away, he said his going for bail – I don't like his chances of getting it.

I don't really have much up to add, therefore I guess I will leave it there for now, and I hope to hear from you again soon.

With best wishes & respect,
Your friend always – Carl

8 January 2009 to Barry Q.[40]

Dear Barry,
I trust this letter finds you and your family in the best of health, and spirits, as it leaves me fine.

I just received your letter dated 6/1/09, and it was my pleasure to hear from you again, as it always is.

As you know at the moment it's only my dad and I in this unit. Its been really good to catch up with him, and spend some time with him, even if it's under these circumstances, as the reality is we'll never get the opportunity to do it again on the outer.

I've been waiting for Matty to return back here with us. I have been assured that Matty will be back here soon. I actually thought he'd be back here today – but as you're more than well aware nothing happens quickly here – unless its bad of course – true?

It's good to hear you're doing some form on training, as it helps the day pass by quicker, and keeps you healthy both physically, and mentally. I've started jogging again, and I've only been doing 30–40 minutes on a much slower speed than I use to jog at, and mate it's been hard. It's amazing how quickly you go backwards once you have a break. I virtually stopped jogging after my mum passed away, which is now 6 weeks ago, as I just couldn't get motivated to do anything. When I go for a jog, my dad rides the bike.

Well buddy I haven't really got much more to add, therefore I'll leave it there for now, and I hope to hear from you again soon.

With best wishes & respect,
Your friends always – Carl

Ps) Please give my best to Tony and Ange

---

40 Name changed for legal reasons.

10 January 2009 to Milad Mokbel

Dear Milad,
I trust this letter finds you in the best of health and spirits, as it leaves me fine.

I haven't heard from you for awhile, so I thought I'd better drop you a quick few lines to say hello, and let you know that I haven't forgotten you.

I see you got 11/8 years, I personally think that was too much, as I said I never in a million years thought you'd get a minimum term of 3–4 years, like all the so called smarties – Solicitors and Barrister tried telling you you'd get, half the time they just tell you want you want to hear.

Than today I seen in the paper, they charged you over that ACC[41] bullshit, I think they give you some extra time for that, but what is anyone's guess, hopefully they don't go too hard on you.

I woke up this morning to see myself on the cover of the Sun, obviously there's not much going on throughout the world, or Victoria, for me to take the cover again, it's a fucken joke isn't it, surely that's story isn't worthy of the front pages, oh well life goes on.[42]

Today I had a visit with Stacey – it was her Birthday today – we had a good visit, it was only a box visit though – but tomorrow we have a contact visit, which I'm looking forward too.

With best wishes & respect, ____________________

41 Australian Crime Commission.

42 That week the *Herald Sun* newspaper had broken news of Carl and George's 'coastal holiday' on Victoria's Surf Coast but the exact location and the purpose of the week-long sojourn was not revealed.

12 January 2009 to Tony Mokbel

Dear Tony,
I was just about to drop you a line, as I hadn't heard from you in a while, but I did tonight, so yeah it's all good.

Peter Morrissey hey – I myself have never used him, but from what I hear he's ok, and tries hard. Mate I hate telling you this, however as I've previously told you, I don't think it matters who you have, you aren't going to get a fair go – and if you're found guilty, you aren't going to get a fair sentence. From what I've been told, if they find you guilty on the Drug matter (company) alone, they want to, and will be asking for you to get the maximum sentence.

I've actually been trying to get a visit with you, so that I can talk to you face to face.

Stacey often sees Dan[43] out the front of the prison, Stacey has been so supportive to me – mate she's been a blessing. I can't praise her enough. I hope Dan is handling things ok – I know it has to be hard on her, and if there's anything I can, or Stacey can do for her just let me know, and it will be done, not that I can do much from here. But Stacey's in the same, or similar situation as her, and she'll be there for her even if it's just for someone to talk too. Just let Dan know if she wants her number, I'm more than happy to give it to her. Stacey doesn't go out at all, or mix with many people. Just let Dan know, and I'll leave it up to you to get back to me if you want her number. Stacey's a hairdresser – she'll even do Dan's hair if she wants her to. Anything to help, or lift her spirits.

---

43 Danielle McGuire, Tony Mokbel's de facto wife.

Hey there was some watch at Emidio's that Stacey liked, but was too embarrassed to get. If it's not too much of a hassle, can you get Dan to pick out a nice watch for her from there, and give it to her when they catch up.

As to whom do you complain to about your conditions, I don't think anyone cares, or listens. They think these conditions are good, for us anyway, and they have the cheek to say we're insane. The problem is both you and I will be kept in these environments for years and years to come; and it's not good for us, and more so our loved ones.

Keep in touch, and I hope to hear from you again soon.

With best wishes and respect,
Your friend always – Carl

Ps) Please give my best to your mum, and also Dan and the kids – thanks

13 January 2009 to Sean Sonnet

Dear Sean,
I just received your letter, and it was my pleasure to hear from you again, as it always is.

I've been expecting to move over your way for the past 2 weeks, however the other day I was told by Mr. Pickering the move might happen soon, and he can't see no reason why it shouldn't, but he wants to wait for Mr. Prideaux to come back from holidays before it happens, and apparently he's back next week. Mate I'm like you though – I don't believe much of what I'm told, until it happens.

I didn't think it would just be my dad and I left in this unit alone – not for this long anyway – Ocka, Dale and Matty were all moved out when Mr. Prideaux wasn't here.[44]

Buddy, you know better than anyone what they're like, when there's not even a problem – they still err on the side of caution, as far as I can work out, the recent media reporting on me have threw a spanner in the works. I've been told that MOU are coming here tomorrow, so you can rest assure that I will be trying to see them, to see what's going on. Once I know what's doing – you'll be the next to know.

Now that Tye's been arrested, I wouldn't be at all surprised if they send him here with me.

I read in the paper the other day GANGLAND Milly got charged for refusing to take the oath at the ACC. From memory he was only following our advice. ☺ My dad was telling me that someone recently got 3 years for not taking the oath at the ACC.

Milly still has to front up on 2 large commercial quantity trafficking charges – which he'll Plea to. Potentially he could end up with another 8–10 years, on top of what he's already doing. The way things are going I'll beat poor old Milly out, you and I might be picking him up – in that red Mercedes of his, before taking him out on our 60 foot Yacht (ha ha). From what I hear Milly has his own boxing training academy at PPP. Believe it or not he's teaching people how to box – what the..........

With best wishes and respect,

Your friend always – Carl

---

44 David Prideaux, former acting/director of prisons and general manager at Barwon Prison, with Rod Wise, acting commissioner, Corrections Victoria, fought hard to prevent Matthew Johnson moving in with Carl. Prideaux and Wise believed that Johnson was both sociopathic and psychopathic.

14 January 2009 to Danny Heaney

Dear Danny,
I just received your letter dated Wednesday the 14th, what the fuck is going on, these days your letters have been making there way to me the same day you send them – not that I'm complaining. ☺

I could only imagine how the tongues are wagging – and when it comes to me, I guess they'll always be wagging – do I care – I couldn't give a fuck – nothing you or I say will ever stop people from talking – behind our backs that is, everyone seems to know what's going on – when they know nothing.

At the moment it's only still my dad and I in this Unit. Matty was due to return late last week, however when that story broke,[45] or they knew it was about to brake, the powers to be put the brakes on. Which threw a spanner in the works, however from what I believe, it should be sorted out sooner rather than later. I've been told that MOU will be here tomorrow to see me – and I'm hoping they have some positive news for me – such as my dad and I will be going to Acacia Unit 3 to be joined with Matty.

If they don't bring someone down here with us soon – I'll be requesting that both you and Tommy come down here with my dad and I – that'd be a good move, what's your thoughts on that one?? How's Tommy handling everything – I know at times he can be a stress head.

Now that Tye has been arrested, who knows where they will put him – if they put him in these environments, which is possible – naturally, I'll be trying my hardest to get him with me. I should have an answer tomorrow as to what they have in store for him.

45 Carl refers to the *Herald Sun*'s story about him and his father leaving prison for a week on Victoria's Surf Coast.

Well buddy, I haven't really got much more to add, therefore I'll leave it there for now, and I hope to hear from you again soon.

With best wishes & respect,
Your friends always – Carl

20 January 2009 to Danny Heaney

Dear Danny,
I just received your letter dated Wednesday the 19-1-09, and once again it was my pleasure to hear from you again, as it always is.

Today my dad and I seen MOU (Vicky Ryan),[46] and she said that Matty should hopefully be coming back here with soon, sooner rather than later – any day now.

Both my dad and I today raised with her, about us going over to Acacia Unit 3, as it has far better living conditions, better access to the Sunlight, whereas here you get virtually none. Access to the Gym, bigger cells, and dayroom, plus pool table, and table tennis table, it would be far better for my dad's health over there then it is here. She said that we wouldn't be going over there anytime soon, possibly in 6 months time – my dad only has 5 months to go. She said Tony has upcoming court cases, and they don't want to unsettle him, however Matty has a murder trial to commence in 2 weeks time, and there happy to send him back here. For fuck sake I've been here for 15 months. I'm more than happy to move over there and share the Unit with Tony. Ange has been there for nearly 4–5 years – he can have a stint here, surely, I am not the only one who has to spend time here? I thought there was going to be a rotation every 6–12 months

46 Vicki Ryan was the effective head of the major offender unit (MOU).

between here and there. 15–16 months ago Ange, Milad, and Horty all asked/requested to be moved over here, and when they got here they didn't like it, so they wanted to be returned back to Acacia Unit 3 – and they were moved directly back there within 2–3 weeks, at mine and Sean expense, as we were moved over here.

Thanks for the cards, there were a few good ones amongst them, a few I've already had before, but that doesn't matter. If any new ones do arrive, can you please pick 10–20 out, and put then aside under my dad's name, and he will order them once you give me the go-ahead.

Well buddy, I haven't really got much more to add, therefore I'll leave it there for now, and I hope to hear from you again soon.

With best wishes & respect,
Your friends always – Carl

21 January 2009 to Beau Goddard

Dear Beau,
Last night I received your letter, dated 16-1-09, and it was my pleasure to hear from you again, as it always is.

GANGLAND Milly – you like that one hey? He doesn't – so keep calling him it, that's what I use to do anyway (ha ha). Let me get this right, he honestly believes that if he gets found guilty on his other charges his facing. He thinks he'll only get another couple of years on top. Yeah right – what medication is he on? He thought he'd only get 3–4 years on the bottom on the ones he just fronted – and yet he got double. Hasn't he woke up and smelt the roses yet?

Actually about 18 months, when I was with him, he was telling both Sean and I that he'd only get 3–4 years. We both said we hope you're right – but personally, we don't think there's any chance in the world of you getting that. Anyway long story short, he bet both Sean and I each a block of chocolate – now since I'm not there to collect, I don't mind if you remind him of our bet and you collect. ☺.

It's good that you've got some youngies coming in to see you, when you have good visits it lifts your spirits.

Well buddy, I haven't got much else to add, therefore I will leave it there for now, and I hope to hear from you again soon.

With best wishes and respect,
Your friend always – Carl

Ps) Please give my best to Chinaman[47] – I have a lot of time for him.

47 Bill Ho.

CHAPTER 4
Three's company

On 23 January 2009, Matthew Johnson moved into Melaleuca with Carl and George. The only dissenting voices to this plan were those of acting commissioner, Corrections Victoria, Rod Wise and acting director of prisons David Prideaux.

Wise sent an email to Penny Armytage, the Department of Justice secretary, on 6 January 2009 expressing concern about the placement of Matty Johnson with Carl Williams. In the email, Wise said: 'There is little doubt that Johnson is capable of causing Williams harm if he were to find out the true nature of Williams' cooperation with police.'

Wise knew that Matty could be offered an attractive financial incentive and would enhance his reputation in the prison if he bashed Carl. He was already facing a 2007 murder charge so, if he was found guilty of that, any further jail sentence would run concurrently. He could effectively kill Carl for free.

In April 2012 the Victorian ombudsman noted in his report into Carl's death that 'notwithstanding these identified risks, [Corrections Victoria] had supported the placement of Mr Johnson with Mr Williams. However, this was conditional on the basis the placement be carefully monitored.'

In 1998 Matty had been involved in the savage bashing of triple murderer Greg Brazel in the Acacia Unit. Brazel had apparently used the metal stem of the seat from an exercise bike to defend himself while his attackers had gone to work on him with a sandwich maker. In light of Matty's past record, everyone should have been especially on their toes.

However, Carl himself held no fears about Matthew Johnson. He had been agitating for Johnson to be placed with him. George trusted Matty as well and so over the objections of Rod Wise the fateful placement was made. It's believed that Johnson knew of the assistance Carl gave police, but as long as it stayed secret, he was prepared to tolerate it.

22 January 2009 to Tommy Ivanovic

Dear Tommy,

I trust this letter finds you in the best of health, and spirits, as it leaves me fine.

I just received your letter dated 21st of January, and once again, it was my pleasure to hear from you again, as it always is.

You said my letters are getting shorter, and shorter. I don't know how you came up with that one, but never the less – whilst we're complaining – I wrote to you on the 6th and you replied to me on the 21st – 15 days later. ☺

My dad will be staying with me now until he finishes his sentence, which is now only 5 months away.

In regards to the papers, media, what can I say, they say and do as they please, they get 1 percent right, and guess the rest. Nothing you or I say will ever stop them, so I try not to let them bother me, otherwise I'll only drive myself mad. I'm over worrying about what others think – people will talk behind our backs regardless. But who are these people – some cunts who hit up other peoples spit, or someone who is irrevelant to my life, and was probably hiding when I was outside, and/or done everything in their power to get people to roll on me. I have nothing to prove to anyone, and to be honest with you I don't care about other people's opinions.

Tom, after spending just over 4 ½ years down here (or 8 years as the Pizza Maker[48] would say), and with my mum passing away, my thoughts have changed a little. I needed, and wanted to spend time with my dad, and every second I spend with him I treasure. Who knows how long he's going to live, naturally we both hope he lives forever, but we know that's not going to be the case. As you know when you're locked up you're out of

48 Carl is likely referring to Rocco Arico, a friend of Tommy's of whom Carl was not fond.

sight, and the old saying is correct "out of sight, out of mind". Look how many people that I've helped out over the years.

As I have previously told you, no-one helped out Roberta, or even offered to help her out with my mum's funeral cost. No-one has asked if my dad or I are ok for our monthly money, no-one gives a fuck. Sorry a couple do, but there are very few. Look at Pizza and what I did for him – paid his legal fees, gave his family money, paid his debts, and on top of that he owed me money. Now he's out, he reckons I owe him. When I seen him at Acacia he was virtually crying at my window, like the little boy he really is – the weak hearted pretender he is. Not to worry.

When my mum was alive, I always knew that she'd always be there to look after Dhakota, teach her right from wrong, discipline her, look after her when ever needed, and just knowing that made my life 10 times easier. Now she gone, and life must go on – but do you know how tough of a pill that is for me to swallow, knowing not only I won't be there for Dhakota but now neither will my mum. And as I've previously said in the above paragraph, I'm sure no-one else will be for her – no-one cares – I know it would be a different story if you were out, but unfortunately you're not and won't be for another 7–8 years and a lot can happen in that time.

You mentioned to let them know, or make sure nothing jeopardizes my placement. Mate in regards to that, as you know better than anyone, they're a law of their own. If they try playing too many games – I will battle to get you to finish off your sentence with me – that's if you want to. I suspect, and was recently told that I'm going to be stuck here for another 10 years – I can't go any further backwards from here, things can only get better.

As you said I should do well at my Appeal – I hope you're right. Let's say I hopefully get the 3 years which I did before I received the 35 years – which I and everyone else seems to think I should, then on top of that I get another 10 – that would leave me with 20 years to go. If that were the case, I'll do it anywhere, here or Acacia – but I want unlimited phone calls, and weekly contact visits, surely that's not too much to ask for.

I still hear from Tash,[49] but not as often as I used to. I haven't heard from her in the last 3–4 weeks, I'm sure she'll write soon. She hasn't mentioned one word to me that you two haven't been talking. Is there anything you want me to say to her? If there is, let me know, and it will be done.

Mate this letter is 10 times longer than the letters you write to me, and as you can see, I reply to your letter the night I receive them.☺

With best wishes & respect,
Your friends always – Carl

24 January 2009 to Tony Mokbel

Dear Tony,
Last night I received your letter, and it was good to hear from you again, as it always is.

I also received the letters you enclosed, regarding your conditions, and placement.

I don't like your chances on getting much, if anything, of what you're asking for. Although I do believe you might be sent to either the MAP or MRC[50] – however I believe if that were the case they'd still keep you in the slot at either one they sent you to – so in my view that could be a backwards step, be careful what you wish for.

49 Natasha Morgan.
50 Melbourne Assessment Prison and Melbourne Remand Centre.

Speaking from experience – I know the conditions that you are currently housed under are far from ideal to prepare, and run committals, and trials from. However, I was forced to run mine under far worse conditions. I firmly believe that it's designed to break/wear you down, and let's face it when the authorities have a formula that's working – they'd be silly to change it.

To give you a little bit of an understanding of what I was up against, listen to this one. I was given a Barrister in January, and told to start a trial in February (the following month), obviously, I made applications for an adjournment – which the Crown supported, and all applications were refused. And this was a double murder I was due to front, with 3 crown witnesses to cross examine. Mate, like it or not, when it came to me the law was thrown out the window, and I think the same thing applies to you.

With best wishes & respect,
Your friend always – Carl

28 January 2009 to Milad Mokbel

Dear Milad,
I was laying here and I thought I would drop you a few quick lines to say hello.

I see they gave you and extra 8 months on top of your 8 years for not participating at the ACC. I thought that weren't a bad result for you, as I thought they might have given you more, and obviously from the media reports you agree with me, as they said you thanked the Judge after receiving the extra 8 months.

I hope that you can beat the other charges you face otherwise...................

Matty's back here with my dad and I, and it's good to have

him back, we don't expect to be here for too much longer. As we've been told that we'll be moving to Acacia Unit 3, sooner rather than later, for that well over-due rotation.

I just got a letter from Sean, and he's been told that he might, or will be heading to PPP soon, maybe he can teach you a few more tricks in boxing.

With best wishes & respect,
Your friends always – Carl

Ps) Please give my best to your mum, Horty, Renate and the kids – thanks.

29 January 2009 to Fabian Quaid

Dear Fab,
Last night I received your letter, and it was good to hear from you again, as it always is.

It was good for Ange that he got bail – although I know absolutely nothing about his case, I personally thought he had no hope of getting it, shows you how much I know.

Faruk is still here, his still in the big Unit, and he still runs only by himself – they don't allow him to mix with anyone – fuck his days must drag.

I haven't heard again from your mate Ray, and I don't really expect too.

Roberta has been busting my balls, asking me to ask you, if you can put her in contact with your friend, who has some shops that might take her shirts, and remind you that she and the kids want to catch up with Ben,[51] so they can take him out for

51 Ben Cousins.

dinner. She said that kids are looking forward to meeting him – but I reckon it's more her, than the kids,☺ if you get a chance ring her up, so she can drive you mad – instead of me (ha ha).

Keep in touch – and I hope to hear from you again soon.

Best wishes & respect,
Your friend always – Carl

29 January 2009 to Sean Sonnet

Dear Sean,
I trust this letter finds you in the best of health, and spirits, as it leaves me fine.

Last night I received your letter, and it was my pleasure to hear from you again, as it always is.

So you could be off to PPP at the end of the year. I see no reason why they won't send you there, and then after you do a couple of years there, maybe Loddon, but I wouldn't be holding my breath on Loddon. The only reason why I say that is because there are a lot of scaredy cats there, but who knows they might send you there, you stick to yourself, and you're not a trouble maker. Once you get somewhere you'll probably wish that you never moved from where you are, as you currently have everything you need at your doorstep, and from what I hear the jails are full of fuckheads, all fucked up from that ICE.

I heard that Gangland Milly is classoed[52] to Loddon, although personally I don't think he'll be going there anytime soon, not at least until he finishes his court cases, his still facing another Traffic Large Commercial Quantity amphetamines, so potentially he could end up with another 3–5 years on top of

52 Slang for classified. The Classo is the Classification Board.

the 8-years-8-months his already serving. And my bet is that he'll also Plea to that, so he'll have to get something on top, and he thought he'd get 3 years, how wrong was his best mate, Nicola.[53] ☺

Fuck how hot is it, mate over here they've had the heaters on, hopefully tomorrow they give us a break and put the air-conditioning on, this is insane.

Well buddy, I haven't really got much more to add, therefore I'll leave it there for now, and I hope to hear from you again soon.

With best wishes & respect,
Your friends always – Carl

2 February 2009 to Danny Heaney

Dear Danny,
One day last week, I received your letter, and it was good to hear from you again, as it always is, sorry I've taken so long to reply.

It's been fucking hot, it's been that hot lately I've had to put my training on hold. You were right down here we have no air-conditioning, we have some vent that blows the air from outside, inside, and it's like a heater – no jokes, it's cruel.[54] Hey, imagine if when I was outside I kidnapped 3–4 people, locked them up and done the same to them as what I've endured over the last

53 Nicola Gobbo.

54 Being prisons within a prison, the management units are sealed from the outside world. The air circulating within the units is only lightly refrigerated in summer and there are constant complaints about the lack of heating in winter. The biggest problem is the constant dust in the air. If an inmate doesn't wipe down his cell every day, he will quickly find everything will be coated with a fine layer of dust. It adds to a claustrophobic atmosphere that contributes to health problems and detrimental psychological effects.

4–5 years – the media would have a heyday, and say that I'm a sick cunt – they would, feeding people through trap doors, getting them to lift there balls, look up there asses, fuck! ☺

Matty's back here with my dad and I, and it's been good to have him back here, his good company. His been back for over one week now, he came back not last Friday, but the one before. However today he starts his trial (murder), – and you wouldn't believe the luck of the draw, his drew Betty KING, she returned early from holidays to take on his trial, its due to go for anything between 4–6 weeks, let's hope he gets a fair go, and has a victory.

Betty still has not sentenced Ange Goussis, over the Lewis Moran murder. He was found guilty in June 08, did a Plea October, and it's now February, still no sentence. I wonder what she'll give him, I'm tipping life with 28 – 30 on the bottom, but the sentence to start from the day she hands it down.

I don't really have much more to add, so I guess I'll leave it there for now, and I hope to hear from you again soon.

With best wishes & respect,
Your friend always – Carl

2 February 2009 to Pauline Laureano

Pauline Laureano is the sister of Renata Laureano, Carl's girlfriend at the time of his 2007 trial.

Dear Pauline,
Last night I received a beautiful card from yourself, which I'd like to thank you for, it was very sweet of you. I was actually wondering why you hadn't replied earlier, keeping me on my toes hey. ☺

So you were saying that you were surprised that I sent you a birthday card – I don't know why you'd be surprised about that – I consider you my friend, and what you and your family, more so Renata, did for me in my time of need will never go unforgotten.

You were saying that the *Herald Sun* came to your place to see if Renata was with me – and she rang them and told them where to go – she should have told them that she's not that lucky – and she wishes (ha ha).

By the way how is that ***fat ass*** bitch? Tell her I asked you how she is, as I always do, but whatever you do don't tell her I called her a fat ass bitch, ok the bitch part you can tell her about – but fat ass, Hmmmm – no, say nothing about that, even though both you and I, know it's the truth (he he). I haven't heard from her in ages.

Well I haven't really got much more to say, so I suppose I'll leave it there for now, and hopefully I hear from you again soon.

With Love & respect – Carl –xoxox-

9 February 2009 to Breanane Stephens

Dear Brea,
Hi ya, how's things? I hope you're ok, and everything is going as good as it can be for you out there, as for me here, I'm fine – no complaints.

Well nothing much has changed in my rather eventful life, same old same old...... just going through the motions and making the best of it. Thankfully, the phones were back on air today, after being out of order for 4 days (since Friday). As you know I love the phone – and I'm lost without it, it's my outlet in here that keeps my sane.

Tonight I received your letter, and the 2 photos that you sent to me, thank heaps Brea for them both – you look so pretty in those pics, some will say you look exactly like your father (ME). ☺ (he he) Thanks for the picture of you and Nick. If he treats you well and makes you happy then I'm happy, but please just promise me that you'll watch boys though. I won't go on, but remember I was once a teenager, and I know every trick in the book, and I'd kill if anyone ever hurt, or disrespected you. Just be careful, that's all I'm saying.

You made my day, and made me so, so happy, when you said that you have 2 pictures of me and you up in your room, I love you so so much Brea.

Last Saturday Jayden's mum came up here with my dad to visit me, she was telling me that Jayden knows you, and he reckons that you and I look so much alike, as I'd say to Kota, we do only I'm better looking. (lmao)

Today I was talking to your mum, and she was saying all of you are coming up here on Sunday to visit Tye. I booked a visit for Penny[55] and Dhakota on Sunday too – it's been ages since I last seen Kota and I miss her so much, Sunday's Valentine's Day, I wonder how many Valentines Cards I'll get this year? The most I have ever got in one year is 4 – not telling you who they were from though, although I think you'd might be able to guess a few of them.

I don't really have much more to add, therefore I guess I will leave it there, and hopefully I hear from you again soon – really soon.

Lot and lot of love,
Now and forever – Carl –xox-

---

55 Penny Brown.

11 February 2009 to Tommy Ivanovic

Dear Tommy,
Last night I received your letter, dated 10-01-09, which you wrote that day – these day the day the mail is coming express post – you've obviously got some pull. ☺

It's good that they moved Matt back here with my dad and I – as his really good company.

I didn't know, or hear anything about anyone having a go at Zarah.[56] However, I haven't talked to her for about 2 months. I took her number off my phone list, because I had to put a few different one on, plus she did a few things that disappointed me – one being not going to my mum's funeral, and also she hasn't been up here to see me just to say hello in 12 months.

I just received a letter from Milad. I was of the belief that the 8 months he just got went on top of the 8 years that his already serving, so he'd now have a minimum term is 8 years 8 months. However, in his letter he reckons they put the 8 months on top of his 11 years, and nothing on top of his minimum term, I don't believe him. Therefore, I'll now ask Shane Tyrell the barrister who was there for him at his sentencing, as his coming to see me tomorrow. I know that Milad still has another large commercial quantity to front. Which he reckons his fighting, but I reckon he'll plea it, so I think that he will end up with a minimum term of anything between 11–13 years, which is a long way from the 2–3 years that he thought he'd only get. Mate the bloke a good for a laugh, and he means well, but his not the full quid, let's face it – his from the first generation of walking upright (ha ha).

56 Carl is presumably referring to Zarah Garde-Wilson.

I haven't really got much more to say, so I suppose I'll leave it there for now, and hopefully I hear from you again soon.

With best wishes & respect,
Your friend always – Carl

Ps) I just told Matt I was writing to you, and he said to say thank you for the card supporting him for his trial, and he also said to tell you to let Max know, the turtle said thanks for giving him a pass.

13 February 2009 to Sean Sonnet

Dear Sean,
I trust this letter finds you in the best of health, and spirits, as it leaves me fine.

Last night I received your letter, and it was good to hear from you again, as it always is.

There hasn't been much happening over here, you know what it's like over here, its the same shit different day, but I guess that's the same everywhere in these environments.

Matty has been going to Court for 2 weeks now – and today he picked a jury for the third time. Now it looks like he should/will finally get under way this coming Monday.

Last night along with your letter, I also received a letter from Gangland Milly, his always the same channel. As you know his at PPP (Waxenby), Julian Knight is in his Unit, and they were going to move Brazel[57] in there too, however the prisoner didn't want him moved in, so they complained to the staff – and stopped poor old Greg's move – what the.................

57 Greg 'Bluey' Brazel.

So Angeeee needed a smoke after his sentencing, I don't know how he never seen that one coming, blind Freddie could've seen that one. I thought he'd get anywhere between 28–35 to start from the day, but if she wanted to be mean she'd give him no minimum, so 30 from the day wasn't too bad – thank god for Angeeee's quick thinking.☺

Well buddy, I haven't really got much more to add, therefore I guess I'll leave it there for now, and I hope to hear from you again soon.

With best wishes & respect,
Your friends always – Carl

13 February 2009 to Milad Mokbel

Dear Milad,
A few days ago, I received a letter from you, and I was happy to hear from you again, as I always am.

There hasn't been much happening here, you know what it's like over here, its the same shit different day, but I guess that's the same everywhere in these environments.

You're right they should just put me, my dad, Tony and Ange all together, in Unit 3 of Acacia. After all they know we're all friends, and are compatible – but like you said, that would be too easy for them.

Last week I received a letter from Fab, who is locked up in Perth. He's sharing a two outer with Troy. As you know, he knows Ray from Sydney, and he told me that Ray recently got bail $1.75 million. I didn't think he had any chance in the world of getting bail, although, when I heard from him, he was extremely confident that he would. I thought he was tripping, so did Jamie and a few others who are up there with him. When I last heard from Jamie, he said Ray's gone mad – he's walking around preparing to go home – and he honestly thinks that he'll get bail – and virtually no-one gets bail up there, but he got it, so good luck to him.

With best wishes & respect,
Your friends always – Carl

17 February 2009 to Wayne Howlett

Dear Wayne,
I received your letter the other night, and it was good to hear from you again, as it always is.

Roberta was telling me that they arrested you over some bullshit allegation. It seems like they never leave you alone. Let me assure you – I know the feeling.

As for Tye, he's not here with me. He's at the remand Centre, desperate city, I believe he's going for bail – which I for one don't think he'll get, and if he doesn't I'll be trying my best to get him here with me.

I don't know if you're aware of this or not, but my dad's now here with me, and its been good to see him, and spend time with him. I treasure every second I get to spend with him, as the reality is I'll never ever get to spend time with him again on the outside.

With best wishes & respect,
Your friends – Carl

19 February 2009 to Danny Heaney

Dear Danny,
I just received your letter, dated 18-02-09, and it was good to hear from you again, as it always is.

I hope that you get something off your appeal – and I believe you will. I still shake my head with disbelief when I think about your case, that drunken cunt tries to kill you, and you end up in jail – what the fuck is the world coming too.

Now regarding Matty's trial, what a nightmare its been for him. His been at Court now for the past 2–3 weeks, and now tomorrow he picks his 4th Jury. He sacked his Barrister (Sean GRANT) – but only on his Barristers advice – as Betty tried to stand over him, and he wouldn't stand for it, so they had a falling out, as she didn't like his opening – long story short, he picked holes in the Crown case, and she said he couldn't do it – what a joke.

A few weeks ago, I had a contact visit with Dhakota and Stacey, and dad was out there on a visit with us, with Kath[58] and Trav,[59] it was a really good visit, it had a good family feeling about it – which is something I haven't felt since my mum passed away. Dhakota absolutely loved the visit, she was running around calling my dad – George, thinking that she's really smart, and that she was cheeky, she's so cute. We have another one of those visits this coming Sunday – so as you could imagine, Sunday can't come around quick enough for me.

I don't have a date for my appeal as yet, I had one, but it was adjourned. We are all hopefully that I will get time off, no I'll rephrase that, we know I will get something off – but what is anyone's guess.

---

58 Kath Bourke.
59 Travis Day.

Unfortunately for me nothing much happens in my life these day – in here its the same thing, day in – day out – its like ground hog day, you know what its like. However, I guess some would say I can't complain, as when I was outside I had enough excitement to last me a lifetime.☺

With best wishes & respect,
Your friend always – Carl

20 February 2009 to Tony Mokbel

Dear Tony,
I just received your letter, and it was good to hear from you again, as it always is.

So when are you getting married???? ☺ All jokes aside if you want my advice, I say go for it mate, if that's what she wants, and it'll make her happy, I believe that's the least you can do for her, and make sure you tell her I said that.

Shane Tyrell is a decent bloke, he's one of very few people that I can say that about, especially in that profession. I talk to him often and he doesn't like the way you're being treated. As you've probably already gathered I have a lot of time for him. I don't know if you're aware of this or not, but he was the only person out of all the Legal profession who attended my mum's funeral, and he has always been there to help me, and my family whenever needed, and most of the time for no fee at all. He will follow your instruction, no matter what they are – and do the best he can for you.

He's not scared of them, and he won't back down. You can't ask for much more than for him to do his best for you, I'd love to say he will win all your cases for you, but you know as well as I do you're up against it, and mate it's going to be hard, tough, and very unfair road ahead for you.

With best wishes and respect,
Your friend always – Carl

Ps) Please give my best to your mum, Dan, and the kids – thanks

1 March 2009 to Rod Collins

Rodney 'The Duke' Collins was a notorious hitman serving jail time for the 1987 murders of Ray and Dorothy Abbey at their Heidelberg West home in Melbourne. He was suspected of having killed at least seven other people, including Mario Condello, and Terry and Christine Hodson.

Dear Rod,
On Friday night, I received your letter, and it was good to hear from you again, as it always is.

You were 100% right you owed me a letter, I didn't write to you earlier – as I thought you might have been busy with your upcoming Committal.

Nothing much is, or has been happening over this side of the building, mate. You know what it's like, it's the same thing day in, day out, in these places, but that's jail. I've just been going through the motions, and doing a little bit of exercise to help pass the time, as well as look after my health.

Some fitness instructor came in here last week. He's something to do with the Geelong football Club. He gave me some workouts to do, they're pretty hard, but they look good. Slowly, slowly, I'll work on them and improve my fitness. He also gave me some things to do on the exercise bike, which I like.

It was good to see Ben Cousins play his first game back the other night. He went ok, it's just good to see him back out there getting a kick, and doing what he loves to do. I like him; he seems like a pretty decent bloke, I hope he has a good year.

Well Tony Mokbel has started the first of his many Committals. He has 8 Committals, practically one after the other, which he doesn't believe is fair – either do I – but that's life. I done it myself – I/myself had 2 drug cases, which resolved into a Plea, followed by 6 committals, back to back, and then a trial, with about 50 mentions in between, so yeah he's not the lone ranger. Once he's finished his Committals, in August he's due to start his first of many trials. Mate, I have more chance of waking up with a genie next to my bed, to grant me 3 wishes, then he has of getting 8 acquittals.

I hope to hear from you again soon.
Best wishes – Carl

2 March 2009 to Tommy Ivanovic

Dear Tommy,
Hey buddy, how's life treating you? All good I hope, as for me I'm fine.

I just received your letter, dated 1st March, and it was my pleasure to hear from you again, as it always is.[60]

Just like out there, nothing much is, or has been happening over this side of the building, mate you know what it's like, in these places it's the same thing day in day out, but that's jail.

60 Some of Gatto's letters to certain inmate associates made their way into Carl's possession. One of those letters mentioned that Tommy Ivanovic would need to watch himself, due to his dishonesty. In his letter to Carl of 1 March, Ivanovic was seeking information on what Gatto had said.

Now regarding Highchair[61]: Chooky[62] lagged you fairly quickly after you told him – and it was about the issue you said. In addition, from what I was told, he said that his loyalty was with them, and the A-Team – not with you. He obviously wasn't shown the same loyalty in return, which bolty bridge[63] played a huge part in.

I didn't know that they pulled Ray's bail – although I was really surprised he got it in the first place.

I see Simon Overland is the new Chief Commissioner, in my opinion that's a good thing.

Re; the contact visit with Stacey - that this weekend was just refused, it was just a little hiccup, as I had already used all my visits for the year. I'm reasonably confident that they'll give me another one later on this month, no one is playing games, from time to time things like that do happen – you know that.

It's Dhakota's birthday on the 10th of March, she turns 8 years old, she's growing up so quickly, she's such a good little kid. Stacey's bringing her up here Sunday to see me, which I'm looking forward too. I don't know what I'm going to get her for her birthday. I think we might get her some bracelet thing that she wants, the same as Stacey wears, it's just hard from in here, with no financial help from the outside. When my mum

---

61 'Highchair' is a name Carl frequently uses when referring to Mick Gatto, based on Carl's perception that Gatto should come down from his 'highchair'.

62 Ali Chaouk, then a Hells Angels bikie, was fighting his own internal club battles, having used some prominent names to dupe people into providing him drugs to feed an out-of-control addiction. This was discovered, which resulted in the club removing his coveted patch while he was in jail. Carl played a big part in his ouster. While awaiting parole in 2018 Chaouk was found guilty of a June 2009 murder.

63 'Bolty bridge' is shorthand for Hells Angels and Melbourne CBD killer Christopher Wayne Hudson and refers to a shooting incident that occurred when a Collingwood AFL player Alan Didak was driving with Hudson over Melbourne's Bolte Bridge on 12 June 2007. It's surprising that these comments were allowed through, given they related to inmate politics and could have created further unrest. It was a sign that Carl was getting some latitude from authorities after his decision to cooperate.

was alive, she use to do everything for me – not to worry my dad will be out there soon, luckily, for me I have Stacey, as she does more for me than I could ever ask for. It's just the people you think should be helping "don't", they don't give a fuck. Mate for all they know, I might not even be getting my monthly money, it's bullshit isn't it, out of sight out of mind.

Re; the police driving you mad, mate you'd expect nothing less would you. I'm guessing they're just chasing up old leads – they quizzed me over countless unsolved things they believe that you played a key part in, from the feeling I got they believe you make the Ice-man[64] look like an altar boy.

Now those letters re; The Don, I can get them for you if you wish for me too, but let's be honest with one another, anyone who needs to see them, to see what kind of bloke he is, has been living on another planet for the past 20 years. I for one think he'll be in here before the years out anyway – that's what my sources say – I guess time will tell.

Keep in touch – and I hope to hear from you again soon.

With best wishes & respect,
Your friend always – Carl

4 March 2009 to Milad Mokbel

Dear Milad,
I just received your most welcomed letter, and it was my pleasure to hear from you again, as it always is.

64 Richard Kuklinski, aka 'The Iceman', was a mafia hitman in the United States who was responsible for more than 200 murders.

Well that was a big sentence, that Betty gave RIZZO.[65] The sentences are getting bigger though – aren't they? If she gave RIZZO 16–13 years on a Plea, I'd hate to think what she'll give Tony if he gets found guilty, after running a trial. I don't know if I've told you this before, or not – but I was told that if they find him guilty on the company charges, the Crown will be asking for the maximum term – life – as they want to make an example of him.

As for Fab, he's locked up over some ecstasy bust. From memory he's charged with something like 45 kilos of MDMA, and Troy, well he's doing 18 months over some bullshit assault, which Heliotis is representing him for. Heliotis is also doing Fab's case too.

I don't really have much more to add, therefore I will leave it there for now. Keep in touch – and I hope to hear from you again soon.

With best wishes & respect,
Your friend always – Carl

Ps) Please give my best to your mum, Renate, the kids, Kabalan,[66] and of course my good old mate Horty – and let Horty know that this year I'm barracking for the blues, and I'm only supporting them for him.[67] ☺

---

65 According to the police, during Tony Mokbel's Greek sojourn, his Melbourne operation, known as 'The Company', was run by Bart Rizzo and Joe Mansour. In November 2008 Rizzo pleaded guilty to three drug charges and a charge of dealing with the proceeds of crime.

66 Kabalan Mokbel, Tony Mokbel's brother.

67 Carl and his father were Fitzroy supporters before the inner-city Melbourne club merged with the Brisbane Bears in 1996. He knew a number of the Lions players personally.

7 March 2009 to Danny Heaney

Dear Danny,
Last night I received your letter, and it was good to hear from you again, as it always is.

I read some article in last Sunday's paper, stating that I'm saying that I'll get this, and that off my sentence, what a load of shit. I don't know what I'll get off, I guess only time will tell, although I hope I get something off, how much though is anyone's guess, and I for one wouldn't dare guess.

Hey I don't know if I told you this, but after my mum passed away Roy Pollitt sent me a condolence card, from the outside – which I thought was really nice of him, he also made mention of those tokens, & said his passed the debt onto me to collect. ☺

With best wishes & respect,
Your friend always – Carl

7 March 2009 to Beau Goddard

Dear Beau,
Last night I received your letter, and it was good to hear from you again, as it always is, it's been a while since I last heard from you.

It's good to hear that Roberta and Rob got out to see you, I was talking to her when she told me she got approved to see you – she was rapt, I know they both speak very highly of you.

In your letter which I just received you were saying that Binse,[68] or badness as he likes to call himself ☺, is going out the back there, and if I know him, personally I don't know him.

68 Christopher 'Badness' Binse.

However, he was here in Melaleuca, when I was here, but I never really seen him, and I certainly didn't talk to him – personally I have nothing against the bloke – but his not my cup of tea, and you don't want to get yourself mixed up with people such as him – hi and bye that's enough. Milad loves him, and he will no doubt go out of his way to be in his company, but in saying that, he loves anyone whom he thinks is someone, and let me assure you Binse is a nobody.

Now regarding my appeal, as yet I haven't got a date, it was put off for obvious reasons. I have a good team put together to represent me for that – which I'll need, as this is my last chance, and I want to have a red hot go at it. We're all hopeful of getting a good result – I have no doubt that I will get something off, but how much is anyone's guess.

Keep in touch – and I hope to hear from you again soon.

With best wishes & respect,
Your friend always – Carl

14 March 2009 to Fabian Quaid

Dear Fab,
I trust this letter finds you in the very best of health, and spirits, as for me I'm fine.

Last night I received your letter, and it was good to hear from you again, as it always is.

By the sounds of things you've gone from the Penthouse to the shithouse – I guess that's a bit of an exaggeration, but you know what I mean. Whilst you're where you are, what you have to try do is get into reading, go over your brief, and just read, and read, and read, it can't do you any harm, don't leave any stones unturned. Mate believe me don't leave everything up to counsel, as they don't read everything. It's your life, and it's in your hands to do everything in your power to give yourself the best possible chance you can of winning. Let's just hope and pray in May, that you go home where you should be, and get yourself out of that shit hole. As I'm sure there's plenty of other holes you'd much rather be stuck in – literally. ☺

I've enclosed a photo of my cousin (Nikki) for you, as you requested, she a top chick, cheeky bitch, her and I are very close, she's always been so supportive to me.

Fab, a good mate of mine (Matt Johnson), who lives in the same unit with my dad and I – is also a good friends with Fat Ang,[69] and he has asked me, to ask you, if you could tell Ang to send him a photo of Ang and Ben together. As well a contact phone number – thanks.

I don't really have much more to add, therefore I will leave it there for now.

Best wishes & respect,
Your friend always – Carl

14 March 2009 to Danny Heaney

Dear Danny,
Fuck all is happening down here, same old, same old, just going through the motions.

By this time next week Matty should be finished his trial, he says its going really well, so let's just hope he gets a good result.

I like you read in the paper about Rod, and that witness re; photo board. Buddy unfortunately for him his going no-where,

69 Angelo 'Fat Ange' Venditti.

the odds are stacked against him, and from what I'm led to believe – he knows it. Let's face it his 63 years–old, and has serious matters in front of him. On top of that when they raided his flat, they found a loaded gun amongst other things, on just that alone he'll get 3–4 years, it'd be different for him if he was in his 30's – 40's, or maybe even his 50's, but the sad reality is his not.

Last week I spoke to Mr. Pridueax, whilst talking to him, I inquired about having a visit with you, Dave and Tommy, but more so yourself, I explained the reasons to him as to why I wanted the visit. He said he didn't have any problems with it, and it made sense. He told me to ask MOU the next time I seen them, which I will be doing. He also said he'd be supportive of it, but as we both know his only one voice, his a pretty reasonable man, where "yes is yes, and no is no", and you can't ask for much more than that, but in my situation, everything goes to the top of the tree. As you know, and I am sure you can appreciate, there is only so much that I can tell you in a letter.

With best wishes & respect,
Your friend always – Carl

16 March 2009 to Tony Mokbel

Dear Tony,
I just received your letter, and it was my pleasure to hear from you again, as it always is. Buddy you reply whenever suits you – as I know you're busy with your cases, I know that you will eventually get back to me.

By this time next week Matty should be finished his trial, he says its been going really well, but he said today there were a few headaches, things didn't all go his way, but so far so good, let's just hope he gets a good result.

I know the frustration you are going through – it's bullshit. What you have to do is try find a Junior barrister who will stick by you, throughout everything – but it's hard, because you have so many cases to go on, one after the other, after the other, and no-one can get their head around them all, with the time limit the Judge expects them too. They just can't prepare to represent you properly. I don't know what to say to you mate. I've told you from day dot, that you haven't got much chance of beating everything, and if by chance you beat one, they'll get you on the next. You're in a difficult situation. Reality is that you're between a rock and a hard place, with Legal Counsel representing you that you wouldn't normally let you represent over a parking ticket.

Stacey's going good. She said your mate rang her the other day, and told her to call in anytime she likes. She was rapt. Tell him I'm so grateful for everything he does for her. She also said when she seen Dan out the front a few weeks ago, she thought Dan might have wanted her to do her hair. If she does – that's no problem at all, that's the least she could do, make one day & she'll not only do Dan's hair, she'll do all of the kids hair too. Apart from that she also does waxing, and all that shit too, she a fully qualified hairdresser. I'll leave that one up to you, and you let me know – but please let Dan know that it's no hassles at all.

I don't really have much more to add, therefore I will leave it there for now, and I hope to hear from you again soon.

With best wishes & respect,
Your friend always – Carl

18 March 2009 to Tommy Ivanovic

Dear Tommy,
I just received your letter, and it was good to hear from you again, as it always is, except for a few things that I will mention in one moment.

Mate, believe me I don't like want they write in the papers either. I actually hate it, as much as you do, if not even more so, but what can I do about it??? I can't stop them, and on top of that, it is what it is. But when I say that, don't jump to conclusions. There're a lot of things that you obviously don't know, that I honestly believed you were made fully aware of. You have to understand I am limited to what I can tell you in a letter, I think I've said enough.

Buddy but believe me – when I tell you this "I honestly could've give two fucks what people are saying, or will continue to say about me". I dare say these people who are talking about me, have wanted to say something about me for a long time – but just have never had the balls to – fuck them, fuck them all. Mate do me a favour and if anyone says anything about me again, which I'm sure they will, tell them to take it up with me, if, or when we cross paths, because I won't be losing any sleep over it, and for that matter neither will a lot of other friends of mine. However, on a separate note if you're going to lose sleep over it, and you need a break, let me know, and if you want – I'll try my best to get you down here with me for a while – it's your call.

As for Penny, she's been rude to Stacey on more than one occasions, and people have been there and seen it for themself, ask Dennis or Maila[70] if you don't believe me.

As for Tash – I haven't heard from her for months, and I couldn't care less if I never heard from her again for the rest of my life.

---

70 Dennis and Maila Reardon.

You also asked me about Highchair[71] – the Don has that letter. I suggest that if you're still in contact with him, or any of his obese A-Team mates – ask them for it.

With best wishes & respect,
Your friend always – Carl

20 March 2009 to Wayne Howlett

Dear Wayne,
Firstly, congratulations on your girl being pregnant, you'd be rapt with a boy on the way. I'm so happy for you mate, I like the names you picked. When I next talk to Roberta, I'll be sure to let her know, she'll also be rapt for you. I think she has a lot of babies stuff – such as bibs, bunnyrugs, ect ect, from one of her many ventures that she started, then got sick of before it got off the ground.

I just I received your letter, with the photocopy of your gym enclosed, and it was my pleasure to hear from you again as it always is. The gym looks grouse. My girl has just started training; I should get Shaune to send her a Gym outfit for a shit shir.

Well what do I have to tell you – Hmmmmm, as I'm sure you're more than well aware, nothing much happens or changes from day to day in these joints. It's the same thing day in, day out, especially when you're around the corner. ☺ They may as well freeze me, and thaw me out when it's time to go home. I might suggest that to them, and see how it goes down. ☺ In saying that, I'm going along ok, just doing a little bit of exercise, and making the most of the time that I'm getting to spend with

71 Ivanovic was still trying to get hold of the letter Gatto (Highchair) wrote concerning his dishonesty. Carl knew that Ivanovic was out of favour with both Gatto and his crew, and the bikies, who he refers to as the A-team.

my dad, although he spends most of his days on my computer, playing spider solitaire, and poker. He's addicted.

One day last week, or the week before, there were people in here looking around – as to where they could put a stove, cupboards, ect, ect, in. As they were saying, they're thinking about making these little units which I'm currently in, and look like being in for a few more years to come, self-catering units. Which would mean we'd cook all our meals for ourselves, which I for one think is a good thing, as then we'd get to buy all our own food, and cook whatever you wanted to cook, for breakfast, lunch, and dinner. That way I can eat to preserve myself – good idea.[72] ☺

As for those Underbelly books – they're all full of shit. Probably the one closest to the truth would be the one Adam Shand wrote – "Big Shots". I don't know if you seen it in your papers over there, but last week, or the week before, Lewis Moran's brother was shot at.[73] Anyway after that he come out and told the truth, that his nephews started all the bullshit with me; about time someone said the truth. They were bullies and good for nothing. It's just bullshit that it took me to put them out of existence, it should have been done a lot earlier, especially with the way they used to carry on and treat people.

I don't really have much up to add, therefore I guess I will leave it there for now, and I hope to hear from you again soon, really soon.

With best wishes & respect,

Your friend always – Carl

---

72 The chance to cook for oneself in a management unit was an important privilege. It could engender an esprit de corps between inmates. And authorities knew the way to an informer's heart was through their stomach. As much as Carl grumbled continually about the food, when they carried his corpse out, he was in the best shape he had been in since his teens.

73 In March 2009, Lewis Moran's brother Desmond 'Tuppence' was shot at while sitting in his car outside his Melbourne home, but survived unhurt. The bullet lodged in the steering wheel.

26 March 2009 to Sean Sonnet

Dear Sean,

I trust this letter finds you in the best of health and spirits, and stress free, as there's no reason to be stressed, kick back and chill. ☺

I just received your letter, and it was good to hear from you again, as it always is.

I knew I wouldn't make everyone happy, but in saying that, when can you? As you said you can't always please everyone all the time, so there's no use in trying. As I'm sure you could appreciate I'm limited to what I can tell you through the mail, I'd like to be able to see you and talk to you face to face, and have a really good talk to you, if you get moved with me I'll talk to you further. I don't why other people are saying things, and throwing there two bobs worth in, when it's got nothing at all to do with them, I guess it's just human nature, anyway fuck them, fuck them all & what they have to say, if they see me they'd probably say hello – there all weak cunts, I've seen it all before.

As you said – I know who my mates are, and they're re the only ones who really mean anything to me. Mate I can think back so clearly too only 4 months ago, when my mum passed away, without going into anything – let me just assure you, in my honest opinion 99% of the population are all full of shit, users, and selfish cunts.

If you want to spend time with me, I think I may be able to get you with me, who knows we might even be able to get Unit 3 – but if that's want you honestly want, let me know ASAP, preferably through Kath, as that way I'll know quicker, or in a letter straight away.

As for the security I have no idea what's going on there, they come through here too, but nothing like it was years ago.

I knew that Drag Queen had finished up, that's not news to me, there's not much I don't know. ☺

I do not have much up to add, therefore I guess I will leave it there for now, and I hope to hear from you again soon.

With best wishes & respect,
Your friend always – Carl

1 April 2009 to Milad Mokbel

Dear Milad,
I just received your letter, and it was my pleasure to hear from you again, as it always is. Buddy, you took your time in replying to my last letter, nearly one month – what the .... I look forward to your letters. I'd love it if you were here with us. I'm forever telling Matty that you're the best company to have around.

When you're next talking to Melanie, can you ask her if she received my letter, which I sent to her address in Dubai months ago. It was a nothing letter, only a letter thanking her for her support. As I've told you before, I like Mel – her heart's in the right place. Let her know that I still want her to visit me the next time she's in Melbourne. It'll only be a box visit – better than nothing. ☺

So Tony's had a few victories, good. I for one hope that he has plenty more to come.

My dad goes home in just over two months – that's providing he gets his parole, which I can't see him having a problem with. I yelled out to him earlier, and told him that I got a letter from you. He said to send you his best, and said that he'll snip you when he gets out, and he'll give it back to you with interest when you get out. I think Horty's been teaching him some tricks.☺

Keep in touch – and I hope to hear from you again soon.

With best wishes & respect,
Your friends always – Carl

Ps) Please give my best to Renate, the kids (little Robbie), your mum, as well as Kabalan, Harry, Larry, and naturally my good old mate Horty.

2 April 2009 to Fabian Quaid

Dear Fab,
I just received your letter, and it was good to hear from you again, as it always is.

I'm very pleased to hear that you've now got Robert Richter representing you, I, personally would prefer him representing me than Heliotis. Let's just hope justice prevails, and you go home. Don't worry if that be the case, than you can rest assure that I will give you a leg up with Nikki, I thought you'd like her. At the moment she's back in QLD, but I think she's coming back to Melbourne soon to live. I've just put her phone number back on my list, so when I ring her, I tell her that I have a good bloke for her (you), the only problem is you have to wait to meet him, as he has one little hurdle to get over (he he). I tell you now she's a good chick, really down to earth, easy going, as well as gorgeous. I've enclosed another photo of her for you, now that's two photos of girls from over there you owe me – & they have to be girls who can, and will, write to me, I'll leave that in your capable hands, now I'll anxiously be waiting for your reply. ☺

Keep in touch – and I hope to hear from you again soon.

With best wishes & respect,
Your friends always – Carl

3 April 2009 to Barry Q.

Dear Barry,
Hey buddy how's things? As good as they can be expected I hope, as for me I'm fine.

Well Matty just returned – not guilty on all counts, that's the best news I've heard for awhile, it's a huge win for him.

Hey I don't know if you're aware of this or not, but today Chris Trail (who represents Matty's Co-accused), let it slip to Matty's Counsel, that whoever his jail Barrister is, whom his getting instruction from, practically or virtually got him over the line, **QC Barry**, his our man, if he can't do it no-one can!!!!! All your good work has finally paid off, it's just good to hear things like that, I bet it makes you feel good, and so it should, you should be very proud of yourself, because both Matty and I are proud to have you as our mate.

As you know, my dad goes home in just over two-month's time, that's obviously providing he gets his parole, and now after today's result Matty could and should be a chance for bail, so that would leave me one out. So I'll have to try and get over there with you 3. So what I suggest would be the best to do is, plant the seed now, and I not only push from this direction, BUT you 3 also push from your end "hard', to let MOU know that you 3 want me over there, and I'll do whatever I can from my end.

Keep in touch – and I hope to hear from you again soon.

With best wishes & respect,
Your friend always – Carl

Ps) Please give my best to both Ange and Tony – thanks

6 April 2009 to Wayne Howlett

Dear Wayne,
Hey buddy how's things? As good as they can I hope, as for me I'm fine.

I just received a letter from your way, with a short message from yourself, and Mick Marlow.[74] He writes to me every now and again, always just out of the blue, he says don't write back to him, as it's only outgoing mail for him. Can you please let him know that I received his letter, and let him know that I said thanks for his support. He seems like a funny bloke.

Nothing much is happening here – same shit, it's fucking freezing here today.

I had a visit yesterday with my girl, a contact visit, which was really good. I think I've told you before, I only get one contact visit per month, so I always have it on the first weekend of the month, I can't wait any longer. Although as of this month my contact visit regime has improved, I now get a contact visit every fortnight – woohoo. Anyway it's a lot better than once a month. Box visits are shit. My girl loves, and looks forward to our contact visits, as do I.

As I told you in my last letter, she's started training. At the moment she's going full steam ahead, getting up every morning and going to the gym at 6.00 am, before she goes to work. I can't

---

74 Michael John Marlow murdered a man in Tasmania in 1990 and is a notorious rapist.

see that lasting too long. ☺ Anyway, I bet her that she wouldn't keep it up for one week. She did, probably only to win our bet. I told her if she did, I'd buy her some boxing wraps, and gloves, so she can have her own.

I don't know if you have them over there at your Gym, but if you do, can you do me a big favour, and ask Shaune to send her some boxing gloves, and wraps, to the following address – [deleted]. Her name is Stacey Vella, she's not expecting them, but I don't want her to be able to call me a non payer (ha ha).

If you don't have them there's no problem, I'll just chase them up elsewhere. If you can, next time when you write back to me, can you please let me know either way – thanks buddy. Thankfully my dad will be home in just over 2 months time, so then he'll do all these odds and ends for me.

With best wishes & respect,
Your friends always – Carl

8 April 2009 to Beau Goddard

Dear Beau,
The Saints are flying – you'd be rapt, I see they were having something to say about Brendon for doing the cuff sign for you,[75] they should get a fucking life. I seen the article in the paper, and Brendon handled himself very well, he obviously looks up to you, let him know I was proud of him. I like Brendon; he is actually my favourite player in the whole completion.

75 St Kilda star Brendon Goddard caused a controversy after one of his goals by crossing his arms over his chest, in a gesture believed to symbolise handcuffs. He admitted it was a tribute to his half-brother, Beau, who was an inspiration to him.

On the Sunday just passed, I had a contact visit with my girl – we had a really good visit, I hang out for the first weekend in the month to come, so that we get to have our Contact visit. I think we needed it, box visits are fucked. Then she came again to see me on Monday, and again today, devotion – dedication – that's what I like to see. She's so good my girl, and I love her so much, she's one in a million, I only wish that I was out there to spend time with her, as I know how perfect it would be, never mind I'd much prefer to have this with her, than nothing.

Well buddy the footy show is about to start, so I'm gonna get going, and kick back and watch that, and Hopefully Sam's come out and does something stupid, his always good for a laugh that bloke.

With best wishes & respect,
Your friend always – Carl

14 April 2009 to Sean Sonnet

Dear Sean,
I hear that the black dog is again snapping at your heels, mate what can I say, personally I believe it's the environment, it's not healthy for anyone. I thought you were telling me that you've got a system to beat it, which I've been anxiously awaiting to hear all about. ☺

Fuck all happening over here, same shit different day.

As you'd probably already be well aware, Matty won his trial. He was acquitted on all charges, and apparently, Betty weren't a happy camper, fucked if I know how he got that result. After all, he even jumped in the box and said he'll plead Guilty to assisting an offender, murder after the fact, and Betty offered the

Jury that as an alternative charge, however they acquitted him on all charges.

Now regarding my running, yesterday I did the quickest 5 kms, that I've ever done, speed 13 from start to finish. Before that, I've only ever done 12 all the way. Now I want to work myself up, and aim to be able to do speed 15 – kms all the way – 5 kms in 20 mins. I only do those runs once or at most twice a week. As I'd much rather do 10 kms, on speed 10 – as I enjoy it more, and it burns more calories.

If you have any program that you believe will help me train me better, can you please write it out, and forward it onto me, any help will be appreciate – thanks.

With best wishes & respect,
Your friends always – Carl

15 April 2009 to Tommy Ivanovic

Dear Tommy,
Hey buddy, how's things? As good as can expected I hope, as for me I'm fine.

I just received your letter, dated the 12th of April, and it was good to hear from you again, as it always is. You took your time in writing; I thought I would have heard from you earlier, better late than never though.

So you're now over all the bullshit, buddy don't do your head in over things that you have no control over, people are always going to have an opinion, but most will keep it to themselves if I cross paths with them, you know as well as I do most people are false, and pretenders. I will keep trying to get a visit with you, if I get one – I get one, but again don't stress.

It's good that you now have that young girl in your life, who knows what can happen, just take it as it comes, and enjoy it whilst it last, the company would be good for you though, you need people to talk to other than the people you're surrounded by.

I haven't heard anything about Faruk getting charged over Dino's[76] murder, but it wouldn't surprise me if he did, and if he does he'll have 3 murders to face, oh well that's life.

Nicola hey. As for her having a hand in getting me arrested, she's gave Allan T. the same advice, as the Don gave him, roll and look after yourself, but for some unknown reason they didn't like it, nor would they believe it when she gave John W. that same advice. It's a funny world we live in that's for sure – I might end up beating them all home.

With best wishes & respect,
Your friend always – Carl

17 April 2009 to Barry Q.

Dear Barry,
Earlier this week I received your letter, dated the 10th of April, and it was my pleasure to hear from you again, as it always is.

You were 100% right – Matty doesn't want to go for bail, or leave, whilst my placement is not settled. I told him to go for it, and if he gets it, to get the fuck out of this place, and stay out. As I'll be alright, hopefully if he gets it, they move both my dad, and I, over there with you, Tony and Ange, and move one of us into the other unit to sleep, but let us run out in Unit 3, like they did when it was me, Sean, Ange, Horty and Milad all over there. I guess time will tell.

---

76 Dino Dibra.

Anyway, Theo[77] is putting the affidavit together over the weekend for Matty's bail application, and filing it on Monday morning, and I'll be ringing him first thing on Monday morning to insure it's done.

What else do I have to tell you; I'll fill you in on what's on the rumour mill. Strong rumour is that the Don, will soon be here, arrested over what, who knows, that rumour has been strong for a while, but is now getting stronger. Faruk will soon be charged with another murder, the murder of Dino Dibra and a few wogs will soon be arrested over some conspiracy to murder plot.

I don't really have much up to add, therefore I guess I will leave it there for now, and I hope to hear from you again soon.

With best wishes & respect,
Your friend always – Carl

77 Theo Magazis, Carl's solicitor.

CHAPTER 5
The end of the affair

On the day of Justice Betty King's sentencing of Carl, on 7 May 2007, there was a very public spat in front of the courthouse between two women who had turned up for the occasion. His former wife, Roberta, had arrived under a full head of steam and was more than a little irritated at the presence of Carl's current girlfriend, Renata Laureano, who was wearing what she claimed was an engagement ring. Roberta was not permitted to enter the courtroom that day, because of the abuse she had hurled at Renata at an earlier hearing, but Renata had to pass Roberta on her way into court and she received another earful.

Carl and Roberta were by now divorced, and Carl had taken to teasing Roberta that Renata was living proof that he could 'still pull 'em even when I'm in jail'. He had even suggested to Roberta that he and Renata might have a child by IVF. She could laugh at this in private but in public she was still Mrs Carl Williams and she wasn't about to forfeit the stage to another woman.

Roberta screamed at Renata to keep away from Dhakota ('Don't go near my daughter, you trashy piece of fucking carnage') but also offered the young woman some advice based on her own experience: 'Stupid sluts like her fall in love with gangsters and think it's all glamour and glitz but they are going to be bringing their kids to jail, running errands for their man.'

Renata must have taken this advice to heart. Roberta later claimed that Renata never visited Carl in jail. Almost immediately it was clear that her relationship with him was over and she disappeared from the public gaze until her marriage to a 'long-time boyfriend' in a glitzy marriage reported widely in May 2009.

Fortunately Carl was able to move on pretty quickly himself. While he was adjusting himself to his new circumstances, he received a letter from a twenty-year-old hairdresser called Stacey Vella, from Kurunjang on Melbourne's western fringe.

Very soon afterwards Stacey became his girlfriend and maybe even his fiancée. In the *Sunday Herald Sun* of 6 September 2009, Liam Houlihan provided what seems to have been a well-sourced account of the Carl/Stacey affair, relying on interviews with her family and friends. This story claimed that Carl had presented her with a resized man's ring containing nine 1.5-carat diamonds, which she had regarded as an engagement ring, even though her father pooh-poohed the idea that they were engaged. Her friends said she had written Carl letters signed 'Stacey Williams' and sent him raunchy photographs taken at a glamour studio. In one, she wore not much more than a man's white shirt, apparently given to her by Carl, with a ring prominent on her wedding finger.

But the prison romance fell apart when Carl discovered his would-be bride had become romantically involved with a Melbourne boxer. The final verdict of Stacey's mum was, 'Carl Williams hooks these kids in to pass his time, then he chases them.'

Most of Carl's letters to Stacey were handwritten, or destroyed by him after they broke up. His computer certainly contained no trace of his correspondence, except that the dates on which he wrote to her in early 2009 are noted in a well-organised running list he maintained under the heading 'Letter to reply too [sic] – 2009'. However, his computer did contain the following love declaration, which was apparently created on 20 November 2008, and surrounded a border of interconnected hearts he called 'Stacey Love Heart Border 1'.

Stacey – Being with you

When I think of how we met I wonder was it fate? Was it chance.

I only know that when I'm with you I have this feeling of completeness that I have never felt before.......

A warm feeling that begins with just a look from you ....

A touch from you and I feel my mind and body begin to melt.......

Being in your arms I feel safer and stronger than I have ever felt.......

You give me the courage to be the real me.......

You look at me and I feel special.......

I don't know why or how we found each other, I only know that being with you makes me a better person.......

Love now, always and forever,

Your man – Carl Anthony Williams –XOX-

19 April 2009 to Nikki Denman

Nikki Denman was Carl's cousin on his mother's side.

Dear Nikki,
I trust this letter finds you in the best of health and spirits, as it leaves me fine.

Well today, I finally got hold of you on the phone, and thank god, I did, as I had a really good conversation with you, I really enjoy talking to you, and I've been hanging out to hear your voice. It was also good to talk to your friend – Bella. I tell you what Nikki, it's strange after all these years being in here talking to someone I have never met before. I feel like I'm slowly losing my communications skills. Usually I could talk under water with a mouthful of marbles, but today when I was talking to Bella – I felt nervous. This place must effect you in some ways, and I don't mean in a positive way either, as it's surely not good for anyone to be housed in here for years and years.

After I talked to you, I rang your mum up and spoke to her for 2 calls. As you said she's been a little bit down, and I could pick it up through her voice too. I hope she picks up, as I love your mum. To me she's my aunty, but I look at her more like a mother figure, even more so after my mum passed away. I don't need to talk to her every day, but deep in my heart I know one million percent that she'll always be there for me. I told her to take no notice of that fat, miserable, depressed cow (Sarah), but I know that it's easier said than done.

Please let Danni know that I'm extremely disappointed that I haven't heard from her, especially after she promised me she was going to write to me. Hopefully she'll be wondering what she can do to make it up to me. Please let her know that I said that's a hard one, especially with me being in here, although a few photos in lingerie would be a good start – of her I'm talking about. ☺

Nothing much has been happening here, same old, same old. As you know, there's only me, my dad, and Matty in this Unit. My dad should be going home in about 2 months time and Matty will now be going for bail – which he should get, especially now after getting acquitted of the murder charge he was facing. Therefore, if those two go home, I'll be trying to get back to Acacia with Tony Mokbel, Ange, and Barry Q., the change will be good. In addition, I get along with all of them well. They've all wrote letters to let me know that they'll support me through anything I do, and they've been pushing from that end to get me over there with them.

It'll be good if I can get back over there as they'll be stuck in these environments just like I will be for years and years, so we can all stay together. In addition over there in the unit they have the Gym, pool table, table tennis table, and more access the the sun – so it'll be better if I can get back over there.

I don't really have much up to add, therefore I guess I will leave it there for now, and I hope to hear from you again soon.

With love & best wishes – Carl –xx-

Ps) I hope you like the photo I've enclosed for you, now it's about time that you sent me a few.

20 April 2009 to Fabian Quaid

Dear Fab,

I just received your letter, and it was my pleasure to hear from you again, as it always is.

When your letter arrived, I knew it was from you, so I was feeling it, trying to work out how many photos' were in there, NONE ! – What the.... Then on top of that, you want to shir me up about these "Pussy Cat Dolls". Tell them, or I should say "Esmerelda",[78] as she's the one who going to write to me. That when she write to me – which if you have any pull, should be very shortly after you receive this letter, that, when she sends me a letter (ASAP), for her to also please enclose a few photos, and an address as to where I can write back to her. You were saying that you told her about me – what did you tell her? I think you'll be on to it straight away, especially after you hear what I'm about to tell you.

On Sunday, I spoke with Nikki, and I was telling all about you – pumping you up of course. I told her you that were a very close friend of mine, whom I've known for a very long time – and I trust and respect, which you fit in a very small category. Anyway she said "I'm surprise that you're trying to set me up with one of your mate, as usually if anyone even looks at me when you're around, they'd get turned on". I said well that's when dickheads are trying to pick you up, this bloke is one in a million. Sit down for this one – so she said when your mate (YOU) is next in Melbourne, and she's settled back here, she'll be more than happy to go out on a date with you you. She said but let him that there's know there's no kissing on the first date. ☺ But then again there could be.

I don't really have much up to add, therefore I guess I will leave it there for now, and I hope to hear from you again soon.

Best wishes& respect,
Your friend always – Carl

Ps) Now please do me that favor, and get Esmerelda to write to me ASAP, just for a laugh, and it'll give me someone else to write to, to occupy my mind. I'll be expecting to hear from you really soon, I'll be disappointed if I don't. ☹

---

78 Not her real name.

22 April 2009 to Wayne Howlett

Dear Wayne,

I just received your letter, dated 18 April, and it was my pleasure to hear from you again, as it always is.

Yesterday I rang my mate's place, where you had the gloves and wraps sent for Stacey. Thanks so much for doing that for me, it really means a lot to me you doing that, and will never go unforgotten. I don't like to ask people for anything, even simple things, because most people say they'll do it, and don't. From my experiences when you're out of sight, to some extent you're out of mind, that is unless someone hits a hurdle and ends up in jail, then they want to write to me and kiss ass – like fuck.

I personally haven't spoken to Stacey since she received her gloves and wraps, but apparently when she opened the package she was over the moon. I also had flowers sent there for her on the same day. She a good chick, really easy going, and her support for me has been unbelievable. Lately though she' been going through a bit of a rough patch. She just wants me to come home with her (I wish I could), or she says that she'll even stay here with me (ha ha).

In addition, the visits are getting harder and harder for her to leave. Because she tries to get here for every visit, and I have 2 box visits per week, and 1–2 contact visits per month, there were a few weeks there when she came out here to see me 3 times a week. It's just too much for her. Then she goes to parties with her friends, and all her friends have their partners there with them, and she's all by herself, because I'm here, and unfortunately the Authorities won't allow me to go.

It's hard, mate. She's only young and, let's face it, I have 33 years to go – I should get some time off at my appeal, but fuck, even if I get 10 off, I've still got 22 to go. I've told her from day dot, if ever she ever feels like she's had enough, talk to me about it, and I'll accept whatever she wants to do. I'm not a selfish cunt – I know whilst I'm here, her life is virtually non-existent, and sometimes that's does my head in. Don't get me wrong, I love her, she's the best – but waiting 33 year for someone, and remaining loyal is a hard task. If the roles were reversed I couldn't do it, could you? (ha ha)

Please, when you're next talking to Shaune, give him my best, and thank him for sending the gloves and wraps to Stacey, if he was the one who you got to do it. And make sure to tell him, if he talks to Roberta, not to mention Stacey's name to her, as one minute she accepts Stacey, and the next she's calling her names. I think in some strange way Roberta likes to think that she's still with me.

I don't really have much up to add, therefore I guess I will leave it there for now, and I hope to hear from you again soon.

With best wishes & respect – Carl

30 April 2009 to Fabian Quaid

Dear Fab,
I just received your letter, with the photos of Esmerelda enclosed, and it was my pleasure to hear from you again, as it always is.

Buddy in one word "HOT" – deal me in – I'd be rapt if you could get her to write to me ASAP. However, if you could pull this one off, I'd be in debt to you for life. ☺ Obviously, with her permission – give me her address, and phone number (landline), so I can put her on my phone list, and give her a ring to give me someone new to talk too, I'd be good for me.

She couldn't have come at better timing – as I have just split with my girl, whom I was seeing for the past for 2 years, and I've been doing it a bit hard lately. I'll fill you in briefly as to what happened, she's had enough, she's only young – 22 years old, and a really good girl – I could speak highly enough about her. Anyway she use to come to see me twice a week, write to me every day, and I'd ring her every morning and for 2–3 calls, and usually every afternoon for a couple of calls. So basically she use to do my time with me, and it got to hard for her, anyway as you could imagine, the the past week, or two has been a nightmare for me. She says that she still wants to come and visit me – just not as regularly, and she also still wants me to ring her at least a few day a week, I don't know if I will, as it only make things harder. She also says that she never wants me out of her life, but she just can't deal with this situation anymore, which although is hard to accept, I can see her point, as the way things were going she didn't have much of a life. We only get one contact visit per-month, and when she leaves, she cries her eyes out, she wants me home with her – which isn't possible, and it's not getting any easier for her to accept, if anything, it's getting harder. And let's face it, as it stands I still have another 33 years to go – all I can say is her company was good whilst it lasted, and I wish her nothing but the best.

So yeh if you could put me in contact with Esmerelda, it'd be fantastic, as I'm sure it would take my mind off Stacey. Hey also when you write back to me, can you let me know what she said when you told her that I wanted to be put in contact with her, and if she know that I've got the photos of her.

So your trial has be adjourned for 6 months, lucky you told me that, as I'd just brought you a good luck card, and I was about to post it tomorrow. It's better to be fully prepared, than under prepared, fuck leaving everything to appeals.

I've already sent Nikki the photo of you – the one you sent me – I had her check it out, and send it back to me. So she's already fully aware of what she's in for – don't worry buddy, as I told you in my last letter, everything is done for you, so basically all you have to do is turn up. But send me a photo and I'll forward it on to her to keep. I talked to her on Sunday, but haven't rang her since, as Stacey has taken up most of calls, or me ringing people questioning them about Stacey – which I have to stop doing, as it only does my head in, but there's nothing much else to do her – but think.

I've heard no more news on those rumors – I hope they're just rumors, I've found that a lot of the time they get started in the hope that people will talk.

I don't really have much up to add, therefore I guess I will leave it there for now, and I hope to hear from you again soon.

Best wishes& respect,
Your friend always – Carl

8 May 2009 to Wayne Howlett

Dear Wayne,
I just received your letter, dated 2 May, and it was my pleasure to hear from you again, as it always is.

There hasn't been much improved on my situation with my girl, she can be so stubborn. On Monday, I had a visit with her, a contact visit, and it was a good one too – just what I needed. Yeah I know in the last letter that I wrote to you, I told you that she weren't coming to see me for a few weeks, but the first week of the month is always our Contact Visit. I guess she weren't going to let anyone else steal her contact visit (ha ha).

Buddy she's wore out, she's had enough, and who could blame her. As much as I love here, I have to let her go – she needs a rest and some space to think about things. I'll give her some space, and if she comes back all good and well, and if she doesn't – I guess it wasn't meant to be. I think she will, I hope so anyway – surely she just can't turn her feelings off like a light switch. I can't anyway.

Today was the first time that I've talked to her after our visit on Monday, and fuck it was good to hear her voice. I've been hanging out to hear her voice badly, but I haven't rang, I've held off. This boring cunt of a joint doesn't help matters, and all we/you have is our phone calls and visits. Oh well, what will be, will be. I think regardless of whatever happens she's be back, even if it's just as a friend. After all, it's more a friendship that we have than a relationship anyway.

Providing my dad gets his parole, he should be out of here in 6 weeks time, I'll miss him when he goes, but I'll also be rapt for him to get out of here. He's been good company, especially after my mum passed away.

When I next talk to Roberta, I'll let her know that you want to talk to her. Buddy if there's anything I can ever do to help either you or Shaune, in any way, just ask and, if I can do it, it will be done. As for the wankers, fuck them and the horse they rode in on.

With best wishes & respect – Carl

9 May 2009 to Milad Mokbel

Dear Milad,
Last night I received your letter, and it was my pleasure to hear from you again, as it always is.

I heard that you and Horty were slotted over some bullshit allegations – what a load of crap. It's bullshit, but what can you do – hopefully with a bit of luck you won't be there for too long. I don't know why they even think you'd have a gun – obviously they haven't seen, or been watching you hit the bag. ☺

Well Matty goes for bail this coming Thursday, and he should be a good chance of getting it. I hope he does, so he can get the fuck out of this cunt of a joint.

Still no news from Melanie, what she's doing with herself, next time when you talk to her, let her know that I said I'm still waiting for her letter, tell her I said she's slack.

With best wishes & respect,
Your friend always – Carl

10 May 2009 to Wayne Howlett

Greeting Wayne,
I just got off the phone from Stacey, and I told her that I received a letter from you the other night, and that you had said to me, that if she needs anything for her boxing training, to just let you know, and it shouldn't be a problem getting it. Anyway she doesn't like to ask for anything, and I know that better than anyone. She likes to try and stand on her own 2 feet. However, at the same time, I like to do try to do anything I can for her, as it makes me feel good, and there's not much I can actually do for her from here.

So I pushed her, and reluctantly she ended up saying that she needs some ankle supports and a chest guard. So if it's at all possible, it would be grouse if you could get Shaune to send them over to her, at that same address I gave you last time. Stacey VELLA [address deleted] and if it's no trouble, can you ask him if he can throw in a pair of shorts for her (small). Thanks buddy – I really do appreciate it and more than you'd ever know.

Nothing much has happened here. I've just been going through the motions, this is a boring cunt of a joint – I've now done 5 years of it. Fuck, enough's enough, these cunts are relentless (ha ha), and they want to keep me here for another 10 years. I might end up with my own table, full with pens, and coloring pencils, making cards all day – what the.................(ha ha). Fuck you've got to laugh don't ya.

Over the past few days I haven't spoken to Roberta, I should get hold of her tomorrow on the phone, and when I do I'll be sure to tell her to make contact with either Shaune or yourself. You should put her number on your phone list, she's usually always good for a laugh. Notice how I said usually. ☺ As at times, she can also be a lunatic.

With best wishes & respect – Carl

11 May 2009 to Tommy Ivanovic

Dear Tommy,

I just received your letter, dated 10th of May, yesterday, and it was good to hear from you again, as it always is.

You sound very happy with Megan – that's good, I'm happy for you, as you deserve to have someone good in your life who makes you happy – you're a good man – and a very good friend. It would be my pleasure to meet her, I seen the photo you sent Matty of her, she's very pretty.

Yeh, lately I have been having a few problems with Stacey, she said to me a few weeks ago that she's had enough, she wants me home with her, which isn't possible. I love her so much, but these last few weeks have been hard to tolerate. As I said, she wants me home with her, and now! Which unfortunately isn't at all possible, she's missing me badly, and after every visit she doesn't want to leave, and when she does, she's just cries her eyes out, as she doesn't want to leave me behind – it's not fair. However she has now decided that it'd be best if we backed off one another for a bit, which I don't want to happen, but I respect her wishes, after all she hold the cards – not me – It'll be a different story if I were out there, but unfortunately I'm not. I hope that she's just going through a rough patch, and she wakes up to herself and changes her mind, and the sooner the better. I usually see her every Sunday, and Monday, but this weekend she never came to visit me. She came last Monday on a Contact visit, and she's coming again this coming Sunday – as she's bringing Dhakota up here to see me. I usually talk to her every day, for a few calls in the morning, and sometimes again in the afternoon, however as the past few weeks she started a new job, where she now starts work at 8.30 am, instead of 9.00, which again makes things harder. I talked to her yesterday for a few calls, and she told me that her feeling haven't changed, she still loves me more than anything, and could never love anyone like she loves me, but she can't stand it how I'm not out there with her. My mum use to be there for her, and they supported one another, now that my mum is no longer here she just feels like she's got no-one, and that her life is falling apart, she a fantastic person, whom I couldn't praise enough. Although I want her to come back to me – badly – I'll accept, and respect whatever she does, let's face it if the shoe was on the other foot, would I be able to do it – I doubt it – would you?? Oh well what will be will be, it's not much use me worrying about things I have no control over.

Give me a couple of weeks for things to settle down a little bit with Stacey, and hopefully she comes around. If they do, I'll get her to bring Dhakota up here to see you, but in the meantime you're more then welcome to get your sister to bring her up here, just contact Roberta, and I can't there being any problem there – it's up to you.

The other day I went to see the doctors, & whilst I was in there I weighed myself, I'm now 86 Kilos, that's the lightest I've been for as long as I can remember, when I got arrested in 2004 I was 113 kilos. I've lost a few kilos over the past few weeks, stressing about Stacey, and I didn't have an appetite, oh well the worst is over.

With best wishes & respect,
Your friend always – Carl

Ps) Maybe Megan has got some friends who could write to me, and help take my mind off Stacey, ask her, and get back to me ASAP on that one, if she has can you get them to write to me, ASAP, and enclose a photo. ☺

15 May 2009 to Barry Q.

Dear Barry,
I just received your letter, dated 14th of May, and it was good to hear from you again, as it always is.

Well first things first – Matty just returned from Court – and unfortunately both he, and Morgs[79] were both refused bail – as she said that they were both unacceptable risks. She also set a new date for trial – sometimes in October this year. So it looks like he might /will be kicking back with me for a little while longer. I wanted to see him get out so bad, but if he had of I would've missed his company, as his really good company – with him nothing is ever a problem, lots of laughing and that's what you need in these places.

---

79 Mark Morgan, a friend of Matty Johnson's since childhood. At their trial, later in 2009, Matty was charged with the murder of Bryan Conyers and Morgs was charged with being an accessory. After the jury retired for 27 hours, they pronounced the pair not guilty.

Now that we know Matty won't be going for a at least six months, and my dad goes home in 5 weeks time. So what I suggest is that we'll try get either you or Ange to move over here with up to give either of you a change. I didn't say Tony, because at this stage they still don't want to put Tony and I together, as believe that I can help him in his matters – which I've already said he don't need my help. Anyway, until his matters (murders) are over, and dealt with they'll keep us both separated, after that I see no problem with them putting us together that's what I've been told anyway. When you write back let me know what you and/or Ange think about the above.

With best wishes & respect,
Your friend always – Carl

26 May 2009 to Barry Q.[80]

Yes Mate,
I just received your letter dated Monday, 25 May, and it good to hear from you again as it always is.

So you could see that I'd lost weight, lately a lot of it has been through the stresses that I've been having with Stacey – Buddy she's gone – what can I say, I've chased little bit, alot more than I have anyone – I don't usually do that – as its against my religion (ha ha). She came up her on Sunday, and is hopefully coming again next Monday on a Contact visit, where we'll talk further, but she'd had enough. But in saying that she still want to stay in my life, and she said who knows, in three months she might realize that she wants me back – 3 months might be

80 Since his letters of early May, Carl had been moved from the Melaleuca Unit to the Acacia Unit at Barwon. For the rest of his life all letters were sent from the Acacia Unit, Barwon Prison.

too long. As I can move quickly – step have already been put in place to fill her shoes, you're either in or out – no breaks – no fence sitting, and no-one is going to dictate to me what's going on, especially some 22 year-old girl, even if I do love her, my daughter will get away with but no-one else.

I hope that they let you come over here for a run-outs, with us, but I think you're more hope of coming here with us after my dad gets out on 20th JUNE, he was granted his Parole. So he only has just over 3 weeks to go now.

I do not really have much up to add, therefore I guess I will leave it there for now, and I hope to hear from you again soon.

With best wishes & respect,
Your friend always – Carl

"We cannot change the cards we're dealt,
just how we play them".

Ps) Please give my best to both, Tony and Ange, and both of their family – thanks.

Postscript Joke

A kid is doing his homework. "Dad", he says, "what's the difference between 'potentially' and 'realistically'?"

His dad says, "That's tough; it's probably easier to demonstrate it too you. So, go and ask your mum if she'd sleep with the milkman for $1 million; then ask your sister the same question."

Two minutes later, the lad is back. "Dad, they both said, for $1 million? Definitely!"

"Well, "says the man, "there's your answer. Potentially, we're sitting on $2 million; but realistically, we live with a pair of slags."

27 May 2009 to Fabian Quaid

Dear Fab,

I wrote to you about 3 weeks ago, asking for you to get me Esmerelda's phone number, with her permission of course. As I need someone to take my mind off the girl who I was seeing – she's done my head in. Do your best to get me the number, and please get back to me ASAP, also as yet I haven't received a letter from her, and you reckon I'm playing with your emotion – kick a bloke while his down won't ya.

I'm glad that you liked the photo I sent you, I thought you'd have a lot of fun with her, she's good value isn't she. ☺

I do not really have much up to add, therefore I guess I will leave it there for now, and I hope to hear from you again soon.

With best wishes & respect,
Your friend always – Carl

28 May 2009 to Milad Mokbel

Dear Milad,

I just received your letter dated 25th of May, and it good to hear from you again as it always is.

Buddy again I need you here with me – woman problem again, after 2 years – what the................. Oh well, it was good whilst it lasted. She came in too often, and it took its toll on her – sometimes 3 days a week. You'd have to have a screw loose to do that for 2 years, wouldn't you (ha ha). She'll be back, I find all the nutty ones, I must be a magnet for them.

My dad was granted his parole, so he's home in just over 3 weeks time, which is good for him, I'll miss him when he goes home, but I'd much rather see him outside, then stuck in this hell hole.

With best wishes & respect,
Your friend always – Carl

2 June 2009 to Tommy Ivanovic

Dear Tommy,
Last night I received your letter dated 28 May, and it was good to hear from you again, as it always is.

As you know my dad was granted his parole, so his home in just over 2 weeks time, which is good for him, I'll miss him when he goes home, but I'd much rather see him outside, then stuck in this hell hole.

Now Stacey – sit down whilst you're reading this, otherwise you might fall over. As I told you we're finished, and as I also said to you a few months ago before she ended it, her attitude towards me seemed to have changed – she stopped writing to me every night, the phone calls weren't the same, and I could feel something wasn't right, but she was going through a rough patch in her life, so I didn't take too much notice of it. But I had a secret suspicion that she was seeing another bloke, as she started doing boxing/ kickboxing, and praising up some young goose. I asked her countless times, and I told her if she was, I'd rather hear it from her than anyone else. But she always denied it, and said I wouldn't do that to you – what do you think I am – so I felt a bit bad for asking. Anyway, after a few weeks my suspicion grew greater and I was doing my head in, so I got Roberta to check it out, who better to do it then her, and find out what was going on between her and the bloke who's name she was mentioning – and within one day Roberta contacted the bloke, and had the bloke admitting to it, without even giving him a Chinese burn. But he said that he never knew that Stacey was with me, he was petrified when Roberta rang him questioning him. As for Stacey, she still denied it for a few days, but after my relentless cross-examination, she buckled and confessed, than broke down in tears, saying I fucked up, what can I do, it was only once – once to many. I now believe that she's seeing another bloke, she admitted to me that she kissed this bloke, but nothing further is going on – bullshit, I will fill you in on more, when I find more out. I've still been talking to her nearly every day on the phone – but things aren't the same, far from it, things finally took toll on her, and she broke, it was good whilst it lasted, what can I say, she said things would be different if I were home, and I guess they would be – the gas girl would still be there too (ha ha ha). Stacey said she still wants to stay in my life, yesterday she came to visit me, and she's coming again on Sunday on a contact visit.

Well buddy, I haven't really got much more to add, therefore I'll leave it there for now, and I hope to hear from you again soon.

With best wishes & respect,
Your friends always – Carl

9 June 2009 to Tommy Ivanovic

Dear Tommy,
Well buddy today my dad was telling me, that he spoke to Kath, and you sacked Megan – finished – what happened? The last letter that I received from you I thought everything was going well with you two, what can you do, in here you can fall into females, who

usually if we were outside they wouldn't get the time of day from us, at the start it's all exciting for them, then reality sets in.

As for Stacey – she's gone. I had my last visit with her on Sunday, it was supposed to be a contact visit, but on Saturday afternoon, Mr. Reid came down here to see me, and he told me that the powers above don't want me to have a contact visit with her, that's happened the last 2 visits in a row. We've been arguing a lot over the phone, and sometimes I lose it. But still I should've been able to have a contact visit with her, as that's what she wanted to have – although we argue, and I lose it, never in a million years would I ever do anything to harm her, they said they understand that, but they can't take the risk, it a duty of care – what the .... She's done my head in, and I kick myself for letting her, enough is enough, I have to snap out of it, as its not health for either of us. You get into a routine, and become reliant upon them, which isn't a good thing to do. After my mum passed away, things between her and I haven't been the same, she use to draw so much strength from my mum, they spend so much time together, and when they weren't together, they were talking to one another on the phone. I told her that I knew it weren't going to last forever, but there are ways to handle things, and she went the wrong way about it. I haven't rang her, and I don't know whether she'll make contact with me again or not, she's pretty stubborn. But she won't forget me quickly, as she has my name tattooed on her inner thigh, what can I say, it was good whilst it lasted, that's the best way to look at it. I must admit that she did put in a good effort for 2 years, so I have to hand her that, it must have been draining on her, but on the same token she put her hand up for it.☺

Your friends always – Carl

10 June 2009 to Pauline Laureano

Dear Pauline,
Well hello there

Sorry I haven't wrote to you earlier – no excuse is good enough, so I won't even bother coming up with one.

I did see Renata in the paper, and I thought that story wasn't even news worthy – they should just leave her alone – she was good to me, and I have nothing but good to say about her, and your family.

As you're probably already aware my dad only has just over one and a half weeks to go, I expect there to be a media frenzy when he gets released. I hope I'm wrong, but you know what they're like. Oh well what can you do – unfortunately for me my name sells papers.

Jenny was right, I am back in Acacia, I have been back here for about 1 month, she's doesn't miss much, good to see she's still keeping tabs on me. I hope she's received the B/day card I sent her, as I haven't heard back from her since. Has she moved on? ☺

Best wishes,
Love & respect – Carl

18 June 2009 to Beau Goddard

Dear Beau,
I trust this letter finds you in the best of health and spirits, as it leaves me fine.

Long time no hear, as you've no doubt seen over the news the last Moran[81] got killed, and see whom they charged over

81 Desmond 'Tuppence' Moran.

his murder, old mole Judy, what a circus, it's a jungle out there.[82] ☺

I've finished with Stacey, mate I don't know what's got into her. I don't know what she was thinking trying to pull the wool over my eyes – she'll have to get up earlier to do that.

Today I was talking to Rob, and he was telling me that you might have a couple of girls who will write to me, and maybe even come in for a visit/laugh. If you do get back to me straight away, and tell them to write ASAP – as I need something to help take my mind off Stacey, she's done my head in big time, never again will I fall into one of them, fuck that for a joke.

Well only 2 more sleeps until my dad goes home, it'll be good for him to get out of here, I'm going to miss his company that's for sure.

I really don't have much more to add, so I suppose I'll leave it there for now, be good or be good at it. ☺

With best wishes & respect,
Your friend always – Carl

23 June 2009 to Jenny Laureano

Jenny Laureano is the sister of Renata Laureano, Carl's girlfriend at the time of his 2007 trial.

Dear Jenny,
What a nice surprise it was receiving a letter from you the other night, I thought you'd forgot about me, as it's been a while since I last heard from you.

---

82 Judy Moran was charged with orchestrating the hit on Des Moran. This is a tongue-in-cheek reference to the theme from the *Underbelly* TV series 'It's a Jungle Out There', written by Burkhard Dallwitz. The first and most successful *Underbelly*, it chronicled Carl's rise and fall.

Well where do I start. I've had a pretty rough last few months, Stacey and I are now completely finished, she's had enough, and who could really blame her, coming here to see me 2–3 times a week. The visits were getting harder and harder for her to leave me here. I always thought in the back of my head it was going to come to this. Lately I don't know what's got into her. Anyway, maybe I was blinded, they say love can do that. As you know I couldn't speak highly enough about her over the past 2 years, week after week she's been so supportive to me, I just always though she's be there. However, after my mum passed away things between her and I did seem to change, I think my mum was her rock. I have to be honest it weren't much of a life for her, what can I say it was good whilst it lasted.

Now that I'm no longer seeing Stacey you'll have to get some girls to write to me to keep my occupied, I'll leave that in your capable hands. ☺

When it rains it pours, on Friday night I was eating my dinner, and the cap, which I had on my front tooth, broke. I'm spewing big time, as it looks horrible. I'm hoping that I get to see the dentist this week, but I don't think they cap it, and if they don't there's no hope that I'm going to let them pull it. I'll have to go through the process of getting my own dentist in here to fix it.

As for a visit, I'll have to organize one for you soon. I just want to see what's going on with this tooth of mine – I don't really want to see anyone with it like this, I look ugly.

With love and best wishes – Carl –xoxox-

26 June 2009 to Fabian Quaid

Dear Fab,
I just received your letter, and it was my pleasure to hear from you again, as it always is.

Still no news from Esmerelda – maybe she's writing me a book, one can only hope (ha ha), I guess she'll write whenever she's ready – which hopefully will be sooner rather than later, everynight when the mail arrives, I'm there waiting by my door expecting one from her, and you said she sounded keen. ☺

As I told you in my last letter, over the last month or so, I haven't spoke to Nikki, as Stacey has taken up all my time, what a mind boggler that was, talk about doing my head in. The other night I received a letter from Nikki's sister Kerry, and she was telling me Nikki's moved back to Melbourne, and she was telling me that her and Nikki want to come and see me whenever they can, so I guess I'll be seeing them soon.

I don't really have much more to add, therefore I guess I will leave it there for now, and I hope to hear from you again soon.

With best wishes & respect,
Your friend always – Carl

Ps) Please give my best to Toto, and tell him I wish him a belated Happy Birthday, and if I were out, I'd get the boxer to give him a lap dance (ha ha)

26 June 2009 to Beau Goddard

Dear Beau,
I just received your letter, and it was my pleasure to hear from you again, as it always is.

Nothing much is happening here, same old, same old, just training, and having a laugh. Since my dad went home, there's only 2 of us here in this unit, me and Matty, luckily his good company, we get along well. I hope that they move someone over here with us next week (Tommy), but they will only put one other person in here with us, because if they put more than one, we'll lose all day – dayroom, cell, and gym access, as we're only allowed to run 3 out here, high security.

Yeh I've heard all about the bullshit what's gone on with Tommy, that's just what it is "bullshit", jail, you know what it can be like, cunts talk like old women, they get 5 % right, and run with it. I heard from him twice this week, and he was stressing out, mate his done nothing wrong, hopefully they move him down here with me, and he can get on with his time.

You were saying that you're in the process of getting some girl (Tracey)[83] to write to me, that'll be good, you're on the ball – photo first. ☺ I hope that I hear from her sooner rather than later, as I enjoy writing letters, that's what I try do to help me pass my time, and keep me sane, some would say it's a bit late for that.

With best wishes & respect,
Your friend always – Carl

4 July 2009 to Beau Goddard

Dear Beau,
Last night I just received your letter, and it was my pleasure to hear from you again, as it always is.

I received that photo, and I think you should get Jess to write to me, instead of Tracey, you should be able to pull that one off;

83 Not her real name.

so I'll leave that in your very capable hands, and hopefully when you get back to me you have some good news. ☺

I haven't spoke to Rob or Roberta the last few day, those two are funny, I like ringing them up and stirring them. I like Rob, his good, his really good with the kids too, and they love him, I'm hoping they both get up here to see me soon as I haven't seen them for a few months now. Every time I talk to Rob, I ask him to get some girls to write to me, and he starts whispering to me in case Roberta hears him, fuck I'm the one who wants the girls for me, not him, fuck they're funny.

With best wishes & respect,
Your friend always – Carl

7 July 2009 to Jenny Laureano

Dear Jenny,
I trust this letter finds you and you loved ones in the best of health and spirits, as it leaves me fine.

Last night I received your letter, and also the card you sent me – your card was really nice, thanks. I was very happy to hear from you again, as you know I always am – quick reply – keep it up, I love it, I've heard that before.☺

You were saying in your letter that you're not going to get girls to write to me, as I have you. I can't eat pasta every night, plus you couldn't keep up with me anyway, and deep down you know it, after all I'm not one of these young Lebo's who needs to be wearing "L" plates (ha ha).

So you reckon that you've been keeping tabs on me, I wonder who's giving you your information, Hmmm that's a hard one to work out.

I promise you that I'll organize a visit for you very soon. I still have to put your mum's phone number back on my list. Long story short is that over the last few months I've been using all my calls on Stacey, but as of today I put a stop to that. I let her come in to see me today for the last time. I bet she tries to make contact with me again. Girls they're hard headed – one taste and they're hooked. What am I trying to tell you for; you know what it's like.

I really don't have much more to add, so I suppose I'll leave it there for now, and I hope to hear from you again soon.

With love and best wishes – Carl –xoxox–

13 July 2009 to Fabian Quaid

Dear Fab,

Still no news from Esmerelda – I have no idea where her letter has got to, you could be right she might have sent it via camel, who knows with these women, and I thought I was good, they play me on a break. ☺

So your happy with Ray's cousin (ha ha), at least I always find the time to try and brighten up your day, and give you a laugh, you're a good man, and I enjoy, and look forward to your mail. I've enclosed a few photos for you that Nat sent to me, so you can have a better look at, I hope you enjoy them.

Fab, a friend of mines son is sick in hospital, his name is David, and his a Richmond supporter. It would really be appreciated, if you could get BEN to get a Richmond jumper signed for him, and forward it to [address deleted].

With best wishes & respect,
Your friend always – Carl

14 July 2009 to Tommy Ivanovic

Dear Tommy,
Last night Matty just your letter, and he said you were wondering why I haven't wrote to you. Mate it's only been one week since I last wrote to you, now you know how it feels, there has been times when you haven't answered my letter for up to one month, so I don't think you're in any position to be complaining. ☺

On Monday, Brendan Money[84] came to see me after he'd spoken to you. I told him I wanted you here with me, he said he really wants to move you on elsewhere. I said I think it's best if he moves on after he spends a few years down here with me. After I spoke to him I rang the boss, and told him its best for my mental health if you come here with me, he said he'd check it out and see what he can do, his coming up here to see me and talk to me face to face on either Friday or Monday. Don't worry I'm doing all I can to get you here with us – that you can rest assure.

I don't really have much up to add, therefore I guess I will leave it there for now, and I hope to hear from you again soon.

With best wishes & respect,
Your friend always – Carl

84 Brendan Money worked in Police & Corrections as deputy commissioner, offender management.

16 July 2009 to Natasha Morgan

Natasha Morgan was a correspondent of Carl's and former girlfriend of Tommy Ivanovic.

Dear Tash,
On Thursday night, I received your letter dated 5th of July, 11 days to find me – what the…nevertheless, it was my pleasure to hear from you again, as you know it always is.

You were saying that you now know how it feels not to get a letter straight back from me, well at least something positive came out of my late reply. See you are just so used to me treating you so good, I've spoilt you (ha ha).

As you know the past few months I've had woman problems. You were close, it wasn't Renata, it was Stacey that I was seeing. Renata was long gone, and on my terms, unfortunately unlike this one. I was seeing Stacey for the past two years. I rotate them around – quick mover hey. Always looking to update them, they're just like car – only problem is I'm not getting to drive them. ☺

She'd had enough, and who could really blame her. She was only young – 22 – she'd been visiting me every weekend since she was 20. In my view, her putting in a solid 2 years was a good effort. Oh well, life goes on – one doors closes and as you know another opens, for who we're yet to see. I have say I fell for Stacey, it's probably the first time in my life that I've had my heart broken, and it's not a good feeling. Let me assure you though I won't be letting it happen again. Sometimes I think that maybe I feel for her because of where I am. I thought that I met the right girl, but at the wrong time, however I know myself, and if I were outside, I couldn't help myself, I would've had 5 girls, and I'd still be searching for more, I love the thrill of the chase. ☺

Just a short one today, as I don't really have much more to add, therefore I will leave it there for now. I'll write you a longer one when I get a letter back from you, which is hopefully sooner rather than later.

With love and best wishes, Carl –xx-

21 July 2009 to Wayne Howlett

Dear Wayne,
Good to hear that you're now at a minimum, I'm happy for you, as it would be much better. Now hopefully you can get Shaune there with you, when you talk to him please tell him I said hello and give him my best – thanks.

You asked how things are with Stacey and I. Buddy we're completely over. I never saw this one coming, not just yet anyway. When she was good, I thought she was the best thing since slice bread. I must admit I did love her, and so much so, honestly I thought the world of her. Maybe everything just got to her – remember she's only 22 years old, and she's a very pretty girl, she's only human, and she need affection.

So now you'll have to get those girls writing to me from over your way. Let them know that I just want someone to have a laugh with, and if they play their cards right, I might even put them on my phone list and from time to time I'll give them a call. Get them to send me photos with their letters; as I have to check them out first. I'd be rapt if you could get on to it straight away.

As you know, my dad is now outside. I try to talk to him everyday. He's going ok – although he needs a hip replacement, but was yesterday told that they don't know if they can do it, as they're not sure if his heart will be able to take the stress of the operation.

I watch all the footy over here, not much else to do in jail is there. When I was outside occasionally, I would go watch a game – that's mainly if I had corporate seats.

At the moment over here we only get access to the one HD channel, which is the 24 hour sports one. Better than nothing.

With best wishes & respect,
Your friend always – Carl

24 July 2009 to George Williams

Dear Dad,
I trust this letter finds you in the best of health, and the highest of spirits, as it leaves me travelling along ok.

I just received your letter, and it was good to hear from you again, as it always is – fuck this phone being taken off me[85] – I've missed not talking to you mate, don't worry when I get it back, I won't be falling into anything again, although personally I don't think I did anything to begin with.

I know you say don't fall into it, that's not my game, and you're 100% right, she's not worth it. As of two weeks ago I took her off my phone and visitors list, I can't be bothered with her, and that's exactly what I told her. But it's easier said than done, especially in this environment, as you don't have much to occupy your mind.

85 Carl refers to his phone being taken off him 'over some bullshit to do with Stacey' in a letter dated 9 August 2009 to Natasha Morgan.

I recently spoke to the coach about your cameras,[86] and he said they'd fix everything up for you – whatever you needed and wanted. If I were you I'd get them to fix up whatever security you think you need, and spare no expenses. After all it's not every day you get people wanting to put their hands in their pockets. ☺

I really don't have much more to add, so I suppose I'll leave it there for now, and hopefully I hear from you again soon.

Love and respect always – Carl

86 In the year and a half following Carl's return from his break on Swan Island, he was speaking to Petra's Steve Smith, whom he called 'Coach', five or six times a week as momentum gathered for the committal hearing for Paul Dale on the Hodson murders. It's clear from this letter to George that police took responsibility for ensuring the safety of George after he left prison by providing him with security cameras.

CHAPTER 6

'In some strange way Roberta likes to think that she's still with me'

Roberta Mercieca was born on 23 March 1969, one of seven children in the family. Her father was a Maltese immigrant who had been a truck driver, but he died in an accident when she was only eight months old. Thereafter her mother ricocheted from one abusive relationship to the next and Roberta suffered abuse at the hands of her mother and her mother's boyfriends, including being beaten with a kettle cord and having her head held underwater in a bathtub. Her mother also once attempted to pour nail polish remover into her eyes. Ultimately Roberta ended up as a ward of the state, dividing her time between foster homes and orphanages.

When Carl first met Roberta she was married to Dean Stephens, a small-time criminal on the Mark Moran payroll, with whom she had three children. But Dean was a violent husband. In her book, *Roberta Williams: My life*, she recalls, 'One night I was so exhausted from sitting up . . . that I fell asleep on the floor. When I woke up, Dean was dragging me around the lounge room by the hair and smashing me in the face and head with a gun.' Later that night, he put the gun to her head and threatened to kill her.

Carl and Roberta started off as just friends and ended up as just friends; most of the time they enjoyed each other's company. She was a highly attractive woman, but she was too feisty and independent to be a typical trophy wife.

Dean willingly gave her money so she could travel and educate her three kids. With her divorce settlement from Dean she set herself up in a luxury house at Hillside, furnished lavishly at Carl's expense; here he could come and go as he pleased. That way he could still spend lots of time with his mum and always have a few girls on the side.

He agreed to have a child with Roberta. Roberta recalls: 'We had planned to have Dhakota and Carl said he would never have wanted anyone but me to be the mother of his child. After suffering severe endometriosis, which I didn't know I had till we had tried for nearly a year to conceive Dhakota, Carl got very frustrated and annoyed. We consulted a specialist gynaecologist Dr Bruce Downing, now retired, and he operated. We had to try straight away. We conceived virtually straight away and Carl was over the moon.'

Their relationship, particularly during Roberta's pregnancy, was turbulent because she could never accept his philandering and at times she confronted him and his girlfriends. Despite this, one night when Roberta was in the bath he presented her with a one-and-a-half-carat diamond ring. He didn't want his daughter, whom they named Dhakota, born out of wedlock.

Their relationship ended following Carl's sentencing in May 2007, but Roberta told the *Herald Sun,* 'I love him to death . . . We only [split up] because he just wanted me to move on.' There is relatively little written correspondence between them, because they spoke on the phone frequently and she visited him regularly at the prison.

26 July 2009 to Roberta Williams

Dear Roberta,
Well as you know, I've had my phone taken off me, and fuck its boring without it.

I know I shouldn't fall in that thing, as she's not worth it. After she last came to visit me, I took her off my phone and visitors list. I can't be bothered with her, and that's exactly what I told her. But it's easier said than done, especially in this environment, as you don't have much to occupy your mind. Plus you know what I'm like, I let people get to me from now on though, I'm going to try my best not to. I have to try and stop myself from always getting to have the last say – after all, look where having the last say has got me. ☺

You asked me how did I meet her, and I told you she wrote to me, and unfortunately I replied to her which I don't usually do. I now wish I never did. The other night I was going through my letters, and believe it or not, I found the first letter that she wrote to me. [He reproduces here the first letter he ever received from Stacey Vella.]

I'm look so forward to seeing Kota today, as I've missed her so much. It's the first visit I've had in two weeks.

I don't really have much up to add, therefore I guess I will leave it there for now, and I hope to hear from you again soon.

Love & friendship – Carl – xx-

28 July 2009 to Danny Heaney

Dear Danny,
I just received your letter, and it was good to hear from you again, as it always is.

You're 100% right mate with Stacey, no matter which ever way you look at it, it still cuts deeps – emotions, they're a cunt of a thing. I did love her, there's no doubting that, and I let her in, which is something I very rarely, if ever do. I always say if you can't turn your back on it, don't get involved. I thought she was good, different, and my mum really loved her, oh well what can you do.

Today I had a visit with Roberta and Rob, it's the first time that I've seen them in a few months, it was good and enjoyable visit, which is what you need in these environments. I can always count on Roberta to catch out someone if they're doing something wrong by me – especially if it's a young female who I have feeling for (ha ha).

One day I was at Scottish Dave's[87] office, Dave and I were walking in the underground car park, when we seen Roberta yelling and screaming, shaking the cage that was separating us, she was calling me all sorts of names. I looked at Dave and said I've been caught. We made our way over to Roberta; she said some slut is texting messages to your phone saying she loves you. Dave said its probably the Police, that's what they do, I looked at him, laughed, and thought best you keep out of it, than she turned on Dave, fuck it was funny, she use to catch me out all the time, and I use to try cover my tracks. Therefore, Stacey never stood a chance when she was on her case.

Down here we get what they call the cooking program, we get it every fortnight, and we're aloud to spend $5.50 per person. In

87 David McCulloch. This occurred while Carl and Roberta were still together.

Unit 3 they're getting the self catering, and apparently once they get it in there and everything's going smooth, we are going to get it in here, how long that'll take is anyone guess. However, when it comes in it'll be good, as we'll get cook all our own food.

I'm led to believe that Tommy will be moved down here with us very shortly, so it'll be good to spend some time with him. He'll be happy down here, he can cut out a few years with me.

My dad is due to go for his operation on Monday; hopefully everything goes well for him, and his heart can take it.

My dad was telling me that a few weeks ago Roy Boy rang him up, he said his only made 2 mistakes, shot the wrong person, and got paid in counterfeit money, at least he can now look back and see the funny side of it. I think his still looking for his tokens, what a funny cunt he is.

I don't really have much up to add, therefore I guess I will leave it there for now, and I hope to hear from you again soon.

With best wishes & respect,
Your friend always – Carl

31 July 2009 to Esmerelda

Dear Esmerelda,
I trust this letter finds you in the best of health and spirits, as it leaves me fine.

Shock Horror!!!!! Thankfully, I finally received a letter from you – with photos enclosed – lucky me hey – they say good things come to those who wait, and as you know I've been waiting long enough to hear from you – one thing is for sure though, your letter and photos were better late than never. ☺ The next time I get photo taken of myself here, I'll send you one, as

I've lost 30 kilos from the ones you'd have access too, so you probably won't recognize me.

In one of the photos you sent me you were in Melbourne (Spice Market), do you come to Melbourne often?

You were saying that you have so much to say, but you haven't found the time to sit down and write to me, best you do hey, because I'd really enjoy listen to you. Fab has really praised you up to me – and now especially after seeing the photos of yourself that you sent me – I'm anxiously waiting to get to know you better, he did say that you talk a lot, and he said that you're a real down to earth girl.

So you googled me hey – Hhmmmm, scary, I can only imagine what you seen. If I were to believe only half the shit that they write about me – I'd be scared of myself, they love to sensationalize everything about me, and unfortunately for me my name sells, so naturally the media love me. ☹ Thank god you haven't seen that bullshit Underbelly series. I heard that just recently they were playing it again in Sydney, do me a favor and don't watch it, as believe me I'm nothing like that. All I'll say if you have anything that you want to know about me, ask me – and I'll tell you the truth, I have nothing to hide, any questions you have I'm happy to answer.

I won't bore you to death with my letter, therefore I'll wait until I hear back from you, which is hopefully sooner rather than later, and when I do I'll write more. When you write back tell me more about yourself – as I'm all ears, and would love to get to know more about you, after all you probably know more about me then I know about myself, after looking me up on the computer. ☺

With best wishes & respect – Carl

2 August 2009 to Fabian Quaid

Dear Fab,

On Friday night, I received a letter with photos enclosed from Esmerelda, it was only a short letter, but it was better than nothing, and now it has started the ball rolling, the photos were good, she's hot, and a few of her friends aren't bad types either, but my focus is on Esmerelda (ha ha).

The last time I wrote to you, I had Nikki coming into see me, she's actually visited me two times in the last fortnight, at the moment she's living at her sisters place which is only 15–20 minutes away from this jail. On the visit I talked to her about you – she's interested, I told her that you were sending me photos of yourself so that I could forward them onto her. As of 2 weeks ago, I lost my phone calls until further notice, over some bullshit allegations to do with Stacey, but when I get them back, I'll ring Nikki, and get her to drop you a line, hopefully I get them back this coming week.

I seen that you went for bail – but I never seen or knew the outcome, I was just waiting to hear from you again, I was hopeful that you'd get it, but I the same token I thought you were up against it.

So Ben is writing a tell all book, that should be a good read. I like it how his always been supportive of you, as I have previously said he seems like a really good bloke, good friend – which as you know they are few and far between when we find ourselves up against it.

With best wishes & respect,
Your friend always – Carl

2 August 2009 to Beau Goddard

Dear Beau,
I trust this letter finds you in the best of health and spirits, as it leaves me fine.

I received a letter from your friend Tracey – at the moment I'm in the process of writing back to her, she seems like a bit of fun.

It's better for you that you've moved to the Unit in which you have, the single cell is heaps better for you.

I don't really have much more to add, therefore I guess I will leave it there for now, and I hope to hear from you again soon.

With best wishes & respect,
Your friend always – Carl

3 August 2009 to Tracey

Dear Tracey,
I trust this letter finds you in the best of health and spirits, as it leaves me fine.

One day last week, I received your letter, with photos enclosed, and it was my pleasure to finally hear from you, as they say better late than never.

I'm glad to hear that you're excited to be my pen pal, its good to hear that I can still excite people even from here. ☺

You were saying that you love facebook, it'd be good if I could get access to that here – as that would help me pass my time – I'd never be off it, but these kill joy will never allow that to happen. I only get one, one contact visit per month, and I'm only aloud to make 32 phone calls per week , although at the present time I'm only aloud to make one phone call per day, as they say I've been a naughty boy, I don't think I'd even know how to be naughty, its not in my nature (he he).

I won't bore you to death with my letter, therefore I'll wait until I hear back from you, which is hopefully sometime soon, and when I do I'll write more.

When you write back tell me more about yourself – as I'm all ears, and I'm guessing you would already know enough about me. If you have any questions at all that you'd like to ask me I'm more than happy to answer them, that way you'll get the truth, rather than some beat story that you'll read, or see on the TV about me. ☺

With best wishes & respect – Carl

4 August 2009 to Esmerelda

Dear Esmerelda,
I trust this letter finds you in the very best of health and spirits, as it leaves me fine.

Hey last night I received another couple of photos from you, you sent 8 in total, but they only give me 6 at the one time – so I got 6 with your letter, and I got the remaining 2 last night, rules hey, I'm not used to living by them (he he). One of the photos was of the Spice Market (your favorite place) how often are you in Melbourne, and if you don't mind me asking, what kind of work do you do? After googling me, I'm guessing that you know more than enough about me, even if most of it is untrue – so I thought that it's only fair if you tell me more about yourself.

The other photo I received was of Susannah who was on Big Brother, and in Zoo magazine, we're not allowed to get the Zoo magazine here, the bloke who owns Zoo actually write to me regularly.[88]

How long are you going to Vegas for? I wish I were coming with you, what a thought. Do you travel overseas much?

I don't really have much more to add, therefore I guess I will leave it there for now, and I hope to hear back from you again soon.

With best wishes & respect – Carl

7 August 2009 to Danny Heaney

Dear Danny,
Last night I received you letter and it was good to hear from you again, as it always is.

Tommy is here with us – his good company, and it's been good to catch up with him, we've been driving him mad, he needs to get a sense of humor. I think that he thinks Matty and I are gone in the head. He said if we were both out the back, people wouldn't know how to take us. He takes things to serious, and worries too much about what others are thinking, but slowly slowly his coming good.

So you liked the story about Dave and Roberta, what a nightmare she could be at times, I have that many stories I could tell you about her, you'd never stop laughing. One night we were out having a drink, me, my dad, Theo the Solicitor, 2 of his workers (females), and a couple of other Solicitors. Anyway, Roberta rang me up and wanted the keys to the city apartment; she said she was coming past to pick them up. Time got away; the drinks were

88 Carl seems to have had intermittent correspondence with Paul Merrill, who was in fact the editor, rather than the owner, of *Zoo* magazine. Roberta had done some bikini shots that were published in the magazine in August 2008.

going down like lollie water. I went to the toilet, and when I walked out one of Theo's worker were there, she was hot, and I had my eye on her, we started talking and one thing led to another, and we started kissing. In comes Roberta – fuck – caught red handed, chairs went everywhere. I quickly got her out of there, took her to her car and thought she'd settled down, how wrong I was, she jumped in mounted the gutter and was trying to run anyone of us down, people were running everywhere, fuck it was funny. That was the last I seen of Theo's worker, and the last Theo seen of her, as usual, Roberta bombed me out good and proper.

I don't really have much up to add, therefore I guess I will leave it there for now, and I hope to hear from you again soon.

With best wishes & respect,
Your friend always – Carl

9 August 2009 to Natasha Morgan

Dear Tash,
I don't know if you know but an ex of yours is now here with me – Tommy. His been here for a few weeks, and it's been good to catch up with him – Matty and I haven't had anyone with us since my dad went home, so as you could imagine since the day Tommy arrived we've been driving him mad. He asked me if I still write to you, I told him I do, and I consider you a close friend of mine, so if he has anything negative to say about you don't waste his time tell me, which I think shocked him a little. He said he hasn't anything bad to say about you, after all it was he who finished it with you.

I've had a boring last few weeks, as I had my phone calls taken off me for 3 weeks, over some bullshit to do with Stacey.

Yesterday I finally got them back. But you know the old saying, "what doesn't kill you only makes you stronger". I haven't spoken to her for about 5 weeks, how time flies when you're having fun – not! Slowly, slowly I'm getting over her though, but in saying that I still have my bad days when I can't seem to get her off my mind, don't forget I'm still only human despite what some people like to think of me, and I had feeling for her.

With best wishes, Carl

10 August 2009 to Fabian Quaid

Dear Fab,
Yesterday I spoke to Nikki for a few calls, hopefully you walk at your trial, and if you do, I reckon you've got her, you'd be impressed with the ground work that I've done for you. In one of your last letters you asked me what she does – she a mother. She was with the father in QLD, he went to prison for a year or 2 and she visited him every week, then when he got out he fucked up and was being rude to her, so she packed up and left, came back to Melbourne, and now she's staying with her sister until she finds her own place. She seems interested in you – I could probably get her to write to you, whatever suits you, or do you want to wait and see what the outcome at Court? Buddy I don't mind hooking you up with her, as she'll be a good catch, but are you looking for someone to be serious with?

Last time I was telling you that after my dad went home, that there was only 2 of us left in this Unit. About one week ago they brought one of my friends here with us, whom I know from outside, Tommy, he is also my daughters Dhakota godfather, it's been good to catch up with him, and the added bonus is that his a chef. ☺ So if we get that self-catering thing that I was telling you that we were getting, we'll be eating like kings, but then I'll have make sure I don't out the weight back on.

I'm waiting on a letter from Esmerelda, hopefully she don't keep me waiting to long, she sounds like she'd be a lot of fun, I wouldn't mind letting her come to visit me when she's next in Melbourne, I'd really like to met her. ☺

You must have other girls over there that can write to me – put them onto me for some fun – let me know when you write back.

Fab, as of Today that footy jumper still hasn't arrived, his out of hospital now, but if you can still organize a jumper for him it'd be good, but if you can't no worries, the address is – [address deleted].

I don't really have much more to add, therefore I guess I will leave it there for now, and I hope to hear from you again soon.

With best wishes & respect,
Your friend always – Carl

13 August 2009 to Beau Goddard

Dear Beau,
I just received your letter, and it was my pleasure to hear from you again, as it always is.

Your 100% right, jail is a funny place – plenty of time to think, unfortunately for me the slot /is worse. With Stacey . . . I just never seen it coming, that's the hardest thing to get my head around. Roberta weren't much help either though, ringing her up a couple of times a month abusing her, telling her that she's going to bash her head in – what normal person wants to put up with that shit.[89] Oh well at least now Roberta will be happy that I've lost her, as that's the last thing she wants some young, pretty, sexy 22 year old being my girl – true? Unbelievable isn't it, I can't win, my punishment of 38 years obviously isn't enough for her. She'll never be happy to see a girl make me happy.

Tommy our live in chef has been cooking our meals – on the weekend he made a nice pizza for us, and then for dinner he made chicken breast filets with steamed rice and some lemon sauce – it was beautiful.

Slowly, slowly, I'm starting to get my visits organized again, what a mess that thing Stacey created. She used to come up here to visit me twice a week, and also bring Dhakota up here to see me twice a month, so when she stopped coming it put a big hole in my visits. I now have a friend of mine Penny bringing Dhakota up here to see me, which is good, as I really look forward to seeing Dhakota.

I don't really have much more to add, therefore I guess I will leave it there for now, and I hope to hear from you again soon.

With best wishes & respect, your friend always – Carl

13 August 2009 to Tracey

Dear Tracey,
I trust this letter finds you in the best of health and spirits, as it leaves me fine.

I just received your letter, and it was good to hear from you again, and just for the record, I enjoyed it.

---

89 Roberta is adamant that this is totally untrue. She comments: 'Carl had to make up shit blaming me for everything when he was angry.'

As of Sunday I got my phone calls back, I'm now aloud to make 32 calls per-week instead of 7, so yeh I'm back in the game. I enjoy using the phone and keeping in contact with a few people outside. As there are only three of us who live in this unit, so it's always good to hear from people, we're in a high security unit, with strict conditions. If you want, when you write back give me your number, and I'll out you on my phone list, and give you a call and have a laugh with you, the only problems is that I can only call between 8.00 am and 3.00 pm, as they're the only hours that I'm out of my cell.

You sound as if you'd be a good laugh, and heaps of fun – it's a shame I'm stuck in this place, as I love having a laugh, and taking the piss out of people, sounds like you do to – nothing better, and I'm good at it – plenty of experience I guess, there's a sucker born every day. ☺

What date is your B/day? Mine is October 13 – I actually got shot on my 29th B/day, good present hey – but some say the return gift was much better.

You were saying that you have some cousins and uncle that live in Broady, that's where I was brought up, then I moved to Essendon and then the city, the city living I enjoyed the most – everything is at your doorstep, club, restaurants, strip clubs, ect, ect.

Thank god you haven't seen that bullshit Underbelly series. I heard that just recently they were playing it again in Sydney and Qld, I'd say in time they play the rest of here in Melbourne – which I'm not looking forward too. They get some parts of it right, like who was killed – apart from that nothing much else is. Nevertheless, they seem to get away with calling it the truth – unbelievable. I don't like the way I'm portrayed, like some braindead imbecile, I should've expect any better, after all I'm not the most popular person in the Authorities' eyes – oh well you can't please everyone all the time, so it's no use trying too. They have me driving cars and socializing with people that I've never even met before in my life.

With best wishes & respect – Carl

17 August 2009 to Roberta Williams

Dear Roberta,
Surprise, surprise, mail just arrived, and I got a letter from you, one letter and that's all I got – one from the loyal ex – looks like no one loves me these days, oh well that's life, at least I know you'll never desert me.

You mentioned Stacey in your letter, and that I shouldn't worry about her – it's easier said than done. I don't really worry about her – I just hate the fact that I let her in. Her getting with someone, to some extent is understandable – but to just drop contact with Dhakota and me after I thought we were so close, and she was sincere, well that's another story. You know me and I never turn my back on anyone I care about, no matter what the problem is.

I haven't really have much up to add, therefore I guess I will leave it there for now, and I hope to hear from you again soon.

Love & friendship, always and forever - Carl – xx-

18 August 2009 to Danny Heaney

Dear Danny,
I just received your letter, and again it was my pleasure to hear from you, as it always is.

Roberta and Rob are supposed to be coming to visit me this week – Thursday, but they're not the most reliable people, I hope they come though, as I always have a laugh with them. I nearly always cause a fight between them, fuch they're funny.

Tommy's now settled in well, after you told me you use to call him Two Guns, we started running with it, we stir him up all day, we double team him, I don't think he'll be going anywhere for a while.

Roberta's in the process of writing some book a tell all – no doubt she's going to say about all the girls I fucked behind her back – play the poor victim – the standard thing, what a joke, what can you do but laugh. ☺

With best wishes & respect,
Your friend always – Carl

21 August 2009 to Roberta Williams

Dear Roberta,
I trust this letter finds you in the best of health and spirits, as it leaves me fine.

What a good visit I had with you all yesterday, thanks for taking the time out to come and see me – I look forward to seeing you. I love it when Brea comes and visits me with you, as we can both gang up on you and give you shit, as you could see, she also loves it, and just for the record yesterday you looked well, a piece of advice – let your hair grow.

When Stacey was with me, she thought that she could say anything to you, and out of respect for me, you wouldn't hit her, or say anything back to her. I use to hate that, and I was forever telling her to treat you with respect. She hated it how I was always there for you, but I'd often tell her if you don't like it, you know where the door is, after all you reached out for me, I never found you.

I haven't really have much up to add, therefore I guess I will leave it there for now, and I hope to hear from you again soon.

Love & friendship, always and forever – Carl – xx-

22 August 2009 to Wayne Howlett

Dear Wayne,
Firstly, congratulations, and please tell your missus that I said congratulations' also to her – thanks.

It was good that the prison let you shortly after the birth, I'm so happy for you. I can relate to you when you say it's a spin out when you look at your baby, and you can see yourself, I still do it all the time, when I look at my daughter. I've enclosed a photo of her (Dhakota) with Mundine for you to keep.

My old man had the operation – hip replacement – all went well – he had it done last week, his now at home recovering. They say he'll up and at em in about 6 weeks time, once he can walk he'll feel much better, his hip was fucked, when he was here with me he was in constant pain all day from it.

Yesterday Roberta came up here to visit me, we only get box visits, but we had a good laugh, I enjoy seeing her, when she's in a good mood, she's great company and a pleasure to be around, its just catching her at the right moment. ☺

I'm anxiously waiting to hear from these chicks that you got to write to me.

With best wishes & respect,
Your friend always – Carl

27 August 2009 to Roberta Williams

Dear Roberta,
I hope everything is going as good as it can be for you out there, as for me here I'm ok – pissed off a bit, but that's life, and I'll survive.

This morning I tried to ring you up, however when I did I was out of calls, then I had another look at your phone number, and that's when I noticed that the authorities' had placed an extra zero in front of the number, which makes it uncontactable. Then Tommy tried his phone – zero in front too. I knew something was up – so straight away, I asked to see someone to see what's going on – and they told me that the Governor will down sometime in the afternoon to talk to me.

When the Governor arrived, he said he had orders from above to take you off my phone, for 3 months, because of some phone call yesterday, when I was talking to you, and you rang Stacey's work, he said the powers to be are saying that your behavior on the phone is unacceptable. I said if Roberta is talking to someone else on another phone, whilst I'm on another phone, what does that have to do with me, he didn't say much, as he himself hadn't heard those calls. Therefore, what I'll do is call him back next week and talk further to him – the Governor is pretty good, and has always been very fair with me. I still can't work out what the fuck those calls has to do with me though. So if I understand correctly. I now won't be able to talk to you, but more importantly my daughters, Dhakota, and Brea for 3 months, because you were talking to, or even abusing Stacey on the phone – surely that can't be right, what are you suppose to do sit back and say nothing. You talking to her has nothing to do with me, the prison, or for that matter anyone else.

I haven't really have much up to add, therefore I guess I will leave it there for now, and I hope to hear from you again soon.

Love & friendship, always and forever – Carl – xx-

27 August 2009 to Beau Goddard

Dear Beau,
I just received your most welcomed letter, dated 26/8, and it was good to hear from you again, as it always is.

Tonight as well as your letter, I actually received a letter from Tracey, she's seem like a nice person, and seems like she'd be good fun. She gave me her phone number and told me to put it down, so I will, and I'll ring there and have a laugh. You mentioned that your friend Stacey, said if I want to write to her, tell her I said if she writes to me, and I'll gladly reply, I should get them both up here for a box visit for a laugh. What do you reckon?

I don't have any Asian girls who write to me, although a while ago there was one who kept writing, she even sent me a photo of herself, but I never replied, as I was with Stacey and back than I never wrote back to any girl I didn't know. I just thought for once I'll do the right thing, and look where it got me. Do you have any Asians write to you? If I get some, I'll be sure to put them onto you, what about ones from the Philippines, Dennis wife Maila might have some, I've never asked. Chinaman must have some girls, what other ones do you have writing to you.

With best wishes & respect,
Your friend always – Carl

Ps) Please tell Chinaman that I said hello, and wish him all the best – I have a lot of time for that bloke.

28 August 2009 to Tracey

Dear Tracey,
Last night I received your most welcomed letter, and it was my pleasure to hear from you again, as it always is.

So you're sick of men, at your age you should have them all on their toes. I know if I were out there now, I'd have all the female species on their toes, and as for men being headfucks, girls aren't too bad at it themselves, but I guess they can only fuck with your mind when you allow them too, that's why I very rarely let to me people in.

The City living is the best – I love it – I use to live at the Regency Towers – which is the adjoined building to the Marriott hotel – on the corner of Exhibition and Lonsdale streets, as I've previously said in the city everything is at your door step, and there are females everywhere. ☺ Where I lived, there was a bar downstairs' and Andrew (Benji) and I, use to go down there and just join in with any party that was happening, we didn't even know them, and we'd get photo taken with them and everything, gee it was a laugh.

Hmmm – the photos you had taken for the Live2ride magazine – I can't wait to see them, so best you send them to me ASAP –xx- ☺

With best wishes & respect – Carl

Ps) If you and a friend ever want to come up here for a visit – just let me know and I'll organize something, I'll leave that up to you, you let me know when you write back – ok.

2 September 2009 to Fabian Quaid

Dear Fab,
I just received your letter, dated 26/8, and it was pleasure to hear from you again, as it always is.

Nikki's good, I spoke to hear today, and I have to ring her again tomorrow morning, as she's going back to QLD for a one week holiday. When she comes back, she said she wants another visit. Before you go home, I'll give you her number, and give her yours – she'll go out for dinner and a few drinks with you – no problems. She's still waiting for those photos you were sending me to forward onto her. I've actually put two photos in this letter of her for you to keep, hope you like them.

My mate's son received that jumper you had sent to him – thanks for doing that – you made his year, you're a good man, and someone whom I'm proud to call my friend.

Your right, Tony's trial is underway – there's a suppression order on it over here – so if you get anything in the paper on it over there, can you please forward it to me – thanks. We're currently in the same Unit – but there's 4 section, his in one part, and I'm in another – we sometimes see one another in the visit centre. We usually keep in contact through the mail – although I haven't heard from him since it got underway. He should win it – but the big hurdle he has to get over is who he is. I don't ask him much about it – as according to him his going home on everything, they should never have brought him back to Australia – so I say nothing, as I believe some people don't like to hear the truth.

No news from Esmerelda – I send her a letter – no reply – I guess she'll write back when she's ready. If you talk to her get her to write and tell her, and I wouldn't mind her coming in for a visit when she's next in Melbourne. What's she do for a living?

You must have heaps of girls over there who can write to me – get onto it buddy for me. Let me know more when you write back.

I don't really have much more to add, therefore I guess I will leave it there for now, and I hope hear from you again soon.

With best wishes & respect,
Your friend always – Carl

3 September 2009 to Roberta Williams

Dear Roberta,
I trust this letter finds you in the very best of health and spirits, as it leaves me fine.

Thanks for coming to see me today, as I really enjoyed the visit, at first you weren't in the best of moods – which given the current circumstances, is understandable – and why would you be?

Bert after talking to you today, I thought I'd write you this letter.

When you're good, you're such a pleasure to be around. I'm the first to admit that when I was outside, there were times when I took you for granted, and hurt you, everyone makes mistakes, and that's one I'll always have to live with, I don't regret many things that I've done in my life – but hurting you – I do. I know that I'll probably never in my life find another person who loved me like you did, but I can also assure you now – that I also loved you – and a lot more then you'd ever imagine to be possible. I could go on and on, but I won't, as I've probably already given you a big enough head already. My point is you meant a lot to me, and you still mean a lot to me, no one will ever fill your shoes – never. I just thought

I'd tell you that, so don't you ever forget it. When Dean said I paid an amount of money for you – all I'll say if that were the case, than you were well under priced, and he got short changed. If he wants to run with that, then I got a barging, and on top of that, I was the most satisfied customer in the world, no complaints from this end. As much of a pain in the ass you could be at times, I for one most certainly have no regrets, and I wouldn't have returned you, not even for all the money in the world. Therefore, when you're down, think of all the laughs, and good times we shared, as there were a lot of them, to many to mention.

Roberta, you were 100% right when you said that there were alot of girls that were jealous, and envious of what you had with me. They were because it was you who I gave so much attention to, who I gave my heart to, who I feel in love with, who I took care of, who I married, and not only let, who I wanted with all my heart to have my child, and you who I came home to. As you're fully aware even Stacey was very jealous of you, she'd often say to me – Carlos, I hate it how Bert had the best of you, she's so lucky, it's not fair – why couldn't I have had those years with you. Well let me assure you – you weren't the only lucky one – because I consider myself extremely fortunate to have spent the time I did with you, and to have the memories that I do, and will always cherish.

I don't really have much up to add, therefore I guess I will leave it there for now, and I hope to hear from you again soon, you said you have a broken foot – not hand, so you can write a letter ever now and again – True? ☺

Love & friendship, always and forever – Carl – xx-

3 September 2009 to Danny Heaney

Dear Danny,
On Tuesday night, I received your most welcomed letter, and it was good to hear from you again as it always is.

I knew Faruk was at trial – and I know John W. is one of the witnesses again him – I've heard one of his mates also turned – some bloke who owed the kebab shop, who they put up to give evidence for Gatto at his trial – saying he minded guns for Andrew. I also heard some person Fizza is a witness – I don't know him, and I don't know what his said. Brad A. isn't a witness in that case, he couldn't be in two places at once, as his giving evidence against Tony – re; Lewis Moran murder, I haven't heard how that's going, but Tony should be a good chance of winning it, fingers crossed for him.

Today I had a visit with Roberta – the first hour was with her alone, and the second hour Rob joined us – as he went to see Sean first. It was a good visit and we had a laugh, when she's in a good mood she's always a laugh – small does are good. ☺

With best wishes & respect,
Your friend always – Carl

6 September 2009 to Beau Goddard

Dear Beau,
I just received your letter, and it was good to hear from you again, as it always is.

I haven't heard from Tracey for a few weeks – the prison have tried to ring her to put her number down, however every time they ring her, they can't get hold of her. So I told her in a letter, that if she wants me to call her, for her to ring up the prison and get her number verified – there is not much else I can do – the balls now in her court – true?

I knew Rob and Roberta had split up – for how long who knows – I like you think they'll get back together and I hope they do, as I think she'd be lost without him. Honestly though I don't know how he puts up with her, and her moods, and I believe he deserves a medal for doing so. I haven't spoken to her – as a few weeks ago the prison banned her from talking to me for 3 months, over bullshit to do with Stacey. Rob actually came up here to see me yesterday with Brea – and it was a really good visit, I like Rob, so do the kids, and his good with them.

I see Roberta's book is due to be released next week, god only knows what she'll have to say in there about me – I can't wait to read it – NOT!! I seen today's paper and that was more than enough for me – what a load of shit. No doubt, she'll be painting herself out to be the best thing since slice bread, and the victim in everything and anything – what a fucken joke.

With best wishes & respect,
Your friend always – Carl

6 September 2009 to Tracey

Dear Tracey,
On Friday, I received your most welcomed letter, with photos enclosed, and I was so happy to hear from you again, as I always am. The photos were fantastic – thanks for them – you looked hot, and I can clearly see why you'd turn for "Jackie McKenzie" Hmmm, what a thought (he he), are you and her friends with one another, and in regular contact with each other, or were you two just put together for that photo shoot? Let me know when you write back.

Is this correct, that all the girls who live with you, also work with you, how many of you girls actually live there. Let me know when you're thinking about moving out – as I know a place in the city where the rents are cheap, they're only one B/room places, but there not too bad, and they're security, only problem is they don't come with car parks spaces, but you can rent a car park close by.

In your letter you mentioned, that in my last letter to you I didn't seem in the best of moods – sorry if I came across like that – nothing was wrong – it might have been that time of the month (ha ha), again I apologize if I came across cold.

So you have a friend who regularly comes up here to visit someone, it would've been good if I knew that earlier, as I would've organized a visit for you, maybe next time. As I said to you in my last letter, if you ever want to come up here and see me, it'd be my pleasure to allow you to have a visit. I only get one contact visit per –month, and two box visits per week. Do you have any idea who your friend visits, and what the duration of her visit are, the reason I ask that is because in different part of this prison, visits are for longer – I'm in the Management Unit – and my visit are only for one hour – where in some other places their visits are for two – three hours. I don't want you coming up with someone, and after you've finished seeing me, you have to wait out the front for hours for your friends visit to finish – get my point.

You wanted to know more about Prison life – as I said earlier I'm in a Management/High Security Unit, and have been since my arrest in 2004, 5 ½ years ago. The regime I'm on, is different then what other people in different section of this Prison are on – we're on a more restricted regime – where was get virtually fuck all.

The unit that I'm currently living in has 6 cells, but at the moment there are only 3 of us who live in here – me and two others. Now what do we have access to here – a Gym – which consists of machine weight, treadmill, exercise bike, boxing bag, chin –up, dips, and sit up station, two small exercise yards, one being no bigger than a tennis court, and the other is half that size, in both yards we get filtered sunlight, as there is mesh covering the roofs. In our cells, we have a toilet, a shower, and we have TV's in our cells, that we can watch whenever we want, and whatever we want, although we only get the free to air channels. As you can see I have my own personal computer – which I'm always on, unfortunately we can't access the internet – although I wish we could – I'd be on that facebook all day and night, that'd make my time go quicker.

The only things that I'm allowed to have sent in besides letters and photos, are virtually – books, magazines, jocks and socks, no movies or anything like that. Other things such as CD's, PC games, Playstation games, runners, ect, ect, we can buy once a month on what is called a special buy, we pay for them, and the Prison go out and purchase them for us.

My daily routine is I get up – we are let out of our cells at 8.00 am – than I usually make a few phone calls, eat breakfast – go for a jog on the treadmill, have a shower. Then I do the weights – eat lunch – mess around with the others here for a while, and/or I make more phone calls – do the weights again, than its nearly time to get locked up for the day – which is 3.00 – 3.30 pm, I usually go to sleep about 10.30–11.30 pm, quite boring these days aren't I?

I put a phone list in last week to have your phone number added to it, so that I can ring you – obviously it hasn't been done as yet, so I'll get on to it first thing tomorrow morning, once it's on I'll give you a ring – as I'm looking forward to talking to you.

I haven't really have much up to add, therefore I guess I will leave it there for now, and I hope to hear from you again soon.[90]

With best wishes & respect – ♡ Carl –xx-

10 September 2009 to Natasha Morgan

Dear Tash,
I've been laying here looking at your photo, which is on my notice board, and I thought what better to do than write you a quick letter. Before I go on I must say you look hot – honestly, you don't look a day older then the last time I seen you, which would've been about 10 years ago.

I don't know what you did to Tommy, but lately he can't seem to stop talking about you – it's like he has an axe to grind with you, I wish he'd just get over it. I hope you don't get angry, but recently I showed him that dirty letter you wrote to me a while ago. I didn't tell him you wrote it, but I think he knew it came from you. Anyway a few days after, he asked me if you've ever wrote me a dirty letter – I said no, but I said that I've been thinking of asking you to, as you're a good writer. He said, I bet you $100 canteen that you can't get one off her. Please, please, do me a favour and write me the dirtiest letter you can, to stick it up his ass. If you do, I'll be in debt to you for life.

Love & friendship – Carl

90 Carl received a last letter from Tracey on 5 October 2009. Its contents are unknown, but he did not reply to it.

CHAPTER 7

'I have the looks, personality, and the women know where I am at all times'

For most of his adult life, Carl had never really known a time when he was without young women at his beck and call. With the departure of Stacey, he was firing off letters in all directions in search of a new companion. Enter 'Kylie'. To protect her privacy, this is not her real name and some details in the correspondence that follows have been altered in order to conceal her identity.

Meantime, he still kept up his regular correspondence with the many other women in his life, not least Roberta.

10 September 2009 to Kylie

Dear Kylie,
Shock horror!!!! I finally received a letter from you, and yes, it was my pleasure to hear from you, better late than never.

Firstly, you don't have to thank me for keeping in touch with your mum, as I enjoy writing to her, and I look forward to receiving mail from her. She's a good person, whom I have a lot of time, and respect for, and I can't say that about many people.

So you're a Collingwood supporter – don't worry I won't hold that against you. ☺ In the Unit which I'm in, there are 3 of us who live here, not Tommy, but the other guy who lives here with us is a mad, fanatical, Collingwood supporter, and I drive him crazy when they get beat – I love a shit stir, and he hates it – got to do something to amuse myself. When the games are on TV (delayed telecast), I listen to them on the radio to get the score, I pretend I don't know what's going on, and bet with him – money for jam – or I should say chocolates for jam (he he).

You asked how I've been? I'm going along ok – I have my up and downs, the same as when I was outside, I guess. As you could imagine – I had a hard time coming to terms with the loss of my mum, as her and I were so close – I use to ring her up every morning religiously, she was not only my mother, but also my best friend, and I miss her so much. Then recently I had a bit of a hard time splitting up with Stacey – normally, I don't let anyone in, as don't I trust many people, but I did her. I had a lot of time for her, and when it ended, she told me a lot of lies, which I caught her out on, and they hurt, all I ever asked of her to be was honest – which I don't believe is much of an ask.

You and your girls want to know how I'm in here, and I always seem to be able to get hotties. Why should that come as a shock? After all I have the looks, personality, and the women know where I am at all times. Believe me I don't just find the hotties, I also find the fruit loop ones, and they can sometimes be hotties too, but these days I can get rid of those ones quickly – and they can't stalk me (he he).

As for there being no good men out there – I can't say they're all in here, I can only speak for myself, and I'm in here. Surely, there has be some good ones out there. Although all the girls I talk to seem to say the same as you "there's no good men out there," maybe you'll have to run a petition to get me out of there – as it seems like I'm the only good one around. I can cook, clean, and I know how to treat women – it's pretty simply isn't it.

Now that Stacey and I are finished, I suppose, that I'll be needing another hottie, I'll have to get my little black book out, and if you come across any out there, don't be shy to put them onto me. You can be my talent scout (he he).

With love and best wishes – Carl –xox-

12 September 2009 to Penny Brown

Dear Penny,
I trust this letter finds you and your loved ones in the very best of health and spirits, as it leaves me fine.

Penny, Tom was telling me that you like to go the Concerts with your daughter. I have a friend out there who owns Mushrooms records, and he use to get all the tickets for me to any Concerts, as his business partner, and friend, owns Frontier Touring Productions, they have a lot of the concerts. I haven't been in contact with him for the last few years. But a few years ago whilst I was still in here, my dad use to ring him for me to get the tickets, but he hasn't rang him for a while. If you want too,

I'm more than happy for you to ring him up, and tell him you're a good friend of mine, and I asked you to ring him, to see if he can get you tickets for any concerts that you want to go to. Ask for 4 tickets, and say that they're for you to take my daughter, and a few friends. If he comes through all good and well, and if he doesn't – well nothing lost – nothing gained. I haven't got his mobile number – so what I suggest you do is ring information, and ask to be put through to Mushroom Records, sometimes he can be hard to get hold of – so if at first you don't get him just keep trying.

I've enclosed a few photos for you that were taken at Dhakota Christening, one of me, Roberta, Dhakota, and Vanessa Amorosi – Vanessa sang at the christening. The others are of me, and my mum, and me and Dhakota. Once you've copied them, can you please send them back to me – as they are the only copies that I have. With the one of Roberta, Dhakota, Vanessa, and me, can you please take Roberta out of that photo – thanks.

Penny, if possible, I'd like you to let people know that whoever writes to me, that I will reply to them, providing they enclose a photo of themself with their letter, after all they know it is who they're writing to, so I feel it's only fair that I can see who it is that I'm writing to. Also, let people know that I enjoy receiving mail, and replying to it – as it helps me pass my time, and beat the boredom the exsists in this place, also let them know that I really do appreciate it when people take the time out to write to me.

I don't really have much up to add, therefore I guess I will leave it there for now.

Keep in touch.

Best wishes and respect – Carl

14 September 2009 to Roberta Williams

Dear Roberta,
Now that I can't ring you, it's so hard to tell you things – so I have to try my best through mail, or messages through my dad.

As you know today I had a visit with Dhakota – and attitude was that bad, I actually left the visit before it was finished. I couldn't put up with her, she was so rude, she wouldn't answer anything I was asking her – and she was just being a bitch, talking down to me like I was a piece of shit – and I won't put up with it – if anyone else talked to me how she did today, they would've copped a backhander.

Roberta all jokes aside she has to lose some weight, she's so fat that it's unhealthy; all she wants to do is feed her face with rubbish, enough is enough – you have to put your foot down now before it's too late, and put her on a diet. I know you might think that I'm overreacting – but I don't think I am, if she keeps putting on weight all the other kids will tease her, and she'll feel uncomfortable doing sports and wearing bathers – just do me a favour, and from now on watch what she eats, get her eating healthy – no more take away or sweets.

Today, she also said that she hasn't been sleeping very well at my mum's place, and she doesn't really want to live there, I know you haven't really got many other options – but myself I don't think I could live there after what happened there with my mum, so I can see where she's coming from. I don't know what you what to do – and at the moments it's just so hard to talk to you. I'm happy to help you in anyway that I can – which I think you already know.

I don't really have much up to add, therefore I guess I will leave it there for now, and I hope to hear from you again soon.

Love & friendship - Carl – xx-

14 September 2009 to Beau Goddard

Dear Beau,
Last night I received your letter and it was my pleasure to hear from you again as it always is.

Yesterday was my B/day, I turned 39, Roberta, Rob, Dhakota and Brea all came up her to see me for it, I had a really good visit with them all, we had a laugh, Dhakota cracks me up with some of the things that she comes out with, she 8 turning 29, she's so cute. I love her to bits, when she comes and sees me she gets all the attention, which she loves.

I hear what you say regarding Roberta, and I don't blame you for thinking like that – however I will say one thing – she always talks highly of you, and has a lot of time for you.

I received a letter from your friend Stacey, I replied to it straight away – I now have a few on the ball, a few really sexy ones from Sydney too – they're smoking hot, and want to come down here to visit, when who knows, they are good friends of close friend of mines, I'll just play it by ear.

With best wishes & respect,
Your friend always – Carl

16 September 2009 to Roberta Williams

Dear Roberta,
I hope everything is going as good as it can be expected out there for you – me here – I'm ok.

Today I had a fantastic visit with Rob and Brea, Brea's such a good kid, and I love her to death, I also have a lot of time for Rob. I see Dhakota never made it up here with them to see me – and that was a good move on her behalf, with the way her attitudes been of late, and she'd want to get rid of her dummy soon, after all she's turning 9 not 2.

Bert, I don't know what's going on with you and Rob, as it's your business, and not mine, but if you need someone to talk to – I'm here for you. However, I will warn you of one thing – if you and Rob, don't, or can't work out your issues – you'd better not go back near that Omar,[91] because if you do, I'll never, ever, talk to you, or have anything to do with you again, and I'll make sure the same goes with anyone I know. On top of that I won't allow you to stay at my mum's place – I may be many things, but I'm not a fool, just thought I'd give you this warning in advance, so the balls now in your court. I'm sick of people taking me for a fool – just because I'm in here, enough is enough, I hope you not only hear me loud and clear, but more importantly you listen to me.

I don't really have much up to add, therefore I guess I will leave it there for now, and I hope to hear from you again soon.

Love & friendship, always and forever - Carl – xx-

17 September 2009 to Michelle Mercieca

Michelle Mercieca is one of Roberta Williams' sisters.

Dear Michelle,
I trust this letter finds you in the very best of health and spirits, as it leaves me fine.

Michelle, I hope you received the card I sent C/- Roberta for you.

91 In March 2007, when Carl and Roberta were in the final stages of their divorce, she announced that she had converted to Islam and had a boyfriend, called 'Omar' (not his real name), of that faith. Carl was never impressed by the presence of Omar in her life.

I just received your letter, with card enclosed, and I was very happy to hear from you, as I always am, thanks for the card – Jess looks really pretty in that picture. Michelle you're always in my thoughts, just as I am in yours. I'll be honest with you, after what happened to Jess did, I've been really worried about you – so tonight, I was really pleased to hear from you, but more importantly to hear that you're coping alright under the current circumstances. You said you hope Jess has gone to a better place, Michelle let's face it, she could've have gone anywhere worse, I agree with you, at times life isn't fair.

I would've been really happy if Jess had of written to me, if I had of known she was locked up, I would've made contact with her first. You know I've always had time for your kids, and it goes without saying that I have a lot of time for you, and that'll never change whether I hear from you every day, or once a year, so please don't you ever forget that.

I just wanted to write you a short letter to thank you for the card, and let you know that I'm thinking of you – stay strong.

Keep in touch, and I hope to hear from you again soon.

Love & friendship – Carl – xx-

22 September 2009 to Kylie

Dear Kylie,

I just received your most welcome letter, with pictures, and jokes attached – and again it was my pleasure to hear from you, as it always is. Thanks for writing back so quickly, as your letters give me a good laugh. In addition, I'm allowed to have dirty jokes – not too dirty though for me, as I'm a bit of a prude (only joking).

From looking at the pictures you sent me – you don't need to lose any weight; you look good as you are – now that's a compliment. I love your smile, beautiful white teeth. Nothing more I love then a nice smile.

Working 7 days a week – you need more fun, and less work. Maybe that's why you can't find guys – or the right ones I should say – as you're working all the time – with your sense of humour, and looks, one would think you'd need to be carrying a stick around with you to beat them all off. ☺

Neighbourly crush – I'll tell you a story. One day I remember pulling up out the front of my parents' place, at the time I was seeing this pretty little blonde girl (Nicole).[92] Anyway, you and Jay were out the front with some boys – you were both only young – and one of the boys said, she's not bad, referring to Nicole. And then apparently Nicole said she heard a female say either is he. I never actually heard it, so I thought she was pulling my leg – now all these years later, I find out she might have been telling the truth (he he).

You reckon my little black book could tell some stories – nah not really. I'm a good boy, if you didn't know that already. ☺ In addition, if it could tell any stories, they might be a bit much for your innocent little ears. I could tell you a few funny stories though – some of them would make me laugh just thinking about them – odd women, that's an understatement, and just for the record I don't put you in that pile – not yet anyway – LOL, right back at ya.

You asked if I get many visitors – beside my fortnightly contact visits that I get with Dhakota – I get two – one-hour, box visits per week, and one, one-hour contact visit per month. I enjoy my visits, as they give me something to look forward too, and get my mind out of this place for that short period of time. When I was with Stacey, she use to take up a lot of the visits, she

92 Nicole Mottram.

use to visit me twice a week, but I enjoyed and looked forward to my visits with her. I've always got people wanting to come up and visit.

As for me getting any time off my sentence, at the moment I still have an appeal pending. I'm appealing the severity of my sentence – and I, as well as my legal team are confident, or I should say know, that I will get something off – but how much is anyone guess – from what I hear it should be about 10 years. The Appeal should come up sometime next year.

I don't really have much up to add, therefore I guess I will leave it there for now, and I look forward to hearing from you again soon – until then "be good, or be good at it."

With love and best wishes – Carl –xox-

28 September 2009 to Kylie

Dear Kylie,
I just received your letter, dated 26 September, and it was good to hear from again, as it always is.

Firstly, I'd better tell you – your letters don't bore me – completely the opposite – I know this might give you a big head – but so be it – without a word of a lie, I love hearing from you, longer the better, keep up the good work.

My B/day is on the 13 of October, not far away now, and I'll now be expecting a surprise from you – I like surprises. ☺ In addition, as for how old I'm turning – I'm turning 39 – sounds old doesn't it? Stop laughing, it's not that funny, I don't feel it though – and whatever any younger guy can do, I can do better – now get your mind out of the gutter, Kylie. ☺

I've got no tattoos – no reason. I don't mind tattoos – just never got any done.

As for men not being able to handle you – for the time being I won't go into that one. Next letter I will though – only after you give me more information and let me know in what way you're referring too (LOL).☺ I've always been out with, and attracted to, stand up girls. They're a lot more fun. I'm not into the robots – never have been.

You asked if I get lots of pen pals. From time to time I get a lot of strangers writing to me, but I don't usually reply to them. I only write back to the people I know, or if someone is a friend of a friend.

Lara, is near Geelong, it's not that far ways, and I can have visits any day of the week – from 9.00 am – 2.00 pm. As I've previously told you, you're welcome to come and see me anytime you want to – I'll be here, I'm not going anywhere soon, not that I know about anyway. But if you plan on coming to see me – you have to let me know in advance, so that I can book the visit at this end, and put you on my visitors list – no rush.

To answer your question – Stacey worked. She is a fully qualified hairdresser. Stacey lived and worked in Melton; she very rarely used to leave Melton – I think she needed a visa to get out of there.

I don't really have much up to add, therefore I guess for the time being, I will love you, and leave you – but I look forward to hearing from you again really soon.

With love and best wishes – Carl –xox-

PS Please give my love and best wishes to your mum – and let her know she can write whenever she likes – I know she has a lot on her plate, she's found me a new pen pal that I couldn't be more happy with.

Postcript Joke

A man decides to have a face-lift for his birthday. He spends $5000, and feels really good about the result.

On his way home, he stops at a newsstand and buys the paper. Before leaving he says to the clerk "I hope you don't mind me asking, but how old do you think I am?"

"About 35" was the reply.

"I'm actually 47, the man says happily."

A little while later he goes to McDonalds for lunch, and asks the man behind the counter the same question, to which the reply is "I'd guess you're 29?"

"Nope I am actually 47."

He's starting to feel good about himself. While standing at the bus stop he asks an old woman the same question.

She replies "I am 85 years old, and my eye sight is going. But when I was young, there was a sure way of telling a man's age. If I put my hand down your pants and play with your penis for ten minutes, I will be able to tell you your exact age."

As there was no one else around, the man thought what the heck and let her slip her hand down his pants.

Ten minutes later the old lady says, "Ok, it's done, you're 47."

Stunned, the man says, "That was brilliant! How did you do that?"

The old woman replies, "I was behind you in McDonalds."

28 September 2009 to Fabian Quaid

Dear Fab,

I just received two letters from you – one dated 10 August, with photo attached, and the other dated 20 September – again, it was my pleasure to hear from you, as it always is.

Mate when Nikki gets that photo of you, she's going to melt – you look well, if I kicked both feet even I'd be interested – but that not my capper.

Esmerelda's back hey – I still haven't heard from her ☹ – maybe someone scared her away from me, because I thought she sounded pretty keen, oh well not much I can do from here. I guess if she wants to write to me she will – I'd like her too, but the balls in her Court. I've been told that we might soon be able to call mobiles from here, if or when that happens, I'll put her number on my phone, that's if she wants me too.

You were saying that lately I've been getting plenty of media coverage over there, same here, and by the sounds of things it the same stories, Stacey. After reading what you did – you now feel sorry for me – so now you're going to get off your ass, and getting some of your girls to write to me. I don't want sympathy – but girls "YES" ☺ – thanks buddy, you're a good man, there's no disputing that. I'll now be waiting with baited breath to hear from them – make sure that you get them to enclose a recent photo of themselves with their letters – thanks. ☺

You asked how often I get to see my daughter (Dhakota), I get to see her twice a month on contact visits, she's growing up so quickly, and at times has an attitude, but with her bloodline you'd expect nothing less would you. I put her straight back in her place if she gets smart with me – I'm about the only one who she listens to though, interesting times ahead for her, at time she's 8 – turning 28. I'm sending my step daughter this coming week to Versace, so my a mate my mine can dress her up for her school formal – no doubt Dhakota will tag along and get some clothes – she say – she's hot, forever checking herself out in the mirror, what a crack up she is.

If you wouldn't mind I'd like a book from my mate,[93] a signed one at that, get him to send me one if you can, it'll be interesting to see what he has to say, if anything about me – although I don't think I'll get a mention – I've never really heard him say anything about me. As you know and I don't hide the fact that I don't have any time for the bloke – and I guess he feels the same way about me – but I think his above running people down, after all we're not kids, Roberta maybe, but I'm not (ha ha).

With best wishes & respect,

Your friend always – Carl

Ps) It goes without saying – good luck for your Trial, that's if I don't talk to you beforehand, but I hope I do.

93 Here Carl is referring to Mick Gatto's book, *I, Mick Gatto*. He probably means 'your mate'.

CHAPTER 8
A contest of narratives

Veteran Melbourne *Age* journalists John Silvester and Andrew Rule were the first people to attempt to piece together what was happening in Melbourne gangland at the turn of the millennium and to shape it into some kind of coherent narrative. They began a series of books, called *Underbelly*, beginning in 1997 with *Underbelly 1: True crime stories*. By 2004 they had reached *Underbelly 8: More true crime stories*. In the same year they also published a book called *Leadbelly: Inside Australia's underworld wars* and sold the TV rights of that book to the production company Screentime, who in turn sold the idea of a TV series to the Nine Network, although the name *Underbelly* was preferred for the entertainment then being developed.

The thirteen-part series *Underbelly* was originally aired from 13 February 2008 to 7 May 2008 and is loosely based on the real events of 1995–2004; it was screened at this time in all states other than Victoria, where an injunction was in place to ensure that the forthcoming criminal trials were not unduly influenced. The first *Underbelly* series proved immensely popular and subsequently there were many sequels, some of them totally unrelated to Melbourne. An updated version of the book *Leadbelly,* now titled *Underbelly: The Gangland War,* was released as a TV tie-in in 2008 and promptly sold more than 200,000 copies.

Clearly there was a quid to be made from spinning the many possible versions of the Gangland War and it was only a matter of time before some of the participants found it lucrative to put their own personal stamp on this battle of narratives. On 1 October 2009 Melbourne University Publishing ventured into what was for them uncharted waters by publishing Mick Gatto's *I, Mick Gatto* and on the same day HarperCollins issued Roberta Williams' *My Life.* As is customary, the books first appeared in shops some days before their official publication day, and quickly found their way to Carl's prison cell. Loyally, he read his ex-wife's version first and was considerably more enthusiastic about it.

Mick's version ultimately sold more than 50,000 copies and Roberta's sold around half that number.

18 September 2009 to Roberta Williams

Dear Roberta,
I trust this letter finds you in the very best of health and spirits, as it leaves me fine.

Over the past few days I've been reading the paper with great interest, as there has been some extracts of your book in there – and after reading what I did, I now can't wait to read your book – NOT!! The million-dollar question is – Do you believe in your own mind – that your book is fiction, or nonfiction?

Fortunately, for me though – I've now learnt how you and I got together, thanks for shedding light on that for me – because that's certainly not how I understood it to be. I can't remember you being covered in blood the first time we kissed one another on the couch at Fitzroy – from my memory it happened after you and I had just returned from shopping at Highpoint.

What's this shit about – I think I'm above going down the Milk bar for you, because tough guys don't do that – I use to go down there all the time for you, and get you whatever you wanted. I use to buy you all the chocolates you wanted, and I can clearly remember going to buy you boxes of cherrie sunday's, redskins, twirls ect, ect, and always a mixture of Ice Creams.

I'd love to know who you were referring to as being my mistress in Brunswick???

Or better still what your interpretation of a mistress is????

I'm not going to go on and on about what I agree with, and don't agree with in your book – however I will say that I believe I'm the only one who has always stood by you, and supported you through anything – & I always will – nothing will ever change that – despite you do some bad things to me. So you should remember that, before you bag me – because once you put things out there, you can't take them back, or correct them.

As for you being depressed – I only wish that there was something that I could do to help you, as I know how you feel. Try putting yourself in my shoes for a moment, after losing my mum, I often feel like I have nothing, & I feel like a bit part of me is missing. The only thing I have to look forward to in life now is seeing Dhakota & Brea – and I know that there will come a time when they both can't be bothered coming into a Prison to see me. So yeh I don't really have a lot to look forward to – do I now, just another 33 more years of this bullshit. Stacey use to make me happy, and unfortunately things with her even came to an end, just as everything does. ☹

I don't really have much up to add, therefore I guess I will leave it there for now, and I hope to hear from you again soon.

Love & friendship, always and forever - Carl – xx-

25 September 2009 to Roberta Williams

Dear Roberta,
I trust this letter finds you in the very best of health and spirits, as it leaves me fine.

Today I had a good visit with Mick[94] – it was good to see him, and we had a laugh, which is needed in these places, his going to come back and visit me again in a few weeks time.

I recently wrote a letter to the General Manager – Mr. Russell Reed in relation to you coming to visit me on a contact visit, he wrote back, and said you can apply to him in writing for consideration to have your contact visits restored on 14th October 2009. Therefore, what I suggest you do is, write to him ASAP, and then hopefully you get them back on the above-mentioned

94 Mick Selim.

date – so we can have a contact visit the day after my Birthday, which is a Wednesday. Make sure you do it straight away don't leave it wait – ok.

What else is happening here – nothing much – it's the same shit day in day out in this joint – the only thing that changes is who Tommy's in love with, and going to marry. ☺

I still have got your book as yet – I'll most likely get it on Monday.

I don't really have much up to add, therefore I guess I will leave it there for now, and I hope to hear from you again soon.

Love & friendship, always and forever – Carl – xx-

29 September 2009 to Natasha Morgan

Dear Tash,
Glad to hear that you liked the photo I sent you – I still think it was a shit one, as I said, I was debating whether to send it to you or not – I was going to wait until I got a better one taken.

Hey, by the flow of mail I've been getting from your way – I think there's a strong possibility you could make some money from hiring out my photo. Over the last week and a half, about four girls have written to me from there – I didn't reply to any of them. The only name I can remember was Carly – and the only reason I remember that one is because of my name – they were all letters of support, and she seemed to the most sensible from of all the letters.

Roberta's book is now out. I read it last night – all I'll say is, "Never let the truth get in the way of a good story." Oh well, as long as she gets a quid out of it. I'd much rather see her making money off my name, than the likes of John Sylvester. One minute she's getting stuck into me, and the next she's saying how good I am – nothing changes.

As for me not listening to you re Stacey – what can I say? I don't usually write back to people I don't know – but she knew people that I knew, and was close friends with, so I didn't feel like she was a complete stranger. Then when she came in to see me, we just clicked, and it was as if I'd known her forever. It was all good whilst it lasted, and I really did enjoy her company. Oh well it's all over with her now and, as you say, it's her loss. Self-catering – we will be provided with a shopping list. I've seen the list and it's got nearly everything you need on it – I believe they get a lot of the things from Safeway's. Once it comes in, what we'll be doing is ordering whatever we want on a weekly basis. It'll be good once we get it. If you could come here, I'd cook you up a good feed – but I think Tommy might get a little jealous. Oh well, you can't make everyone happy all the time, so there's no use in trying.

With love and best wishes, Carl –xx-

29 September 2009 to Beau Goddard

Dear Beau,
Late last week I received your letter, and it was good to hear from you again, as it always is.

Spewing I was barracking big time for the Saints to win, they had their chances, and they missed some else goals, which we both know you can't afford to do against Geelong, or more importantly in a Grand Final.

Brendon tried his heart out – and I believe he can hold his head up high; I'm a big fan of his, his my favorite player. That was a good letter you wrote Brendon, the one they published in the paper, by the sounds of things you must have been a pretty handy footballer yourself.

I see on Friday, Tony was acquitted on the Lewis Moran murder – it was a good win for him – although I still think they'll catch up with him in the end of the day – on the drug matters. They'll give give him a bigger sentence when they do eventually find him guilty – you know what they're like.

Today Faruk got found guilty on the Victor Peirce murder,[95] interesting days ahead – he still has to front over PK's murder,[96] and the strong rumor is that they are going to charge him over Dino Dibra's murder – initially he thought he'd get bail – then he was told he'd 100% beat in at the committal, then trial – now what appeal?

John W. was the main witness against him – and John only got pinched after Allan T. rolled – and we know who not only told but also supported Allan on rolling, it bet his ass is twitching now.

I heard in the Peirce trial that the defense were trying to say that I ordered that murder – what a load of crap, A) at the time of the murder I was in prison, and B) when Victor was killed I never even knew Andrew.

No news from any of the girls – I don't know what's happened with Tracey – she send me a photo of her, and another girl which was in the magazine live 2 ride – the other girl is super hot. Tracey was saying that she's a penthouse pet, her name is "Jackie McKenzie", see if Stacey knows her, she's the one I want, if you can pull this one off I'll be in debt to you. ☺

With best wishes & respect,
Your friend always –

---

95 Faruk Orman was convicted of driving Andrew Veniamin to murder Victor Peirce, in May 2002.

96 PK is Paul Kallipolitis, who was found murdered on 12 October 2002 in his West Sunshine home.

29 September 2009 to Milad Mokbel

Dear Milad,

I trust this letter finds you in the best of health and spirits, as it leaves me fine.

I just received your letter, and it was good to hear from you again, as it always is.

I heard yesterday, that on Friday, Tony was acquitted on the Lewis Moran murder – it was a good win for him – and I bet it a big weight lifted off his shoulders. I always said it was a weak case against him – full of lies – but I worried about him not getting a fair trial because of who he is – luckily for him though he never had Betty. As you said he still has a few more hurdles to get over – and hopefully in time he does, as you know I have all the time in the world for Tony – his a good man, and one I'm proud to call my true and trusted friend. I still think they'll try there best to catch up with him in the end of the day – on the drug matters, but all he can do is fight on, and that you can be assured he'll do. ☺

Last week I finally had the pleasure of meeting Karina[97] – she's not a bad sort either – she came up here to visit me with Roberta – she drove Roberta up here to see me, as Roberta doesn't have a license. She was saying that lately she's been having a few dramas with people saying who she was, and wasn't sleeping with – I didn't take too much notice – but it was something about Danielle. I said I'm not interested in bullshit, all I'll say is Milad has always spoke highly of you – I'm always looking out for you – now where's Melanie??? ☺

With best wishes & respect,
Your friend always – Carl

97 Karina Cacopardo.

30 September 2009 to Nikki Denman

Dear Nikki,
I trust this letter finds you in the best of health and spirits, as it leaves me fine.

I've been trying to ring you up at Kerry's, but I haven't been able to get an answer.

I don't know how things are currently going with your love life – but I do know that Fab is still keen on you. He has his trial starting early next month – if he wins – his out, and he reckons his keen on taking you out – he wants me to put in a good word for him. Apparently, he is on face book, someone must be running a site for him – his full name is FABIAN QUAID. He asked me for your full name, so that he could make contact with you on facebook, but I wouldn't give it without talking to you, if you say it's ok, I'll give it to him, and he can become your friend on there. ☺. He sent me a picture of himself, to send to you – which I've attracted to this letter – his the one in the middle, his a really good guy.

Just a short one today to get this photo to you as I promise him I'll send it to you as soon as I received it.

Keep in touch – a letter would be nice. ☺

With Love & best wishes – Carl –Xox-

5 October 2009 to Kylie

Dear Kylie,
I just received your letter, dated 1 October – 3 pages – good work – I've got a smile for ear to ear – thanks to you – and it was my absolute pleasure to hear from you again, as it always is.

You made me laugh when you said you rang the prison, I'm not allowed to have shirts, or anything like that dropped off, or sent in. I'm in one of the Management/High Security Units, and what we can have is different to what other people in other sections of the prison can have. We're only permitted to wear RED clothing – and none can be dropped off – the prison supply us with it all – I don't know what's with the red – maybe it's makes a better bullseye – only joking. I'm only permitted to have jocks, socks, books and magazines dropped off to me – I don't need anything though – your letters make me happy enough. As for you jumping out of the box – well I'm not even going to entertain that subject. Good try. ☺

You ask how it feels to be getting old. What are you getting younger, smartass! I honestly feel younger now than I did 5 ½ years ago, so I don't think that I'm in a position to answer your question. Anyway, your beautiful mother said I don't look my age – do you agree???? If so how old do you think I look? Remember to be nice, as you'll be coming to visit me soon – you promised.

You asked if I ever thought I'd have more kids – I would've liked to have more kids – I would've liked to have had a boy. I always thought Dhakota was going to be a boy – but I wouldn't swap her for anything in the world – I love her with all my heart, she's everything to me.

Sneak away and come and visit me, sounds good, actually it sound like we're being naughty – so you've got yourself a deal. ☺ Lara isn't that far – you don't need an overnight trip – you're funny, you talk like I'm on the other said of the world. As for making a good impression on other people here – when you come to visit me you won't see anyone else. As box visits are held in cubicles, and the contact visits here where I am, are not in the main visit centre – they're in a room, with just me and the visitors.

Obviously with box visits there's no contact, as there is a glass separating you from one another. However, with contact visits, there is contact and you don't have to keep your hands to yourself – they are contact visits. I am permitted to have 1 contact visit per month – that doesn't include my visits with Dhakota, and box visits I'm aloud to have 2 per week.

Do I have a thing for your mum? She's a beautiful person, and one whom I'm proud to call my friend. When all us boys were younger, we all thought your mum was so hot. You know what it's like thinking a person in the neighbourhood is hot (LMAO).

I don't really have much up to add, therefore I guess I will leave it there for now, as I suspect you're had more than enough of me for now – true?

I look forward to hearing from you again very soon.

With love and best wishes – Carl –xox-

9 October 2009 to Roberta Williams

Dear Roberta,
I trust this letter finds you in the very best of health and spirits, as it leaves me fine.

I just received your letter, and it was an absolute pleasure to hear from you.

Bert, don't worry I miss you just as much as you miss me – if not more, so you're not the lone ranger in that department.☺

I miss not being able to talk to you – even if at times, you get me angry, and drive me insane – and I feel like pulling my hair out – Arghh. I guess we're so use to each other – and always being there for one another – that's love I guess – do you agree? (LMAO) that stands for laugh my ass off. ☺ I love you Bert, and I always will, nothing will ever change that, and you know it. I know you also love me with all your heart – and no one will ever take my place in your heart. I wish I was out there with you – I'm just looking forward to getting my phone calls back with you, so that I can hear your voice every morning. I know you have Rob, and as you know, I really like Rob, his good – but at the end of the day Rob's not me.

It was good to talk to Dhakota today, she's so cute – she worried about her money, she makes me laugh.

I know what you mean about the length of my sentence – tell me about it – when you think about it, it can do your head in – that's why I try not to think about it too much. I just try taking one day at a time, and plod along, try not to think too far ahead; otherwise I'll drive myself mad. Hopefully when my appeal comes up I get 10 years off – one can only hope – if that happens then there will be some light at the end of the tunnel.

39 years old next week – getting old hey – but I'm still younger than you are, and whatever any young guy can do, I can do better, and longer – I'm sure you'd agree with that – even if you don't, just agree with me, as it'll boost my ego. ☺

Tonight I got a card from my dad – and he said that he wishes I were outside so we could go and have a steak together for my B/day, I wrote back to him and said, I wish that too, but we'd both probably get no steak, as Kota would eat both ours meals – fat guts she is. ☺

You know I hate B/days. I just wish it would hurry up and pass – as this is my first B/day without my mum, and I miss her like you wouldn't believe. As you know I keep a lot inside – but I can tell you – one year's nearly past and it hasn't got any easier. Not one day goes by when I don't think about her – if there was anything in the world that I could do to bring her back, I would do it at the drop of a hat – and I mean anything, I loved my mum so much.

From what I read in the paper about the Don's book, he has a bit to say about me, even though I don't even know him. He reckons I'm not the brightest – says a lot for him. If I turned all their lives upside down, his included, and I had them all ducking for cover – with no brains – imagine what I could've done if I had half a brain – true? He can say all he wants about me; the proof is in the pudding. ☺ He also nominates me as being responsible in one way or another, for his mates murder – Munster's[98] –, which still remains unsolved, oh well nothing ceases to amaze me these days. I've always said the blokes no good, and nothing will ever change my thoughts. When I met the big dog in the casino he was like a little girl; scared for him life, I was actually embarrassed for him.

I don't really have much more to add, therefore I guess I will leave it there for now, and I hope hear from you again soon, or better still see you in the flesh, not quite in the flesh, although I wish it was – in person you know what I mean. ☺

With love & respect,
Always & forever – Carl –xoxox-

12 October 2009 to Karina Cacopardo

Dear Karina,
I trust this letter finds you in the very best of health and spirits, as it leaves me fine.

You asked me to write you a letter, so here I am – I don't like to leave people waiting, especially you – after all I aim to please – so your wish is my command. ☺

It's been really good talking to you lately – I really enjoy, and look forward to my calls with you – you're funny, and you give me a laugh, which is needed in places like these, so thank you.

---

98 Graham Kinniburgh.

I thought I'd get a card from you tonight – with photos enclosed – no such luck, ☹ hopefully tomorrow night, one can only hope.

Just a short one today, I will write a longer one after I hear back from you, the balls now in your court.

With Love & best wishes – Carl -xox-

13 October 2009 to Kylie[99]

Dear Kylie,
Tonight I received a card, and letter from you – thank you, you sure do know how to put a smile on my face – so again thank you for that. I only wish I was out there, as I'd return the favour to you – with interest. ☺

I'm glad you liked your two letters within the week, you felt special hey – and so you should, because you are, be careful you don't topple over. Hey, just curious, how many times do you read my letters? Make sure you answer that question when you write back!

I wouldn't mind being your dentist – you could come and see me any time you liked – I'd be more than happy to give you a drill and a clean, and don't worry it wouldn't be rushed one either, I'd take my time, and neither of us would want it to finish. I'd make sure you were one happy customer. After all, the better I treated you, the more chances there are of you returning – and I could say with confidence you'd be back. ☺ As I said, I think you've met your match, and I think you know it. (LOL)

I know there have been some stories about me having IVF – take it from me – none of its true. I don't know here they get it

99 Edited version of a five-page letter.

from – I've also read about Roberta saying that I was planning to have IVF babies with other girls – it's never ever been discussed, so I hope I have answered your question.

You asked me when my release date is – well at the moment it's too far away to even think about.

You said you'll give me one week to catch up with all the important people, then you'll expect me to take you out for dinner, what if I wanted to take you out sooner, because you were already in my company, as I seen you as one of those important people? You also said that most months you're a vegetarian, what happens if this was one of the months that you weren't, what would you order?? Especially if there was nice hot, juice meat on the menu, are you wet – I'm mean is your mouth watering? Or shall I just order for you, would you be needing cutlery?? I agree with you, I'm sure you could take me out and show me a good time, but I also quite well know without going into any details, that I could give you the best time of your life, and a time you'd never ever forget, leave it that for the moment. ☺

What hussies can I have come in on a contact visit to see me? I don't want hussies! I told you – when you come in, you can come in on a contact visit. But nah, you'd obviously prefer a box visit – scared hey? ☺ The contact visits are just normal visits, held in a room, but no glass separating us. If you want to touch, hug, or kiss your visitor, you can – nothing else. Therefore, there's nothing to clean up afterwards. Overnight visits – sounds good – hey, wouldn't that make life easier. In years to come, when I eventually move onto a medium security prison, you can have 6 hours visits in a room, with your own privacy – as you put it, quality time.

So on that note, goodnight, and sweet dream – MWAH! ☺

I look forward to hearing from you again very soon.

With love and best wishes,

Lots of hugs and kisses – Carl –xox-

13 October 2009 to Esmerelda

Dear Esmerelda,
I trust this letter finds you in the very best of health and spirits, as it leaves me fine.

Surprise, surprise, amongst many letters, and cards, which I just received for my B/day, there was a letter from you – thank you, it was very nice to hear from you again, I thought you'd forgotten about me. Also thanks for the pictures; you look hot, absolutely gorgeous. If you can, and wouldn't mind, can you please print me out some on photo paper. The ones at Ceasers Pool, Rehab at palms (white bathers), ☺ and a few of you at Vegas, there one shot with and your one of friends, in Vegas, she's also hot, I checked back through the other photos you sent me awhile back, and I think her name is Lou – thanks – Mwah.

Now first things first, you don't have to worry about me sending your letters to anyone, as that would never happen. I'd like to make myself clear on something's, I get a lot of media attention, which I for one don't like – and never have, but unfortunately my name sells paper. From time to time, I do get letters (fan mail) from weirdo's, who I don't know, and I have never ever met, which I do laugh about, and if you read what some of these weirdo's had to say to me – you'd laugh too. ☺

Now I'll explain something to you – which I don't have to, but I choose to, so you don't get the wrong idea about me, I don't usually care what people say, or think about me – but you seem like a nice person, therefore as strangely as it sounds, I care what you think of me. I don't make fun of peoples emotion. I don't let many people in – as I'm very guarded, I have a lot of time for Fab, and he speaks very highly of you, so that's enough for me, as a friend of Fab's, is a friend of mine. Once you get to know me, you will realize that I am the best friend you could ask for – there's not much I wouldn't do for my friends, and I don't say that lightly.

Just so you know, when you're in Melbourne you're more than welcome to come and visit me any time you like. Just let me know in advance, so that I can put you on my visitors list, and make sure I leave space for a visit for you. If you don't know how to get here to the prison, I'd even organize for someone to drive you. I don't know how well you know Melbourne, or who you even know here, but if there is anything I can do for you whilst you're in Melbourne – just let me know, and if I can do it, I'm more than happy too. I don't know what Clubs you go to when you're here, but I'm sure you'd be well looked after, again if there is anything I can do for you – I'll do it.

I've never been to Vegas – it was somewhere I always wanted to go – but for one reason or another I never got there, maybe when I get out. ☺

I hope that I didn't bore you too much, and I look forward to hearing from you again really soon.

With best wishes & respect – Carl –xox-

Postcript Joke

A New Zealander walks into the lounge room with a sheep underneath his armpits, and his wife was sitting on the couch. He says, "That's the pig I have been fucking."

The wife says, "That's not a pig – that's a sheep honey."

He replies, "I wasn't talking to you, I was talking to the sheep."

14 October 2009 to Kylie

Dear Kylie,
Well here I am again – I hope you've now got a smile on your face. After all, you said I can manage to do that to you – even whilst these days there aren't many who can manage to do that. I guess it's just one of my many secret talents.

I was going to write you a handwritten letter, as some people say it's more personal. But I could think of far better ways of getting more personal with you than a handwritten letter – true? (LOL). If you want a handwritten letter, that's not a problem – you know I aim to please, and your wish is my command. ☺

After I finished writing your letter last night, which took me hours to write, I tried to get to sleep – no such luck, as my mind was working overtime. And guess who was on it. That's right "YOU" – so I hope you're happy with yourself, interfering with my much needed beauty sleep.

Then when I finally did get to sleep, at about 1.30 am, I slept like a baby. However I woke up at about 6.30 am, which is the usual time for me – and you were back on my mind. I was in bed completely naked, and .... – let's just say it would have been nice if you were here in my company, although if you were, I'm not quite sure if you could've handled it. This time it's ok to let your mind wonder, Kylie. ☺ You are bad!

Its lock down training today – the staff here are doing some sort of training, so we have to get locked in our cells. Which means I get locked up at 11.00 am, which is now – and then I get let back out of my cell at 1.30 pm – 3.30, then I am locked back up again. I don't mind it – the days goes quickly. Whilst I was out this morning, I made a few phone calls – then I jogged 10 kms on the treadmill. After that I ate some porridge, and now half the days over.

I rang my dad's place this morning, and whilst I was on the

home to him your mum called in – so I got to say a quick hello to her. Made my day – I spoke to her for a few minutes, and it was really good to hear her voice. Are you getting jealous? (he he).

Just a short one today in case you go to the letterbox, as I'd hate to see you go there, only to be disappointed. I hope I made you smile. ☺

With love and best wishes – Carl –xox-

15 October 2009 to Horty Mokbel

Horty Mokbel was the brother of Tony and Milad Mokbel, Carl's long-time associates.

Dear Horty,
I just received your letter, dated 12th of October, and it was good to hear from you again, as it always is.

I will tell you what happened long story short re; statement, I made one statement, and that was against Dale and Rod, Dale is a copper, and like you said fuck him – and Rod is 63[100] – 64 years old, and he looks like being in jail for ever. So long story short is at the end of the day my statement won't affect him. I'd like to tell you more, but it's so hard through the mail, as I said it was one statement, and that's all. Hopefully I should get a good reduction at my appeal, one can only hope.[101]

Milad won't handball Melanie to me – I have more hope of waking up tomorrow morning with a Genie beside my bed, wanting to grant me 3 wishes, there's no chance of him parting

100 Rod Collins died of cancer in Barwon Prison in 2018, at the age of 72.

101 It was believed at the time that Carl had made more than one statement against Rod Collins. Collins told inmates that he could show them at least two statements.

with her. After all this time, I just finally met Karina, not through him though. She drove Roberta up her to see me, as Roberta doesn't have a licence. She's not a bad sort – funny, and good to have a laugh with.

Roberta's books out now, one minutes I'm the best thing ever, and the next minute I'm the biggest cunt in the world, who makes her sick – what can you do – I expected to get a bit of a pay, but luckily for me though that her and I are on the same sides, because if I weren't god help me. ☺

If you get out I will do my best to get you any girls you want – the bloke who owns Zoo magazine always writes to me – his got the best ones, plus I have a few good ones who write to me from Sydney. If you get out, which I hope you do, I'll put you on the phone, if that's ok with you.

I don't really have much more to add, therefore I guess I will leave it there for now, and I hope hear from you again soon.

With best wishes & respect,
Your friend always – Carl

16 October 2009 to Natasha Morgan

Dear Tash,
Hey, you missed my B/day, 13th of October, not to worry, and another bone to pick with you – I never get any kisses off you at the end of your letters. ☹

I just finished reading Gatto's book, or 235-page statement – whatever you want to call it – and what a load of shit it is. He nominates me as being responsible for countless unsolved murders. After his mate copped it, and I met with him at the Casino, he was like a little girl. Scared for his life, I was actually embarrassed for him.

He and his mates have never been my cup of tea. They all drink with coppers, they are all non-earners – forever lashing people, and trying standover, and bullying the harmless. On top of that, they were all bad snipers. They all used to get around in their suits with their sunglasses on, like they were good sorts, but with nothing at all in their pockets. We used to refer to them as the Professional Desperates, whereas on the other hand we were dressed in trackies, with our pockets full of cash. ☺

He rang Roberta up after he read her book, and tried being smart to her, because she gave him a pay in her book. What she said about him was the truth. So she gave it to him with both barrels. She said, "Fuck you, you weak dog – I'll say whatever I want about you. Who do you think you are ringing me up, trying to tell me what I can, and can't say about you. It's all the truth, and you're only acting up now because Carl's in jail – no comeback.

So you're going to get me a few girls. 2 years is a long wait though, it'd want to be worth the wait. I'm already over Stacey, and I'm ready to move on – off one bus and onto another.

With love and best wishes, Carl –xx-

19 October 2009 to Kylie[102]

Dear Kylie,

I just received your letter, dated 16 — October, you said I would get it today, and I did, I knew you weren't just a pretty face. 5 pages – OMG – you certainly do know how to please your man.

You want to hear one of my confessions – I read your letters in bed, completely naked, and then lay there and think about

102 Edited version of a four-page letter.

you – that's enough information for the time being – maybe to much – if you want to hear more, well you give me more, babe the balls now in your court. ☺

If I were outside now. I'd come to Phuket with you, *(that's if you'd wanted me too*). We could go shopping, I could sneak into the change rooms with you, and make sure that whatever it is that you're trying on looks good on you. Who knows what else I'd get up to in there – after all, you live for the moment. ☺

I'd sunbake with you, massage lotions all over your body, paying special attention to the top of your legs to make sure you didn't get sunburnt, jump in the pool with you to cool off when needed (*which would be often*). I'd take you out for dinner, have drinks, out, and/or back at where we were staying – for the time being I'll leave the rest to your imagination, now let your imagination run wild, as mine is now, and will be again later – cold shower needed. (LMAO)

I wasn't mocking your red top idea, take a photo for me, red top, and red knickers – sounds good to me.☺

We can't have dirty magazines – Ralph and FHM are far from dirty.

If I were outside, and we had a fight, do tell me just what it is that I could do for you, or too you, to make it up, and say that I am sorry? Please answer this question in your next letter – lay all your cards out, and don't be shy. I'll be anxiously waiting to hear your answer to this one, and maybe my hands might be under the sheets – wish they were yours. ☺

Now visits – good to hear/or I am relieved to hear that you're more than happy to have a contact visit. I only get one contact visit per month, (*not including my visits with Dhakota's*), and the other are box visits. Good to hear that you won't be just coming to visit me once too – I'd expect nothing less. I don't want you cum once, ideally I'd like you to be continuously cuming,

cuming multiple times, after all once I got you to cum, I'm sure you'd want to cum again, (*hands above the sheets babe*). ☺

Dentist? – Kylie at the drop of a hat, I'd be yours. And I cannot only talk the the talk, but more importantly I *can* walk the walk, and you know that's something that I wish that I could show you now, I'd give you something hard to hold too – my pleasure – you could do whatever you like with it – I suspect there'd be a lot of breathing through your nose. (LMAO)

I hope you enjoy reading this letter, as much as I enjoyed writing it too you. Now let your imagination run wild, close your eyes and think of me being there with you, OMG – what I'd do to you! However, keep in mind whatever you can do, I'd do much better.☺

With love and best wishes,
Lots of hugs and kisses – Carl –xox-

20 October 2009 to Roberta Williams

Roberta,
I won't ask how you are – because honestly at the moment I'm in a filthy mood, and it'd be false of me to ask, and I'm not false – far from it.

Today I was talking to Rob – and he told me that you and him were arguing, because he heard that you've apparently been talking with Omar, and god knows what else. I don't know if that's true, or someone is just making it up – but rest assure I will be checking into it, and I will find out the truth. In addition, if I find out its true – I'll never ever have anything to do with you again in my life, and I warned you of that one month again. I have a funny feeling that it is true – because I know you better than anyone does – and you cannot be by yourself. I told you awhile back if you go back there – I'll completely wipe you, and I mean that. On top of that I'll kick you out of my mum's place – I'm not a fool, and I refuse to be treated like one, and I certainly won't have scum like that going to my mum's place, she'd be turning in her grave if she knew he was in there. I know you and I aren't together anymore, and who you get with isn't really any of my business – but I don't want scum like that near my daughter. I don't trust him around children, and I don't like what he did to Brea, on top of that when you were with him last time, he didn't want Kota to have anything to do with me. I could rent my mum's place out, but instead I let you stay there for nothing. Bert I refuse to do my head in over shit – so if I find out your with him, even talking to him – I never have anything further to do with you – that I promise you on my mother. I'll wipe my hands with you, not that you'd care about that – as I know I mean nothing to you anyway, I never have.

If you want to have anything to do with Omar, I guess that's your business, but as I said he won't be setting foot in my mother's house, no way will I sit here and accept that, it just won't be happening.

I hope that you not only hear me loud and clear, but more importantly you listen to what I said – because I can assure you I mean what I said – I've lost enough in life, so there's not much I really care about these days, which I think you already know.

I wasn't going to say anything – but I got a lot of B/Days cards this year, as I always do – but this year I never got one from Dhakota, she's only 8, so I can't blame her for that – but I blame you, when my mum was alive I always got a card from Kota. I also never got one from you – obviously, you're too busy to send me a card, after all what could you gain out of sending me a card.

I have nothing further to say, so goodbye.

Carl

20 October 2009 to Milad Mokbel

Dear Milad,
Well hello there buddy, how's thing? All good I hope – as for me here I'm fine, no complaints.

Thanks for the B/day card.

Now Melanie – Hmmmm – you'll have to get her to come up here to visit me, before I'd even think about entering into a trade now – Karina is hot, and reliable. ☺ She came up here to visit me again last week, now I know why you didn't want to let go of her. ☺

I just finished reading the Dons book – what a fucking joke. He puts me down every chance he gets too; and he also talks shit about Tony, he is a complete fucking imbecile. I've never had anything to do with the bloke in my life – never even said hello to him if we crossed paths – that is accept for when he was playing detective, and was virtually begging me for his life, when he wanted to see me in the Casino – he even changed that story. Brad A. has nothing on him.

My dad enjoys his conversation with you – after he talks to you, he tell me what happened – but I find it hard to understand him, because all he does is laughs.

I don't really have much up to add, therefore I guess I will leave it there for now, and I hope to hear from you again soon.

Keep in touch.

With best wishes & respect,
Your friend always – Carl

Ps) Please give my love and best to your mum and family – tell little Robbie I miss him.

21 October 2009 to Kylie

Dear Kylie,
I trust this letter reaches you in the best of heath and spirits, as it leave me fine.

I bet once you get my last letter that I sent you, you'll be writing back to me wanting to know about my dream that I had about you. However, I don't know if I'll tell you – again, I might get you too excited – and you might not be able to handle that. I wouldn't want to get you too excited when I'm not out there to satisfy your needs – as that'd only be a teasing you, and I don't think it'd be fair if I did that to you. ☺ What's you view on that? (LMAO)

I have a hypothetical for you, I get released, and I've already caught up with everyone I had too. You and I are now out for dinner, the night is ours, the food is delicious, drinks (*alcohol)* are going down like water, and we are really enjoying each other's company to the max. What happens after dinner? I'm in your hands (*there's no such thing as no*), now answer that, and be totally honest, don't be evasive or shy. I can't wait to get these hot pictures that you are going to send to me, hopefully I'll get them soon, with the answer to the above hypothetical, if you answer that honestly, then and only then might I tell you about my dream. ☺

With love and best wishes - Carl –xox-
MWAH –X- one big extra kiss for you – lucky you hey. (LOL)

22 October 2009 to Milad Mokbel

Dear Milad,
I just received your letter, dated 19-10, and it was my pleasure to hear from you again, as it always is.

I just send you a letter 2 days ago – now you owe me 2 letters, ok I'll reluctantly settle for Melanie, and one letter, the balls in your court. ☺

I've been talking to Karina regularly – she's good value – she's funny and good to talk too, she makes me laugh. She's actually coming up here again to visit me next week, or the one after – most likely the one after, at the start of the month – you know how the contact visit system works here, only one a month. ☺ I always tell her that you speak highly of her; which you always have, I think she's got a good heart, and she means well. You wouldn't believe what a small world it is – I went to school with Karina's brother – we were in the grade – primary and high school, and I've known her father for years.

Now what's going on with Melanie???? Are you going to give her to me or not. Clare I'm not even going to waste my time trying – there's no hope of you giving her to me, after all you wouldn't even give me Mrs. Pitchford, so what chance am I of getting Clare???? ☺

This trade you wanted, consider it a done deal, even thought we both know you've got me, I'm going to end up with a few rookies, and you're getting a seasoned campaigner, the cream of the crop – she's just expensive to run, but moneys no object to you – so good luck to you. ☺ Now Ella and who – that's right Natasha, by the way who are they both – oh forget it – it doesn't really matter anyway, as I guess in time I'll find out out, I'll take anything – after all there has been times when I've settled for 5 cents in the dollar – if you don't believe me ask Horty. ☺

Keep in touch.

With best wishes & respect,
Your friend always – Carl

Ps) Please give my love and best to your mum, Renate and the kids thanks.

22 October 2009 to Kylie

Dear Kylie,

Hello me again.

Well what's happening out there – anything exciting? I hope you're behaving yourself – you'd want to be – or else – I just might have to give you a spanking. (LOL)

When I, or we, are let out of our cells, in this Unit – we have what is known as a dayroom, which the cells are connected too. The dayroom is about 15 metres long, and 7 meters wide, it has a little kitchen, washing machine, dryer, treadmill, exercise bike, and we also have a table tennis table in here. During our out of cell hours, we can access all of those things plus two little exercise yards where we can get some sunlight – in both yards there are telephones, which we can also access during our out of cell hours. As you know we are permitted to make 32 – 12-minute phone calls per week – if you were home, I could ring you.

So you've started power walking – that's good, try to keep it up every day, if the one you walk on has incline, hills – try that – as it burns a lot more calorie then walking flat – and it tones you up.

Now the pictures, they're good – actually they're better than good – you look hot, what are you worried about sending me pictures, snap out of it, the more the merrier. I liked the pictures one of you leaning against the wall – what I've give to be that wall. ☺

By the way, when are you going to get organized to come in and visit me?

That's all for now, can't spoil you too much. ☺

I hope to hear from you again soon.

Love – Carl –xox-

22 October 2009 to Karina Cacopardo

Dear Karina,
What's cooking good looking? Unfortunately, there's nothing to exciting happening on this side of the wall that I can tell you about – unless of course I make it up. ☺

I spoke to you today – thank god, my daily fix – I don't know how I'd survive without it. As I said to you today, for some unknown reason I've been thinking a lot about Stacey lately, although I'd never let her back into my life again, from time to time I still miss her – and I hate that feeling. I haven't spoken to her now for 3 months – shouldn't I be well and truly over her? Maybe I need another girl in my life to help take my mind off her.

We didn't get mail last night, as yesterday it was the Geelong cup, and I believe it was a public holiday up here – or it was in the Prison anyway. So hopefully I'll get an extra big load tonight – I like it when I get mail – it gives me something to do replying to letters, I haven't had and weirdo fan mail lately with girls writing dirty letters, maybe if I were out they'd throw the knickers at me – or wishful thinking you reckon. (LOL)

Just a short one today – to say hello, you now owe me 3 letters – so get off your ass and write me a letter BITCH! ☺

With best wishes & respect,
Your friend always – Carl

24 October 2009 to Kylie

Well hello there,

Last night I received your letter, brief letter at that, nevertheless I was very happy to hear from you again, as I always am – three letters within a week, I feel special – am I??? – I'm also feeling the love! (LMAO)

As I told you nothing exciting happens here these days, no shit, I'm really very boring, not by choice though. However I don't mind making up stories for you, about the excitement I wish I had here – since I don't get any – if you're lucky my story might even involve you – "*WARNING*" I have a vivid imagination, but if you're up to it – I don't mind sharing it with you. One problem I can foresee before doing that is you'll have to set the boundaries for me – that's if there are any. (LMAO) In addition, you have to promise me you'll read it in bed, and you'll let your imagination run wild – stop blushing, my imagination is running wild now.

Trav is a good friend of mine, and as you know he has been for years – we've always been close – his also good with my dad. When my dad was in prison, Trav always use to go up and see him – and make sure everything was ok. It makes my life a little bit easier in here knowing that I have a genuine friend like him, I don't let myself get close with many people – as I think most people are full of shit.

You're sneaking feeling, is 100% spot on about Tommy doing all the hard stuff regarding the cooking here, his the chef, and he enjoys doing it – so who am I to stick me head in and complain. Ok if I were doing something that I enjoyed doing, and it gave me enjoyment doing it, and you loved what I was doing – would you stop me – nah I didn't think so, you could give me hand though – that would be appreciated. ☺

I look forward to hearing from you again soon, very soon.

ME –XXX-

24 October 2009 to Esmerelda

Dear Esmerelda,
I trust this letter finds you in the very best of health and spirits, as it leaves me fine.

What going on out there – anything exciting??? If there is, please do tell. As there's nothing much happening in here, it's quite boring – it's the same thing day in day out in this joint, it's like Ground Hog day. I wish I could tell you that something exciting has been happening here – but if I did that, I'd be making it up.

Today we had what is called the cooking program – we get it once a fortnight. We're allowed to spend $5.50, per-person – that's $16.50 between the 3 of us who live in this Unit. We got chicken breast fillets, potatoes and salad. Therefore, Tommy who is one of my friends who lives in here with me – who by the way is a qualified chef, made chicken Parma, chips and salad – yummy, better the prison food – which is eatable but nothing much to write home about.[103]

The Spring racing carnival is on down here in Melbourne at the moment – I thought you might have made it down to for it. Cox Plate today – which I myself think is the best day of the Carnival myself, along with the Oaks, when I was outside I made it to those two meting religiously. It's funny watching the girls at the races, before the first race, their hairs, and makeup is perfect, a lot of them get around thinking they are Paris Models. Come the end of the day they're carrying their shoes, spewing

103 Complaints about food were strategic. Inmates knew that each official complaint had to be investigated and it gave inmates a sense of control and leverage over an otherwise unyielding system. Occasionally, there were protests when a particularly poor meal was served but these were generally half-hearted. Meals were an important part of getting through the monotony of the day. It's not that food was poor but there was always a sense of there being not quite enough food on the plate; especially for crooks who had lived high on the hog on the outside.

in the brushes, god only knows what they've gotten up to for the day. The majority of them most certainly aren't the princesses, they like to try and portray themself out to be at the start of the day, far from it. And if you can't see that by the end of the races – then you will if you go to one of the pubs around the area, there's a lot of filthy skanks around that's for sure.

As I said to you in my previous letter, from time to time, I get weirdos writing to me – last week one wrote me the most filthiest letter that you could ever imagine. I've enclose a picture which she sent me of herself – I think someone's is trying to play a trick on me – she said I'm the most sexiest man in prison – should I take that as a compliment – (ha ha) – I was thinking of putting her onto Fab. ☺

Keep in touch, and I to hope to hear from you again soon.

With best wishes & respect – Carl –xox-

Postcript Joke

A young blonde woman in Sydney was so depressed that she decided to end her life by throwing herself off the Harbour Bridge. She went down to the bridge and was about to leap into the frigid water, when a handsome young sailor saw her tottering on the edge of the bridge crying.

He took pity on her and said, "Look, you have so much to live for, I'm off to Europe in the morning, and if you like I can stow you away on my ship. I'll take good care of you, and I'll bring you food every day." Moving closer, he slipped his arm around her shoulder and added, "I'll keep you happy, and you'll keep me happy."

The girl nodded Yes. "After all what do I have to lose?" Perhaps a fresh start in Europe would give her life a new meaning.

That night, the sailor brought her aboard and hid her in a

lifeboat. From then on, every night he brought her three sandwiches and a piece of fruit, and made love to her until dawn.

Three weeks later, during a routine inspection, she was discovered by the Captain. "What are you doing here?" the captain asked.

"I have an agreement with one of the sailors, who's stowed me away,' She explained, "I get food free, and free passage to Europe, and he's screwing me."

"He certainly is," the Captain, said. "This is the Manly Ferry."

25 October 2009 to Roberta Williams

Dear Roberta,
I trust this letter finds you in the best of health, and the highest of spirits, as it leaves me just dandy.

As you know today I seen Dhakota and Penny, it was a good visit – Bert, Dhakota's starting to put on weight, she's got a big stomach – she'd better start to watch herself, otherwise she might end up putting too much on, and then she'll find it hard to get off, start watching what she eats.

Bert I think it might be a good idea if you take Kots to a dietician, I'm serious – she's eating much more calories than she's burning off – which simply means she's going to put on weight. You know I love my daughter with all my heart – I'm not being mean saying this, I say it because I care, and I do love her – she's eating out of boredom. I don't want her weight to become a problem for her – she's a beautiful looking girl – but you know if they put weight on they can quickly lose their looks, and I want her to always be stunning.☺

I don't really have much up to add, therefore I guess I will leave it there for now, and I hope to hear from you again soon.

Best wishes - Carl

26 October 2009 to Kylie[104]

Hello, Hello,

I just received your letter, and it was my pleasure to hear from you again, as you would expect it to be – nothing new about that.

You were saying, that you'd like to go overseas to live – whereabouts??

Years ago – I went overseas a few times, one time I went to Dubai, Greek Islands, and then on to Turkey, I cut my trip short, as my brother was still alive, and he was getting out of control here, so I came back, even though I was younger than him, he use to listen to me (*sometimes anyway*). I've been to Bali a few times. I always wanted to get to the States – never got there though, as from 1999 – 2004, I always had outstanding Court cases to front, so the authorities didn't let me leave the Country, I had to hand my passport in as that was part of my bail conditions.

I have no idea what I'll do when I get out – it's too far away for me to even think about.

What I said is if I were out I'd come to Phuket with you, *(that's if you'd wanted me too)*, I would've liked to. Question is, would you have wanted me to???

If I were out would I have recognized you – you would've caught my eye that's for sure, and I would've known who you were once I started talking you. But from the moment I first saw you, I doubt it if I would've known that you were Kylie who use to live in our suburb, but to think that I wouldn't have said hi to you, if I knew who you were – are you alright?

If I were out at one of the clubs, I would've brought you into my company and had a drink with you – what type of person do you think I am? When I was outside I use to love going out to the Clubs to party.

104 Edited version of a four-page letter.

You've got yourself a deal girl, or pact whatever you want to call it, big question now is will you be able to handle it? So when I get out we'll go away together for one week. What's this shit, who knows if we'll still be in touch with each other by then – why wouldn't we be – the only way we won't be, is if you cease contact with me, after all you're the boss aren't you. if you try to do that I've have to stalk you through your mum – nah I wouldn't do that, as much as I'd miss you, I'd have to respect your decision – I sincerely hope that it never comes to that though.

You said that you have a feeling that I live for the moment, just like you do, how does it go "dance like no one is watching, love like you'll never be hurt, sing like no one is listening, and live like its heaven on earth." I've always lived for the day, I had heaps of fun doing it too, it can be good, but it can also get you in trouble, look where it's got me, oh well who am I to complain, I'm still alive aren't I?

You don't think I could keep up with your imagination – well big mouth, how about you stop talking the talk, and start walking the walk – go on try me, please, pretty please! I can read your letters in bed, with one hand under the sheets, whilst I let my imagination run wild, so now you know that, surely you wouldn't deprive me of some satisfaction. ☺

I love the new Vanessa Amorosi song, next time I hear it I'll take more notice of the words. I'm a big fan of hers, I think she a great singer. I had Vanessa Amorosi sing at Dhakota's Christening – she was good and very down to earth, she was holding Dhakota in her arms whilst singing, and she was dancing with her and the other kids on the stage. It was a great night, we and it in the Casino, where they hold the Brownlow medal.

I'm going to miss you when you go to Phuket – I just hope you have a good time though, and that you think about me lots (*constantly*).

By the sounds of things, I won't be getting to see the semi-nude shots. ☹ When you come to visit me, you can't bring them in here with you, then take them home – you can't bring anything in with you. You can send them in, and then I'll send them back out to you – hint hint!

Greens are green clothing, T-Shirts, track pants, tops – as you know where I am, we wear red clothing – when you leave here, Management/High Security Unit, and get cleared into a lower security place, you wear green tackies and tops – white or green T-Shits – and black or green shorts.

I'm just short of 6 foot – just for the record – I don't go for tall woman – I like the shorter ones, easier to throw around the bedroom. (LOL)

You said you've achieved your mission, because you're in my thoughts and dreams – you didn't even want to know about my dream – must say I'm disappointed about that. ☹ You said now you have to work out how to keep yourself there – a little tip for you – don't go worrying yourself as I see no problem there. You could always spice up your letters, keeping in mind I will be reading them in bed. ☺ No need to watch me – so please do get carried away with your thoughts. (Hint Hint)

I look forward to hearing from you again very soon, and hopefully seeing you too.

With love and best wishes, lots of hugs and kisses – ME –XOXOX-

CHAPTER 9

Living the dream

Carl knew that everything he wrote and sent out through the mail was first read by Barwon's postmaster, Charlene. Among other things, it was her job to keep an eye out for any sexually explicit material; normally, if she encountered this, the offending letter would be marked 'return to sender'. But clearly, after he took his fateful decision to cooperate with Victoria Police, the controls on Carl Williams' correspondence were relaxed and so his letters to his various correspondents became progressively more sexually explicit. If he was momentarily embarrassed by the knowledge that Charlene would be reading all this, after a certain point he obviously no longer cared. The imaginary romantic world he created in his letters to 'Kylie' was a refuge in which he needed to dwell in order to retain his sanity.

28 October 2009 to Kylie

Hello, hello,

I just received your letter – it was good to hear from you again, as it always is.

So now you want to know all about my dream – what took you so long to ask about that. (LOL)

Details are fine with you are they? Ok I'll cough up some info for you – I get the message loud and clear, I've teased you enough. ☺

Now relax – and I'll tell you what I can remember about it, now don't hit me if I offend you. As I can't control my dreams, and after all it was you who said you wanted to know about it, so I can only hope that I now don't get myself into trouble for being honest, and telling you the truth. ☺

You and I were away on holidays somewhere, and it was hot. It could've even been Phuket – who knows – I'm not quite sure where we were – as my dream is sketchy at best. All I know is it was hot weather.

You and I were sunbaking – I jumped in the pool – and shortly after you joined me in there – we were messing around with one another – we ended up hugging – and one thing led to another, and we were kissing – passionately (*and for the record you were a really good kisser*). Unfortunately, it was still the middle of the day, so there were people still in the pool. ☹ I was standing, you had your legs wrapped around me, and we continued kissing.

You then cheekily put your hand down my pants; and needless to say, I was rock hard. I told you I was horny as, and that you're going to cop it hard later, can't wait and I'll be holding you to that was your response, before I knew it I'd pulled your bikini bottoms to the side, and I was now inside you – (*heaven on earth*), you were in shock, the look on your face was priceless. You went to kiss me, but instead you cheekily bit me – you said you're unreal, this feels so good though, but why here, although I know that no one can see what we're up to, I still I feel a little uncomfortable, as I can't have my way with you like I want to with an audience here. You said lets go upstairs to the room and finish off what you've now started, but before leaving I quickly pushed myself into you a few times. Now for obvious reasons, and to save myself embarrassment, I couldn't jump out of the pool straight away. We both hopped out and made out way over to the lift – that's all I can remember as I woke up. ☹ I hope you enjoyed my dream, or what I can remember of it anyway. Now the least you can do is tell me what would've happened, if you had of gotten me upstairs where you wanted to get me, and don't be shy, I can't wait to hear your response.

Well that's all from me for tonight – and I look forward to hearing from you again very, very soon.

With love and best wishes – ME –XOX-

MWAH - MWAH - MWAH

29 October 2009 to Ange Goussis

Evangelos 'Ange' Goussis, a former boxer and associate of career criminal and enforcer Nik Radev, was convicted of murdering Lewis Moran and Lewis Caine in 2004 and sentenced to life imprisonment.

Dear Ange,
I just received your letter, dated 27/10, and it was good to hear from you again, as it always is.

Nothing new is happening over here that I can tell you about, same thing – as you know nothing changes in these places – unless of course it's bad.

As you know my dad had the hip replacement done – and he said it's the best thing his ever done – tell your mum if she's finding it hard to get around, it might be worth her having it done – I don't think the recovery's that bad. Tell her I said hello – she's a good woman – I wish I had of met her when I was outside. I hate seeing her sitting in the cubicles waiting for a rotten box visit – this system honestly stinks. Its bullshit I know, and I know how helpless you must sometimes feel seeing them all hurting – I use to feel like that with my mum, they're strong, but everything must take its toll on them – after all they're only human.

Yesterday I had a contact visit with Roberta, it's the first contact visit I've had with her in a few years, and it was good to see her. Last Sunday Dhakota came up here to see me with my friend Penny. Dhakota has started doing taekwondo, she does it twice a week – it'll be so good for her if she sticks to it, as she's starting to put on weight, and needs to do some form of exercise to keep fit.

Chooky – Hmmm, when his Plea? I hear the author – Sylvester's half brother, has been having bowl movements from 5 cents pieces – 50 cents pieces – interesting days lay ahead. I wonder if his giving him the same advice as he gave Allan T. – I think NOT!

Last night I seen that imbecile Chopper[105] on TV, promoting some DVD he's bringing out, and he was bagging Andrew and I. He's now saying how he survived the Gangland War. Whose side was he on, because he most certainly weren't on my side, and I never once seen him popping his rotten head up saying that he was against me. I don't know why he wants to rubbish us – maybe he has to drop my name for some much-needed publicity.

---

105 Mark 'Chopper' Read.

I don't even know the brain-dead imbecile. He is a no hoper, and a very ordinary individual at that.

I never heard the goose say one bad word about Andrew or I when I was outside. That's the usually story though – all talk when Andrew's dead, and I'm doing 3 life sentences in prison. Let's face it, I suppose that could make some big, hard, tough person like him grow a heart, knowing he's never ever going to see either of us. Oh well, if that make him sleep better, good for him. ☺

With best wishes & respect,
Your friend always – Carl

PS. That girl who you see visiting me is Penny. Her and I have been friends for years – she's not my girl. So tell Beth to get me one of her friends. ☺

30 October 2009 to Kylie[106]

Well hello there.

I just received your letter – and I now have a smile from ear to ear, I love it when I hear from you, it really does make my night – thanks –Mwah. I agree you do have natural charm, read on, more to cum later. (LOL)

Correct – if you don't behave yourself you have me to answer too, not that I could punish you how I'd like to from here. ☹ I might send you to the room and tie you to the bed – I dare say if I could give you the punishment that I had in mind for you, you'd never behave, yeh I guess you could say it'd be more pleasure, then punishment, leave it to your imagination.

---

106 Edited version of a four-page letter.

I'd love to give it too you hard and fast – in what way you ask? – Everyway, and every position – don't worry I'd let you have your way and be on top, so you have yourself a "deal", shame we can't turn it into reality – NOW! If we could I'd make you cum continuously, and you'd never want it to end – enough for the moment.

Have you decided on your Plan yet? When you do, can you please share it with me.☺ You're in my good books, and you know you are, so just keep doing what you're doing, and you'll remain in there forever – which I hope you do. I did say to you a while back that some women have ulterior motives, and I believe that was in regards to people I don't know who sometime write to me, and me not answering there letter, as I don't know if they have ulterior motives or not. You don't fit into that category – far from it – and I've never looked at you like that, so get that one right out of your head. I think you're a very genuine person, who is very sincere, and a true friend to the people you care about. Do I have a plan – it's hard with the length of my sentence to have a plan, like anyone though I do enjoy company – but what girl is going to stick around and accept my predicament????

I do wear bottoms if it's freezing cold, not for any other reason but to keep warm. The officers can see in my room anytime they like – as there's like a little window on my cell door where they can look through if they wanted too, I can see them if they look through though, as they have to move a curtain sort of thing – they don't do it – unless they have too, I wouldn't care if they did anyway.

We do our own washing here – we have access to a washing machine and drier during our out of cells hours, so we all do the washing. It's no one in particulars job.

December sound good for me – you are more than welcome to come in and visit me whenever you like. I think you can visit here virtually any day except for Christmas day. Don't worry you won't be taking anyone visits, I know it can be a little bit daunting visiting here especially for the first time – so you visit when you feel like you're up to it – no pressure from me – OK.

Thanks for saying I'm special – you are Kylie, I get along really well with you, and you make me laugh, I wish I were out there so we could really enjoy one another's company.

You said that, you think I'm dangerous and you really should keep your distance, how could you say that, dangerous in what way???

So you reckon, that I should feel free to make up the excitement that I wish I had in here, and you'd like me to share my vivid imagination with you – fantastic news, it works both way though don't it? No boundaries – and you'll promise you'll read it in bed – OMG – what I'd give to be out there now. You wouldn't be reading one of my stories, as you'd be involved – Kylie there's nothing I wouldn't do to you, I'd explore your body with my hands & tongue, I'd tease you to the max, up until you begged me to be inside you – then I'd make mad passionate love to you all night long, in every position you can imagine. I'd let you take control, and ride me, whilst I was holding your hips, and looking deep into your eyes, and I can guarantee you now there'd be no place you'd rather be, when you're taking all of my deep inside you. Just a taste of what's to cum – if you want more – give a little back, and I'll give you a full on story about what I'd do to you if I were outside with you, your call Kylie. ☺

You also said you don't believe that I'm shy, you said that' shit if you're ever heard it – that's not nice Kylie. I tell you now I wouldn't be shy if you were here with me now, I'd kiss you, then I'd gently bite your neck, and I'd have your pants off you within no time – I'm getting hard just thinking about it (*imagination is running wild*) – I'd wreck you Kylie – so I'll leave you on that thought – enjoy! ☺

I'll leave it there for now, and I look forward to hearing from you again soon, very soon.

MWAH

ME –XXX-

30 October 2009 to Esmerelda[107]

Dear Esmerelda,

I just received your letter, with photos enclosed, dated 28 October, and it was my pleasure to hear from you again, as it always is.

Correct, my B/day is on the 13th of October, isn't it rude to ask someone there age? (ha ha) How old do you think I turned??? – I turned 39, but I don't feel it though – when I came to prison I was 33 – now I am 39, and I now feel 10 years younger than what I did then, and everyone says I now look younger too – I strongly believe prison preserves you, I hope it does anyway. ☺

I couldn't agree with your motto anymore, "if you don't have nothing nice to say, they say nothing at all." That's what my mum use to always say (*god rest her soul*), she was forever trying to defend me, that's one of the many things that I loved about her, hey you know what, I feel so comfortable talking to you about anything – so thanks.

I told you your last letter, that you were the *"FIRST"* of many that I replied to that night – so you were the first – No. 1, so

107 Edited version of a three-page letter.

I don't know why you were asking who was the first I replied to – as it was "YOU" – feel special do you now – so you should. ☺

My daughter's name is Dhakota, she's so beautiful, she's in year 3. Everyone says she's the spitting image of me. I've enclosed 2 photos for you – one of me and Dhakota (*taken when I was outside*), and another one just of Dhakota, which is a recent one of her, you can keep them both, give me your opinion when you write back – if she looks like me, of not?

You asked if I have any other kids, besides Dhakota – my ex wife (*Roberta*) had 3 kids before her and I got together, and I virtually brought them up – so I look at them like my own – I'm very close with Brea, she's the middle one – she' 15 – she turns 16, on January 10, same day as your B/day.

I can only imagine how much you'd be hanging to get your licence back, after 12 months without it you would be lost. When you get it back take it easy – don't lose it again.

You said you liked the quote that I sent to you, and you can relate to it. "*I've learnt that it takes years to build up trust, and it only takes suspicion not proof to destroy it'!* Sounds like you're better off without the guys that you have been with, they obviously have issues. I find once the trust is broken in a relationship that's the begin of the end. If there's no trust in a relationship, there is nothing, I wouldn't even want to be friends with someone I didn't trust.

It would've been good if I had of met you when I was out, you seem like a nice person – genuine, and sincere, with a good heart, people like you are hard to find, very rare in this day and age.

I wish that I had emails – save me waiting nearly 2 weeks for a turnaround letter from you, I'd hear back from you immediately – that would be nice, and make my day. ☺

I don't have much more to add – I look forward to hearing from you again soon – really soon hopefully.

MWAH!

With best wishes & respect – Carl –xox-

31 October 2009 to Fabian Quaid

Dear Fab,
Last night I also received a letter, with photos, from Esmerelda, buddy she's hot. She also seems like a really nice person, I like her, I wish I had of met her when I was outside, you have to put in a good word for me. She was telling me in my letter, that she sent both you and I a letter at the same time – and I replied to her, before you did, so she rang your mate up going mad, that you hadn't replied to her – she's funny.

I just finished reading your mates book, or 235-page statement, as anyone seems to be calling it. What an absolute load of shit it was. He puts me down every chance he gets too, I never thought he was that type of person, anyone would think I stole his bone, he obviously has an axe to grind with me – how convenient, chooses to grind in now when I'm doing 3 life sentences. I've never had anything to do with the bloke in my life – never even said hello to him if we crossed paths – that is accept for when he was playing detective, and was virtually begging me for life. I always avoided him and his gang at all costs – like the plague, as they've never been my cup of tea – they were all non earners – always lashing people, and trying to stand over and bully the harmless, not my type of people.

Re; Faruk's case, despite what you hear – I know 100% that Robert Richter weren't at all surprised with the result, a bloke here spoke to him before the verdict was handed down, and he thought Faruk would be found guilty. I also don't think the only evidence was John W., one of his mates, some goose from the kebab shop turned on him and gave Crown evidence, which didn't help him. I also know there was some damaging text messages between him and Andrew, plus a few other bits and pieces. I hear what you say about him getting his other matter adjourned until his appeal is finalized – I myself tried that after I was first convicted, I don't think they (the Crown) will allow him to do that – although I wish him all the best in trying. I think they'll want to keep the pressure mounted on him – I'll be very surprised if they let him get him way – I hope for his sake – I'm wrong.

With best wishes & respect,
Your friend always – Carl

1 November 2009 to Milad Mokbel

Dear Milad,
Today I was talking to my dad, and he was telling me that you'd rang him, and you told him our deal was off – mate, a deal, is a deal – you can't be half pregnant. ☺

If you had of followed through with our deal – and not reneged – I was going to surprise with a few other girls, that I was willing to pass onto you – only because I'm a good bloke, and I love you. Take a close look at the back of this page – good sort – she's from Sydney – so is the other one – they work together – hmmmm – rethinking things are you now? Well don't waste to much time thinking it over – as my deal won't be around forever – I'll be waiting to hear back from you. ☺

By all media reports, it looks like Ange might have another blue to front – let's hope for his sake he doesn't get charged – although I think when they put things out there like they did – they aren't too far away from Charging.[108]

Just a short one today.

Keep in touch.

With best wishes & respect,
Your friend always – Carl

Ps) Please give my love and best to your mum, Renate and the kids thanks.

2 November 2009 to Kylie[109]

Hello hello,

You made me laugh, when you said you don't know whereabouts O/seas you'd like to live as at the moment it's a little hard for you to keep away from the letterbox – how sweet. Now that you're starting to open up a little bit – so best I do too. I wait for my mail to come every night, hoping that I will receive a letter from you, and when I do, I have a smile from ear to ear. ☺

I didn't continuously get into trouble from 1999 – 2004 – I was arrested in November 1999, got bail in February 2000. I was arrested again, I think in April – May 2001 – got bail in June 2002 – I was always on bail so I couldn't leave the country.

You right, I don't have plans at the moment – because if I start spending all my time thinking about my plans when I get out, I'll only drive myself mad, as I still have so long to go before that's even possible. Maybe I'll find myself a good loyal woman, and

108 Ange Goussis was charged with the murder of Shane Chartres-Abbott in August 2012 but there had been media reports suggesting it was imminent for at least two years. He was acquitted.

109 Edited version of a four-page letter.

make some plans – if I was with someone I trusted, and I had faith in, that they'd be around for a while, who knows plans might be made, I'd obviously have to know they were serious. I think I might be opening up a bit too much to you – am I???

So you would've wanted me to come to Phuket with you if I were outside – Hmmmm, you're making me happy tonight, saying all the right things, all the things that I want to hear. I would've loved to come to Phuket with you – we would've had the time of our lives.

I would've taken you shopping, showered you with gifts, sunbaked by the pool with you, took you out for dinner every night, had drinks with you, and just enjoyed your company to the max, and if you let me, made mad passionate love to you all night long. (LMAO)

I said I don't know if I would've recognized you as being your mother's daughter, but you would've caught my eye – you know exactly what I mean. Would I have made a move?? Would you have??? Would you have wanted me too?

Would you have flirted with me – would you have sent signals, to let me know that you were interested, and I was a chance if I had of? I dare say we would've connected – and there would've been chemistry. Anything could've happened who knows we might even had found ourselves staying at Crown Towers (*if we were at Heat*),[110] we might not have even made it there – who knows. ☺

I never knew that you were a dancer at the Mercury Lounge[111] ..... I always used to go there – and sometimes cross to Heat, but I'd never stay anywhere for too long. I went to the Mercury Lounge a fair bit in 2003 – I don't know how we never crossed paths – wish

110 The Heat Nightclub was in the Crown Entertainment Complex. It closed in 2005.

111 A nightclub at Melbourne's Crown Towers.

we had of – I bet you do too – although you had a boyfriend. didn't you, so you would've been off limits. ☺ TRUE???

As I previously said to you, if I'd seen you out, and I knew who you were – boyfriend or not – I would've brought you into my company, and had a drink with you – what would've, or could've happened after that is anyone's guess, but I most certainly would not have ignored you, that you can take to the bank. Who said if you were there that there'd be any competition – after all I thought you said you'd be able to do everything to satisfy my needs – so what competition would there be?? ☺

Whilst we're on the subject – you said you'd satisfy me – I dare say you would too – confidence – I love it! You asked me, what would I like to hear about – I'd like to hear all about how you'd intend on doing to me to satisfy me, if you were giving the opportunity too. What would you do to me???? Don't be shy in answering that, and in full details too, after all I told you all about my dream – hope you're still talking to me after it – fingers crossed. (LMAO)

You did brighten up my day – by saying, you adore thinking about me, it's nice to know that you're thought of, or loved, as sometimes it can be a lonely experience in this place. I don't say your songs are gay – as I think it's nice, that a song can remind you of me.

Who said there's going to be glass separating us when you come to see me – is that a hidden message? Is that what you want????

I don't know why I have to explain something's to you "twice" – I can't just get myself off over anybody, can you? I'm being totally honest with you. Sure I can get myself off – but I don't, and wouldn't even try unless I'm thinking about someone I have some sort of feeling for – you're a shift bitch, and I'm right onto you – do you think I came down with the last shower? You're just trying to get info out of me – why don't you cut to the chase and ask me some tough questions. (LMAO). Do you get yourself off?? Do you think about me whilst you're doing it – now you answer me, fairs fairs KYLIE!

You askcd mc what's my typc – loyal – honcst – short – dark hair – fiery – tomboyish, do you need any more hints???? Do you know anyone who fits that criteria, MATE? ☺

My favourite colour is red, they often show footage of me on the TV wearing a red DKNY jumper, and I think I was wearing that on the day Andrew was killed.

You were saying that the semi-nude photos can be my welcome-out present, but in person, Kylie, you're getting me hard thinking about it, you are, ok, you have yourself a pact – you won't be semi-nude though, you'll be totally nude, deal or not????

Kylie when you come to visit me – before you see me, you go through a metal detector, and they scan you with some wand, so I dare say if you have piercings, it might be best if you take them out before visiting. By the way where are these hypothetical piercings?? It's not that great of an ordeal you have to go through to visit me, you'll be right the first time you'll be nervous – then I' sure you'll be fine.

Well by the time you receive this letter, you'll know all about my dream – I can't recall you asking me 55 times to tell you about it. I'll a little worried – after you read it, I hope I'm still in your good books, and I hear from you again – time will tell – fingers crossed. Now you can spice it up – how – use your imagination – remembering that I read your letters in bed, and I get myself off, over the right person – hint hint (LMAO)

I look forward to seeing you soon, and hearing from you even sooner.

ME –XOXOX-

3 November 2009 to Roberta Williams

Dear Roberta,
I trust this letter finds you in the very best of health and spirits, as it leaves me fine.

Cup day today – I only had one bet, and I did no good, Cup days is too hard to pick winners, anything can win.

I hope everything works out with your driving bullshit,[112] you can't afford to drive anymore – I couldn't handle you going to jail – it would really mess with Dhakota's head, that little girl has already been through enough. I don't know how she's go without you – obviously she could stay at my dad's place – probably even Tommy's mums place – Mary and Vera would love that, and I guess Maila and Dennis would have her too, so I don't think she'd be short of somewhere to stay but she loves, and relies on you so much.

My legs are killing me tonight – as yesterday I ran uphill on the treadmill for 1 hour, and today I did a 1 ½ hour jog – I'm trying to lose my stomach – I haven't got far to go now, but its hard work. I have to be stricter on my diet – which is hard as I enjoy eating some shit.

I spoke to Kerry today; and she had some gossip for me – Dean her brother was out, and ran into one of Nicole Mottram's friends. Nicole Mottram has moved overseas, she now lives in America, with some 50 year old bloke who has plenty of money – and she just had a baby to him, a baby girl.

Mail just arrived, and I received a letter off Plugger,[113] his at

---

112 In early July 2009 Roberta was stopped by police near a booze bus in Preston, in Melbourne's north. She faced possible charges of driving while suspended, using an unregistered vehicle, failing to surrender her driver's licence and making an incorrect left turn.

113 Jason 'Plugger' Paisley.

the MAP[114] (Spencer Street), he said to say hello to you (Bertie Wrout),[115] he said he dropped off, as he was running hot.

I'm looking forward to seeing you next week, it'll be good.

I don't really have much more to add, therefore I guess I will leave it there for now, and I hope to hear from you again soon.

Love & friendship, always and forever - Carl – xx-

5 November 2009 to Milad Mokbel

Dear Milad,
I just received your letter, dated 1-November, and it was my pleasure to hear from you again, as it always is.

Buddy, Karina's not my girl – she's just a friend – my apologizes if I hit a nerve. ☺

You would received the last photo I sent you – she's from Sydney – she's a friend of one of my mates from up there – she writes to me – and she wants to cum (*that's how she spells cum – not me*), to visit me too. ☺ I think you'd want to come back to the table now – as I know you you're a very intelligent man, the money you made speaks volumes for your intelligence. ☺

MOKBEL: Claire and all above have stayed loyal to my stable or so they say.
RESPONSE: *completely untrue – and you know it!!! A few months after you were arrest, Clair was seeing another bloke, there were countless times when Zarah was trying to ring her for*

---

114 Melbourne Assessment Prison, once known as the Melbourne Remand Centre, is the initial reception and assessment prison for men in Victoria.

115 Carl was allegedly involved in the attempted murder of Herbert Wrout, the long-time friend and driver of Lewis Moran. This is an in-joke between Roberta, Rob Carpenter and Carl: Bertie Wrout refers to Roberta herself.

you – why was that – because she was being so LOYAL???? – I think not. Natasha she was with bloke, Derek (ring a bell).☺ Melanie well do I even have to go there, I like Mel – but not the loyalist of people – I'm now getting upset hearing these bitches lie to you.

MOKBEL: None of the above have children, so "No" stretch-marks! Also no Baggage
RESPONSE: *having children doesn't necessarily mean you have to have stretch marks, as Roberta's had 4 kids and doesn't have one single stretchmarks, and she has six-pack – the baggage – agree*

MOKBEL: All of the above are as pretty, if not prettier then Karina.
RESPONSE: *I can't comment on this one, as I haven't seen them, but Karina reckons that she shits all Melanie in look and body, and Mel is better than Natasha, and I have no reason not to believe her – if you disagree and thinks she's lying, sent me a photo of the all and let me be the Judge.*

MOKBEL: Most importantly, all are under under 26 yrs, so that mean everything is pointing NORTH not SOUTH
RESPONSE: *I though Melanie would've been 26 yrs, or older, when is her DOB????*
In addition, the older ones, have all had plastic surgery – I can assure you nothing heads SOUTH, plastic surgery can perform miracles

---

I don't really have much more to add, therefore I guess I will leave it there for now, and I hope hear from you again soon.

With best wishes & respect,
Your friend always – Carl

Ps) Please give my best to your mum, family and HARRY! – thanks

7 November 2009 to Wayne Howlett

Dear Wayne,
Last night I received your letter, with photos enclosed, and it was good to hear from you again, as it always is.

I still haven't heard from Angela, maybe she sent her letter by camel. (LOL) I guess she'll write when she wants too. I've now got a few new ones writing to me – which is good, as it keeps me occupied, a mate of mine put one onto me from Sydney – she's ok, seems like a nice chick, and is sexy as – I've enclosed a photo of her for you to have a look at – when you write back give me your thoughts. It's a picture of her doing a photo shoot for the clothes place she works for.

It would be good if I were permitted to write a book, and get my side of the story out there, the truth, especially after weak mutts such as Gatto make so much bullshit up – but unfortunately, the jail will not allow me to do that, oh well life goes on.

With best wishes & respect,
Your friend always – Carl

Ps) Please pass on my best to Shaune and to your family

9 November 2009 to Kylie

Hello there,

Finally, hip hip hooray – I just received your letter – and it was good to hear from you again, as it always is, first letter I have received from you since last Monday – 7 days. ☹

Maybe after telling you about my dream, I weren't in your good books, I had a secret suspicion that might happen – but you asked me to tell, and I was honest. I now know not to answer all your questions in full detail, that if I don't want to scare you away – which I don't and never want to happen.

Again, I will do my best to answer all your questions, even though you don't answer mine. ☹

My next girl isn't classified as a rebound girl, not to me anyway, what would make you say that?

Re; engagement – what happened is I gave Stacey a ring – I would say we weren't really engaged, as neither of us we're planning on getting married – it was more of a friendship ring, but she use to mess around and say that we were engaged. I'm not saying I didn't have feeling for her, because I did, but we weren't planning on getting married.

So you say you would have been able to satisfy me, piece of cake you reckon. Do you think I am easily satisfied?? As I have previously asked you, what would you do to satisfy me???? I'd like to hear all about it, so please do tell me how you'd intend to satisfy me, and what you would do to me – if you were giving the opportunity to. Don't be shy.

No more dreams I would like to discuss with you – I've learnt my lesson, one bitten twice shy. After I told you about my last one I never heard from you for one week.

I'm glad to hear that I make your night, as you do the same for me, and you know it. So you're happy you got all your answers – told you too much didn't I??? Maybe it's time for me to take a backwards step back into my shell, and keep things to myself. (LOL)

I look forward to hearing from you again soon.

ME –XOXOX-

Ps) I hope you have a really good and safe holiday, which I am sure you will. In addition, I hope you think of me a lot whilst you are gone – and miss me heaps – because I'm going to miss you – don't forget me will now.

9 November 2009 to Beau Goddard

Dear Beau,
Fuck it's hot here, and we still haven't reached Summer yet – still have another week of this heat wave to go, do you have air conditioning up there – we don't here.

The picture gangland[116] showed you were of a girl who writes to me – she's a good sort, she lives in Sydney – nothing's going on though, just a few letter and photo here and there, she also wants to come down and visit me, but I'll play it by ear. She's good friends with a close mate of mine – if I were different story, and that's what she says. Everything is a competition with that bloke – his funny bloke though, how's he settled in up there??? He is the only bloke who has a harem in his own mind, but in reality, I don't think he actually has one girl. ☺ Who is he getting around with up there??

I thought you were kept up to date with my situation – its so

116 Gangland Milly, a name for Milad Mokbel.

hard to fill you in through the mail – it relates to one matter – that's it, I hope I've shed some light on things for you, fuck what anyone has to say – no one I know cares, and that's all that really matters to me – true?

With best wishes & respect,
Your friend always – Carl

9 November 2009 to Roberta Williams

Roberta,
I was really looking forward to seeing you today; I have been for the past week. As I have a lot of things that I'd like to discuss with you – but as I expected, you failed to make it up here. You said you were sick, and you planted that seed a few days before you were even due to visit, so it didn't really come as any great surprise to you never got here today – not to worry, after all what can I do or say, worrying won't change anything. I just hate looking forward to something, only to be let down – story of my life these days, I guess I just have to face reality, times have change, and these days I'm not much use to anybody – what do I have to offer from here, I guess it's hard to accept, but I honestly believe it's the truth. I remember the days when if you said you were coming, nothing would stop you – how you've changed as a person from those days, you use to be so caring and reliable.

Tommy was also looking forward to seeing you, we'd organized for you to see me for one hours, whilst Penny was seeing Tommy, then after you'd seen me, you could've joined there visit for 15–30 minutes, to say a quick hello. As he said, he has not seen you in five years. How time flies when you're having fun – not!

Over the past few weeks, I have written you a few letters – which you haven't even took the time out to reply too. I have no doubt if you go to jail soon – over these driving bullshit charges you have to front up on, which I sincerely hope doesn't happen – you'll write – as you'll have nothing better to do – so pass your time writing, and talking shit to Carl.

Yesterday I had a pretty good visit with Penny, Brea, and Kota. Kota was in the shits as the vending machine wasn't working, when I came out there she said I might as well go home – there's no food – little brat she is, she came good though. We ended making a deal about her dummy, if she doesn't get rid of her dummy by Christmas day, I can get rid of her rabbit, I bet she doesn't stick to it.

I want you to do me a favour, and give my dad some money for me, so when Christmas time arrives I don't have to ask you for money. As I really hate asking you or anyone for money, I thought I'd have my own money this year, as before you moved into my mum's place, I intended on renting it out – if that had of happened I would've had my own money, and wouldn't feel like a beggar asking you for money.

Keep in touch – Carl

10 November 2009 to Kylie

Hello hello,
I trust this letter finds you fit and well, as it leaves me just fine.

I just received 3 letters from you, and you made my night – I've read them over and over – I loved them, I love hearing from you KYLIE, you are the best babe. ☺

I'll answer one letter tonight, and then another tomorrow night. Only problem with that is I don't whether the letter I will send tomorrow night will reach you before you go away, but it'll be there for you when you return – wish I were in person. ☺

Now regarding the visit – what I'll do is book you in for Monday the 23rd at 1.30 pm, as that'll give you plenty of time to get here, but if you get here early, they usually just let you in, and we'll get one hour from the time the visit starts.

About my dream, thanks for given me the heads up for the future. ☺

You said, if one of us is going to be the responsible one, you say it sure as hell won't be you – looks like we'll be having a hell of a lot of fun. (LOL)

Gee what I'd give to be out there now with you. I would've thought you'd be mad to stop in a moment like that – how right I was. ☺ I wouldn't have been stopping either – nothing would've stopped me – that was a dream, not reality. ☹ I could've have cared who was there – as there was nothing they could've seen anyway. Kylie I don't start something and not finish it – you should know that, so you'll always be a happy chappy with me – believe me you! You're 100 % right I wouldn't have been embarrassed getting out the pool, because I would've have been getting out – plain and simply. (LMAO) I would've been making love to you in there, and I would've been making you cum multiply times – that I promise you. Whilst I were inside you, you would've had your arms wrapped around me, and bitting my neck and shoulders, my hands would've been holding your hips, and firmly placed on your bum – pulling you into me – and I would've been hitting you hard too – you never would've wanted it to end.

You made me laugh, when you said if they didn't like the show, too bad, they can leave. As for ideas – I don't think you need any help – I'm actually sure you don't, but I'll help you anyway, just because I'm a good bloke. We stayed in the pool, finished off what I started – and carried it on upstairs in our room, I can't wait to hear you response on this one, I'm getting hard just thinking about it, wish you were here with me now – I'd give it too you long and strong. ☺

My hypothetical, I loved you're ending, you could go lower and lower, and you know it – you know I'd never tell you to stop – never ever, and why would I – I'm not mad you know. Don't worry as much pleasure as you'd give me, I'd make sure that I gave it back to you tenfold – that I promise you.

You finished off your letter by saying you were going to have a long COLD shower, wash your hair, and have the wet look that I am thinking about. If I were there Kylie, you have the wet look alright. I'd have you that wet, dripping, soaking, you'd be saturated, and I'd gladly clean you up – do you reckon I would – or wouldn't??? And in which way??? (LMAO) I'd have your legs over my shoulders, and I'd hit you in places that have never ever been hit before, you'd be kicking yourself thinking he's been so close and yet so far all my life – (LOL) leave you on that thought – I think I'm in need for a shower now – hope you're happy BABE! ☺

I look forward to seeing you soon, and hearing from you even sooner.

MWAH! MWAH! MWAH!

ME –XOXOX-

11 November 2009 to Kylie

Hi there,

How are you going? Good I hope – as for me, I'm fine.

You were saying that your mum said that I've traded her for a younger model. The other day when I was talking to Kath – Kath said to me "Susan was here the other day, and she said you've left her for Kylie", I'll always have time for your mum, she's a great person – best mother in law anyone could even have.☺

You said you are sure that I have hundreds of girls that would want to stick around and wait for me – don't be so sure – not true, I'm not a player – although you think I am. You said you were sure there'd be some strange ones in the mix – If I were out there now I'm sure there would be some skanks throwing themselves at me – looking for some fame or notoriety, or like you said even to fulfil their fantasy. I wouldn't have be interested though. Before I came to prison I used to go out clubbing, and I've seen skanks like that trying to pick me up – I weren't interest though, does nothing for me but make me laugh – they look cheap.

Kylie, if I got out of her tomorrow – I wouldn't forget you. I don't forget the people who mean something to me – I'm not that type of person, I will be making up for lost time when I get out, with one certain person – I'd be turning my dream into reality with her – that's all I'm telling you for the time being.

I got you super frustrated with my remarks – good!!!! Just what I wanted to hear – as that's exactly what I was trying to do to you – mission accomplished – now you know how it feels, its good though – keeps the flame alight. Imagine how frustrated I could get you, if I had my way with you. Having you completely naked, with you lying on your back, me holding your hands above your head – putting myself inside you, only to take it back out, rubbing the head of my ----- up and down your -----, making sure I would just be slightly entering you. Then putting myself slowly but surely inside you – deep inside you – hitting you in all the right places, whilst I was kissing your soft lips – oohhh la la, sound like fun don't it – deal ???? ☺ (LMAO)

Kylie you said I'm special, well so are you, and I'm so happy you're in my life, now my only battle is keeping you there, which I hope I have plenty of success in doing.

Do I wanna see you do a trick?? Of course I do – what tricks can you perform??? If you can put it in your mouth, taste it and then swallow it, you know you can handle it – you'll have to try that – gotta love a girl who swallows.

I'll leave it there for now, and I look forward to hearing from you again soon, very soon.

MWAH

ME –XXX-

12 November 2009 to Danny Heaney

Dear Danny,
How's things buddy, as good as they can be I hope – as for me I'm fine, no complaints.

I don't know how Bert and Rob are going. I don't think they are an item anymore though, I know he still sees her often, but I don't think they live together anymore. I talk to Rob a fair bit on the phone – the only time I get to talk to Bert is on a visit – as the prison has banned her from talking to me on the phone for 3 month – over stuff relating to Stacey – that 3 months is up in 2 weeks time – 27th of November. I can and do ring there, but Bert's not allowed to hop on the phone and talk to me – if she hops on, they'll terminate the call – childish I know, but what can you do? I talk to Dhakota every morning before she goes to school, which is the main thing for me.

Two Guns has been depressed lately, he can't handle the heat, fucked if I know how he worked in a kitchen. (ha ha) His always doing his head in worrying about what others are thinking about him, as you could imagine, we wind him up all day. I told him most people would've even be bother talking about him, after all who's he, as his irrelevant to most people's lives – should of seen the look on his face – priceless – what the .... he should be the topic of everybody's conversation – the next Don.☺

I hope that you will get your leaves soon – it'll be good when you do, give you something to look forward to – the time would fly then.

With best wishes & respect,
Your friend always – Carl

Ps) Tommy and Matty both said to give you there best, as they always do.

12 November 2009 to Jason Paisley

Jason 'Plugger' Paisley, a notorious criminal also known as the 'Trial from Hell' crook.

Big Pun,
How's things buddy, as good as they can be I hope – as for me I'm fine, no complaints.

One day late last week I received your, I was surprised to hear from you – I was spewing that you're locked up again – but nevertheless I was happy to hear from you.

CONGRATULATIONS – YOU'RE GOING TO BE A DAD. ☺

So you found yourself a gook, seems to be the in thing these days – Stacey, now you. What's the world coming to. (ha ha)

I told Bertie Wrout that you passed on your best to her – she said say hello to you and tell you to get fucked. She'd find a fight in an empty house – good old Bertie.

I don't really have much more to add, therefore I guess I will leave it there for now, and I hope hear from you again soon.

With best wishes & respect,
Your friend always – Carl

13 November 2009 to Nikki Denman

Dear Nikki,
I trust this letter finds you in the best of health and spirits, as it leaves me fine.

I just received your letter, it's been awhile, and I've really missed not talking to you – so as you could imagine I was very happy to hear from you – but sad in another way to hear you've already moved back to QLD, as now I won't get to see you very much. ☹ I just hope things work out for you how you want them too. Listen to what I say – you are a good catch for anyone, so don't settle for second best – because you deserve nothing but the best, and I mean that Nikki.

Now that you're back in QLD, you'll have to get Nicole to write to me, surely she's back from New Zealand now. Get onto some girls for me – I promise you, that I'll be nice to them – give me a chance – talk to Helen and ask her to get some for me – I'll leave it up to you – I've begged enough – and I don't normally beg to anyone for anything.

Roberta's is supposed to be coming up here to see me this coming Monday – on a contact visit – by herself – I might be a chance – what do you think?☺

I think her felling for me are still as strong as ever – can't blame her though, as I tend to have that effect of girls. ☺ Nah those days have been and gone for me – as long as we get along good, and have a laugh, once bitten twice shy for me, I'm not that much of a gluten for punishment. (LOL)

I don't really have much more to add, therefore I guess I will leave it there for now, and I hope hear from you again soon.

With best wishes and respect,
All my love – Carl –xoxox-

13 November 2009 to Milad Mokbel

Hey Milad,
I see you have come to your senses – and you want to deal – Melanie, now I will be anxiously waiting to hear from her, and once I do, you'll be hearing from the blonde bombshell *(Crystal),* good, as I prefer the dark haired one myself. You must have some photos of Mel that you can send to me in the meantime. Tell her that I said if she wants visit me when she's next in Melbourne, she more than welcome too, box visit only. I like Mel, I reckon she's ok.

I heard that Claire once did a photo shoot for Zoo, any truth???

With best wishes & respect,
Your friend always – Carl

14 November 2009 to Kylie

Hello.

I hope you enjoyed your holiday – you had a good time, and that you thought about me constantly whilst you were gone – if that were the case I'd be one happy chappy, as I'd be winning ☺

It was so good to talk to you today – I was rapt – I was hanging out to talk to you, the 2 calls flew – could've talked to you all day, not telling you anymore as you'll get a big head, if you haven't already got one. (LOL)

I loved stirring you up today on the phone, it was fun, after our call I did what I said I was going too – man of my word – wish you were here to give me a helping hand. I bet you do too.

What am I going to do with myself this week – Hmmmm – I hate to admit it but I'm going to be lost without you, Oh I'll get two letter from you hopefully that should tide me over. Only 9 more sleeps until I get to see you – can't cum quick enough.

A joke for you excuse the language

Q – Why don't tampons talk?

A – Because they're stuck-up cunts.

16 November 2009 to Kylie

Greetings,

I just received 2 letters from you – which I'm very happy about – so thank you very much, that made my night again – Mwah!

I spoke to your mum yesterday – yeh I did – what did we talk about??? – Hmmm – wouldn't you love to know, maybe

I'll tell you, maybe I won't – I'll just have to wait and see how you play your cards, by the way is there anything you like to tell me??? – I'd rather hear it from you then anyone else. (lmao) It's always amazed me – that when you're not even looking to find out info – how it sometimes just falls into your lap. ☺

You asked if I could have a shower whenever I liked – I have a shower in my cell, so the answer is yes, I can use it anytime I like, any hour, thankfully we don't have shower restrictions here, not yet anyway. At some of the other prisons, they have brought in some restrictions – like 3-minute showers, then the water cuts out, so you can't use it again for another hour, give it time and they'll introduce it here.

As you know, I love a women who has confidence, *(I love yours),* I seriously can't stand blokes who try and tear women down – I believe any bloke who does that has serious issues – I'd like to see them try bringing men down, and not women, wouldn't happen – I consider that a flaw in their character, not the woman's. Roberta is for so thankful to me for giving her confidence, when I first got with her she use walk with her head looking at the ground – I hated that – needless to say, I quickly snapped her out of that.

I don't mind long nails – yours, I believe I'd enjoy – you digging them into my back whilst I'm giving it to you hard, what man wouldn't love that?? Running them up the top of my legs – followed by your tongue, in return – I'd kiss you all over, making sure that I did not miss a spot. Don't worry, my tongue could get into all the hard-to-get places. Do I still want to be your dentist – is the pope a catholic? If I'm drilling and cleaning you, count me in. ☺

ME –XOXOX-

16 November 2009 to Roberta Williams

Dear Roberta,
I trust this letter finds you in the very best of health and spirits, as it leaves me fine.

Roberta thanks for coming into visit me today, as I had a fantastic visit with you, I really enjoyed it, and it lifted my spirits. Today's visit with you was the best visit that I have had in a long time; I really needed it, again thank you – Mwah!. It was so good getting to spend some time alone with you, it's hard leaving though, and watching you leave, today's visit brought back memories. I had a lot of things that I wanted to talk to you about – we got through most of them, the time just went so quickly, they say time flies when you're having fun, and today was no exception. You'll have to make more of an effort to get up here more often – I know it's hard at the moment as you don't have a licence. However, it would be good if you could get up here once a fortnight, once with you and the kids (*Dhakota would love that*) – and once by yourself, or with Rob. I have a lot of time for Rob, his a good guy. It was very nice of him to bring you up here today, and let us have some alone time – we needed it – I can talk more open when it just you and I there – I know you can too.

You might think that I have a lot of people, but honestly I don't – I have you, my dad, and the kids, you are the people who I trust with anything, and everything, and each and every one of you will always be there with me, and vice versa. Lately I've really been thinking about my mum heaps – and I miss her so so much – Bert in a lot of ways she use to give my so much strength – you know how close her and I were. She use to make me laugh, when she always use stick up for me all the time, against you – the Don – anyone – she'd always have her say. I just wish that I could bring her back, even if it were for one day.

Today when you and I were talking about the possibility of you getting with different people – you said I should know you're not like that, as I said to you today, the Bert I knew has changed over the past 5 years – but today was the first time in a long time that I seen the old Roberta appear. Bert you have to think before you do anything, as you have to be a positive role model for the kids – more so Dhakota.

By the way – You are a "bitch" – you've now got me thinking of you overtime tonight – all good thoughts of course – remember though, pays back are a bitch, & as you're fully aware – I have a long memory. ☺ Love you Roberta.

Love & best wishes, always and forever - Carl – xx-

17 November 2009 to Kylie

Hello hello,
I thought I'd write you another letter, so there are heaps there for you when you get home, since I can't be there to greet you, but in a perfect world I would've cum with you, as well as in and over you. (lmao). I hope you're happy to hear from me, another day has past, which means one less until you get home – 6 more sleep until our visit – can't cum quickly enough.

Are you more adorable on the phone, or in your letters – that's a hard one – both – you're now starting to warm up in your letters – and I'm loving it. ☺

So my dream never offended you – good to hear, I didn't think it would, as you said it was only mild, plus you asked me to tell you all about it. However, when I didn't hear from you I thought something was up, sometimes I guess I think the worst – this environment can do that to you. I now hope the steamy story that I wrote to you doesn't offend you – and I hope you like it, if you do, next one I'll go a little further, I still have a lot further I can go, write one back to me, and give me something to work with – a few hints. ☺

Agree – your idea sounds good, actually better than good, get you dirty again, so that we could have a shower together. Imagine the water running off us, whilst I had you up against the wall, with your legs wrapped around me, or the water hitting your back whilst I had you bent over, and I was holding your hips and giving it too you hard = sound like fun. ☺

Yeh, I wish I were the first to discover your talents, I wish I even knew that I were a chance too (*that wouldn't been a nice start*), so don't you now go reminding me of anything – I never even knew – this is the first I've heard of it. Suck it – I'll give you suck it alright. If I had my head between your legs – I'd suck it – and I'd suck it until you cum all in my mouth. Then I'd just tease you by running the head of my cock up and down the lips of your pussy – now you kick yourself – because if you were forward enough years ago to send me the vibes – and if I had of known, the above would've been happening years ago – again kick yourself – I know you are. ☺

Night babe

Thinking of you and missing you heaps

MWAH!

ME –XOXOX-

18 November 2009 to Kylie

Hello there,

What's cooking good looking???

This morning I tried to ring your mum's place, to say hello, and to see how you were going – no answer. Then a few hours later, I rang my dad's place. My dad said to me your mother in law's here, no need to guess who he was referring too (*your mum was laughing*) – then my dad asked me if I wanted to talk to her – I did. Naturally, I asked her if she's heard from you, and how you were. She said you were going ok – and that you had rode an elephant. I think that you would've preferred to be riding something else though – hint hint – it's attached to me. ☺

I don't really have a lot more to say, so I suppose I'll love you and leave you for tonight.

MWAH!

ME –XOXOX-

20 November 2009 to Kylie[117]

Hi,

Phuket belly – what the...................... I hope you're now ok – and it didn't ruin your holiday. As I told you in one of my previous letters, I spoke to your mum when she was at my dad place, and she said you were ok. Then the next day when I phoned my dad's place – Kath jumped on the phone, and said to me, Karen rang

117 At the end of November, Kylie made her first visit to Carl in prison – a contact visit. After that their correspondence became less frequent and less intense. She suffered ill-health over Christmas and later claimed that her 'course' was demanding more time from her.

back last night, and said Kylie is in hospital in Phuket – with Phuket belly. I wanted to ring your mum so bad to see how you were, but I didn't, as I didn't want her thinking things, and start questioning you when you got home.

I don't know how you got Phuket belly, but I just hope you are ok, I guess we'll talk more about it when I see you, that's if you are fit enough to make it here, if you're not I fully understand.

Nothing much has been happening here, naturally, it goes without saying, I've been missing your letters, but I'm travailing along ok, just counting down the days until I get to see you. I hope our visit goes well – by the time this letter reaches you, you would have had the visit with me, I hope you enjoyed it, and you want to cum back.

Just a short one tonight – don't complain – it may be short, but it's better than nothing.

I hope to hear from you again soon – and see you in the flesh even sooner.

MWAH!

ME –XOXOX-

CHAPTER 10

The Williams family Christmas

Carl and Roberta had quietly split in early 2004, when Carl was locked in mortal combat with his enemies. But soon after he moved into a high-rise apartment in the city with his number one henchman, Andrew 'Benji' Veniamin, Roberta moved into an apartment a few floors below. This arrangement suited Carl as he wanted to be near Dhakota while also being unaccountable to his wife. Carl needed Roberta, but he also needed some space of his own. It was an unusual set-up to say the least, considering that Benji was rumoured to have been sleeping with Roberta, which she has always denied.

Over the six years Carl spent in Barwon Prison, Roberta was by far his most constant female visitor. The reason he seldom wrote to her was that she was usually prepared to make the three-hour round trip to Barwon to see him. Carl wanted Roberta to move on from him, but he still relied on her. They had survived the crucible of the Gangland War and that would always bind them together. After Roberta had been through years of abusive dead-end relationships, Carl was the first man to encourage her to believe in herself and she would always love him for that, despite their differences. Even after their marriage ended, their relationship could at times be playful.

However, as Christmas 2009 approached, Carl—in between chatting up his women—found time to adopt the conventional role of head of the Williams household. He continued to be concerned about Roberta's health and yet he felt he had the right to treat her as a truant daughter, who was tempted to fall into bad company and was failing to pay appropriate rent for the roof over her head he had provided.

This was to be a most unhappy Christmas.

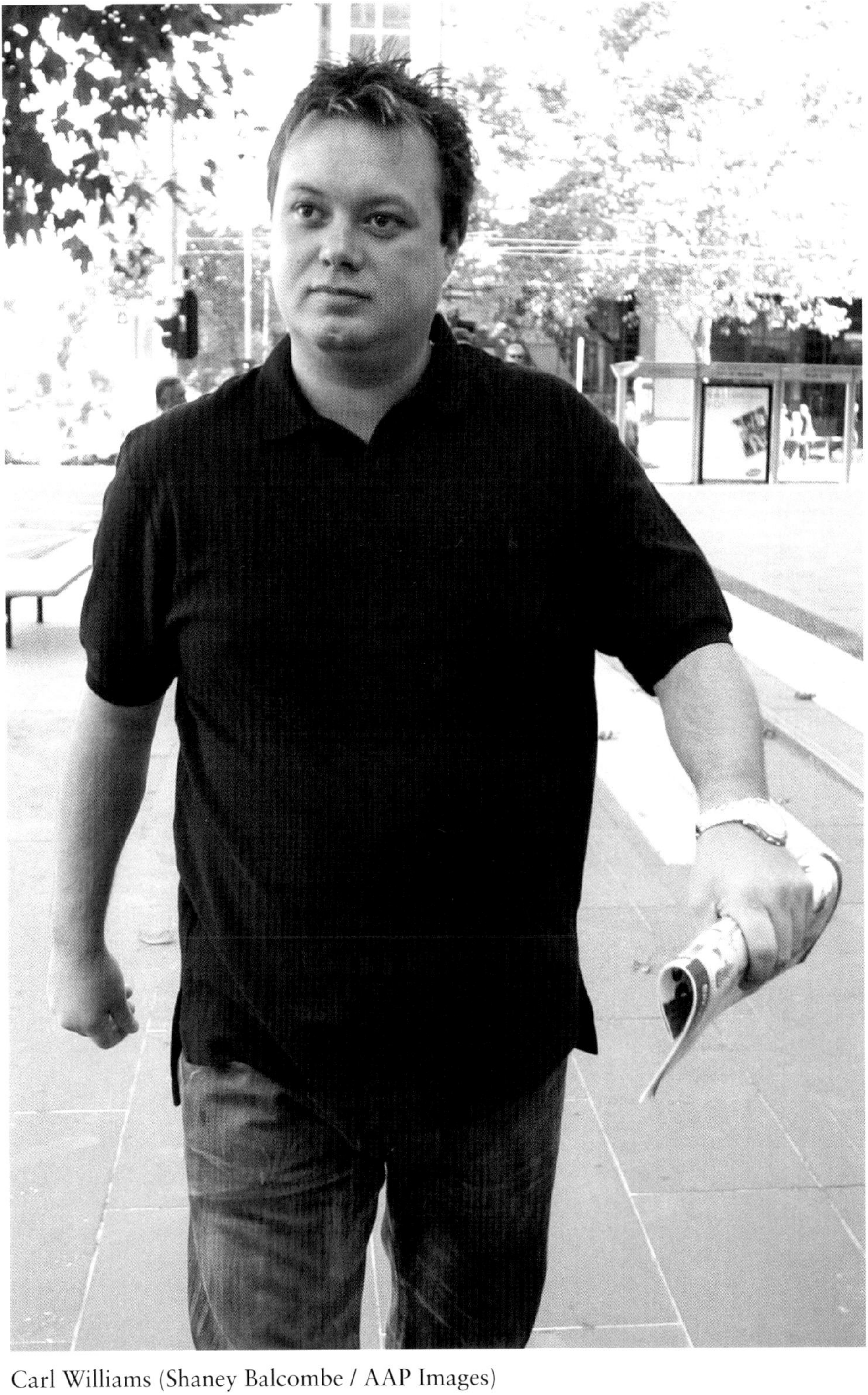

Carl Williams (Shaney Balcombe / AAP Images)

Mark Moran was found fatally shot in this white ute in Combermere Street, Aberfeldie, a north-western suburb of Melbourne, on 15 June 2000. (Simon Dallinger / Newspix)

Jason Moran attending the Coroners Court in January 2002 for the inquest into the murder of Alphonse Gangitano, former head of the Carlton Crew. (Shaney Balcombe / Newspix)

Judy Moran arrives at the car park in Pascoe Vale Road, Essendon, where her son Jason and Pasquale Barbaro were shot in June 2003. (Peter Smith / Newspix)

Mick Gatto (second from left) arriving at St Mary Star of the Sea Catholic Church in West Melbourne for the funeral service of Jason Moran. (Mark Smith / Newspix)

Carl with his three-year-old daughter Dhakota and his wife, Roberta, outside court on 2 December 2003 after being granted bail. (Jessica Lee / Newspix)

Police gather outside the Brunswick Club on Sydney Road, Brunswick, where patriarch Lewis Moran had been shot dead. He was the 23rd victim of the gangland wars. (Craig Borrow / Newspix)

Roberta speaks to the media outside the Melbourne Magistrates' Court on 10 June 2004 after Carl's dramatic arrest by the Purana Taskforce. On her left is her sister, Michelle. (Jason South / Fairfax)

Carl's great friend Andrew 'Benji' Veniamin (right) with Paul Kallipolitis. Benji was killed by Mick Gatto in a pizza house in March 2004. A jury ruled that this was in self-defence.

Tony Mokbel leaves the Victorian Supreme Court, Melbourne, in November 2005 after being freed on bail ahead of his trial for alleged cocaine trafficking. (Stuart McEvoy / Newspix)

Ange Goussis outside the Melbourne Supreme Court, where he was sentenced to twenty years in prison for the murder of Lewis Caine. (Stuart McEvoy / Newspix)

Principal cast members of the first series of Nine Network's *Underbelly*. From left to right: George Kapiniaris (George Defteros), Les Hill (Jason Moran), Simon Westerway (Mick Gatto), Gerard Kennedy (Graham Kinniburgh), Gyton Grantley (Carl Williams), Martin Sacks (Mario Candello), Vince Colosimo (Alphonse Gangitano), Kevin Harrington (Lewis Moran) and Callan Mulvey (Mark Moran). (Rob Baird / Newspix)

The entrance to Acacia Unit at HM Prison Barwon. (Alex Coppel / Newspix)

Star AFL footballer Ben Cousins with Fabian Quaid at the Anthony Mundine–Nader Hamdan fight at the Sydney Entertainment Centre on 27 February 2008. (Graham Crouch / Newspix)

Wayne Howlett at his Xtreme Physique gym in Hobart. (Kim Eiszele / Newspix)

Mick Gatto and Nicola Gobbo on either side of Ray Towell at the Flemington funeral service for legendary Legal Aid stalwart Stephen Drazetic on 10 October 2008. (Angela Wylie / Fairfax)

Roberta and Dhakota at the funeral of Barbara Williams at St Therese's Catholic Church, Essendon, on 2 December 2008. Kota holds a picture of Barbara as a young woman. (Craig Borrow / Newspix)

The body of Des 'Tuppence' Moran is removed from the scene after he was shot dead by two gunmen in a cafe on Union Road, Ascot Vale, on 15 June 2009. (Ian Currie / Newspix)

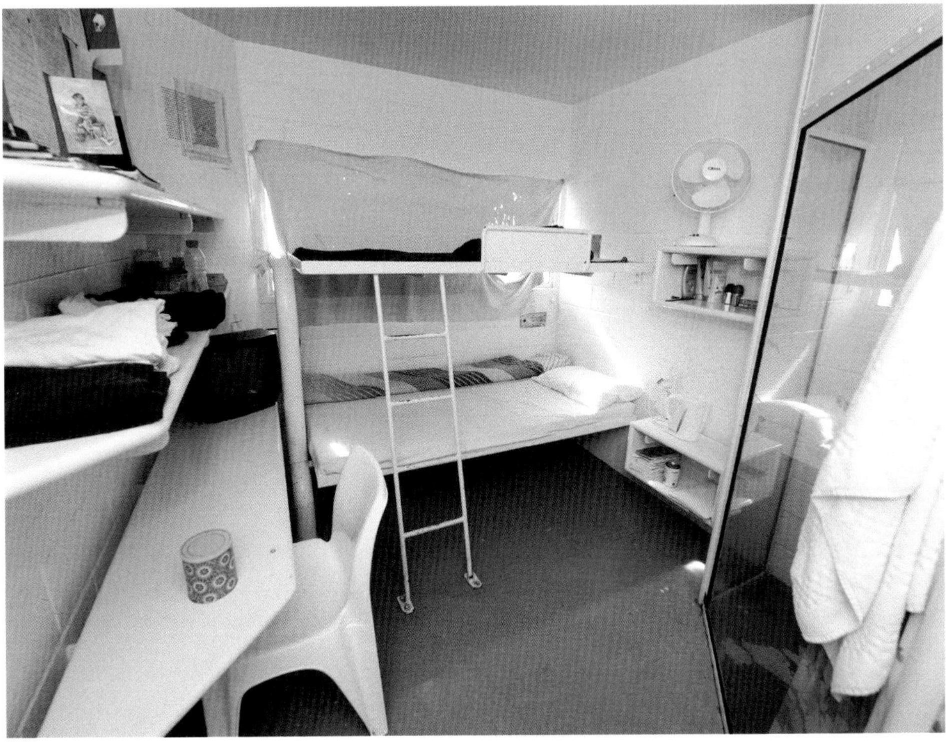

Inside a cell in the Acacia Unit at HM Prison Barwon. (Alex Coppel / Newspix)

'Little Tommy' Ivanovic, the former pastry chef who was one of Carl's two cellmates in Hotel Acacia at the time of his death.

A prison still from 19 April 2010 showing Matty Johnson standing and holding the stem from an exercise bike. He is behind Carl, who is sitting at the table and is about to be bludgeoned to death.

Carl's gold-plated coffin emerges from St Therese's Catholic Church, Essendon, at his funeral service on 30 April 2010. (David Caird / Newspix)

Danielle and Breanane Stephens at Carl's funeral. (Nicole Cleary / Newspix)

Dhakota arrives at Carl's funeral with her mother. (David Caird / Newspix)

The hearse, followed by the family in a stretch Hummer, leaves St Therese's Catholic Church. (Fiona Hamilton / Newspix)

George Williams attending Matty Johnson's committal hearing on 8 December 2010, where Matty was charged with Carl's murder. (Mike Keating / Newspix)

Rocco Arico, who was the first person Tommy Ivanovic called from his cell after Matty Johnson had bashed Carl to death. (Eugene Hyland / Newspix)

Matthew Charles Johnson arrives at the Melbourne Supreme Court on 8 December 2011 for sentencing over the murder of Carl Williams in Barwon Prison in April 2010. (Aaron Francis / Newspix)

21 November 2009 to Roberta Williams

Dear Roberta,

Fucking hell, what do I have to do to get a letter off you????? You name it, and I'll do it, can't wait to hear your reply on this one.

Only 6 more sleep until we get out calls back – yippee – I can't wait. ☺

I seen my dad today, he came up with Penny – 9.oo am visit – Penny was up at 6.30 am, expecting him to be there any minute. (ha ha) They were here early *(naturally with my dad driving*) what time they got here, I have no idea.

Penny told me that she contacted Emidio on behalf of Danielle, for me – no problems. Dan can go there and get an outfit – which she is, either tomorrow, or Monday. His good that bloke, he always does whatever can can to help me make sure my kids always look the best, but come to think of it – they make the clothes, the clothes don't make them – just like I do – don't you agree??? – Hhmmm – You do, thank you – you're so sweet, butter wouldn't melt in your mouth – think I've taking this one too far – Ok then I'm lying, we both know steak would melt in your mouth (lol), but nevertheless I still love you, and just for the record I always will.

What else – ohhhh, I have heaps to tell you – I've been thinking about you lots especially after our fantastic visit – but sorry I'm not telling you about my thoughts in a letter, because if I do, you'll have it in black and white to show everyone my true felling. ☺ Sorry Roberta I'm not falling into this time, nah nah nah Roberta. (ha ha)

I don't really have much up to add, therefore I guess I will leave it there for now, and I hope to hear from you soon.

Love & best wishes, always and forever - Carl – xx-

23 November 2009 to Roberta Williams

Roberta,
I guess I might have been out of order today, when I asked you where you were the other night, when Dhakota had to go stay with Adam, whilst you went somewhere late at night for an hour or more. Yesterday when I asked you where you went, you said that you went to see one of your friends (Jody), from Sunshine, some girl who you grew up with. Then today you said that you went to the Chemist to get some eardrops for Mia, (if that were true, god only knows why Dhakota couldn't have went there with you) – when you gave me different answers, it reminded me so much of when Stacey use to lie to me. If you had nothing to hide, you'd just tell the truth, not tell me two different stories – which makes me think that you obviously do have something to hide, what it is I have no idea, nor do I really care. I just can't handle being lied too, as it gets me really worked up – I'm not an imbecile and I don't appreciate being treated like one, plus I'm always honest with you, so I guess I just expect the same in return from you – one would think that's not too much to ask for.

I suppose at the end of the day, where you went is your business, and if you were seeing someone, again that's your business, not mine – true? After all what you do, and whom you see in your life, isn't any of my business, and vice versa. I just thought if you were seeing someone, I'd like to hear it from you first, rather then hear it off someone else – like I always do.

Bert, I don't know what you are up to out there, but if I were to take a guess, I'd say that you are either seeing someone, or you have your eye on someone, I know you to well. As I've previously told you, if you get with someone else besides Rob – I won't accept them being near Dhakota, nor will allow then setting foot in my mum's place, (which ultimately means A) you'd lose me, not that that would worry you – and B) you'd have to look for somewhere else to stay). I know I've told you this before, and I hope you clearly understand me. You can't just go from bloke to bloke, as I don't want Dhakota seeing you with a variety of men. Honestly I don't even know why I waste my time talking to you, as I for one know that anything I say to you, just goes in one ear, and out the other, because at the end of the day you'll do as you like, my opinion means absolutely nothing to you, it never has.

Just a short one, to let you know how I feel, as I couldn't talk to you on the phone and explain myself – hope you understand where I was coming from.

Keep in touch

With best wishes & respect,
Love & friendship – Carl –xx-

24 November 2009 to Milad Mokbel

Dear Milad,
I just received your letter, dated 17-11-09, and it was good to hear from you again as it always is.

I sent you that photo for you to keep – I didn't want it back, I'm not an Indian giver. You think she's attractive – I dint like her much she has a friend who I like 0 dark haired girl – they said they both want to come down here and visit me soon, I'll play it by ear.

I don't really have any news for you – I hear that Rocky is running things out there, says a lot for the others out there – no time for that bloke, his a piece of shit, and a fucking scared little Wessel. I hear his in regular contact with Little Shane (your mate). I know Fab from Perth is currently fronting his trail over there, I think Con Heliotis is doing – last I heard from Fab (*a few weeks ago*), he was extremely confident of going home – I don't take much notice of that though – don't think he knows much. I hope he wins though – as I've always said he not to bad bloke.

I liked your response, it gave me a good laugh, reminded me off a Barrister – never let the truth get in the way of a good story. Buddy, I tell you honesty though, with a word of a lie, Roberta doesn't have one single stretch mark on her body, even after 4 kids, maybe some cellulite, but no stretchmarks, the air brushings weren't for stretchmarks, that I can guarantee you, I only hope Dhakota has her genes in that department. So no buddy my memory isn't playing games on me.

Claire, your right Karina does know her, and she said she's very pretty, but I've never doubted that. You know me, I like Mel – yeh she's made mistakes, but I can relate to her the best – I have a soft spot for her – and personally I think she's genuine.

With best wishes & respect,
Your friend always – Carl

24 November 2009 to Sean Sonnet

Dear Sean,
Well thank god it's finally cooled down a bit the last few days – which is a relief, as it cooled the cells down a bit – I'm sure the heat will be back again soon though, and only stronger, I'm tipping this summer we'll hit 50 degrees. Years ago when I was in Dubai it was 50's, wondering if Jason would be out there with his oil all over him in that heat, you'd have to be half mad to do that these days, with skin cancer.

The other week I got a letter from Plugger, his pinched again, over some aggravated burgs, his at the MAP – after I received a letter off him, I heard Tye's there with him. He told me to expect him here soon – when he was out, I use to talk to him sometime on the phone.

I was happy to hear that you had a good visit with Rob, I agree with you – he is a good bloke – when he was visiting you, Roberta was over here visiting me, on a contact visit – it was the first contact I've had alone with her for years. It was good to see her, added bonus was that she was in a good mood, ☺ – we had a laugh, she wants to come and see you too – I guess when you get your calls back with her you'll organize something.

With best wishes & respect,
Your friend always – Carl

26 November 2009 to Beau Goddard

Dear Beau,
Last night I received your letter, dated 17 of November, and it was my pleasure to hear from you again, as it always is.

I don't really get any girls writing to me from my facebook page, I don't think a lot of people like writing letters these day, and then waiting a week or two for a reply – if you could email different story. If we could email I dare say I'd have them all going, and if that were the case I'd be more than happy to share with you.

I got a letter off Milad the other night – and all he was going on about was all the girls he has, apparently he does well with the girls, if you don't believe me just ask him. ☺ He seems to like it up there; he'd have all the crumbs talking to him – what I'd pay to be a fly on the wall. (ha ha)

You were saying that you don't talk to many people up there, you're better off like that, when I've been in the mainstream I never really talked to many people – most of them are halfwits – that's jail though.

I see Faruk got sentenced yesterday – 20–14 years, I thought he done well – wonder if he thinks the same – after all he thought he'd get bail – then beat it at committal – than he thought 100% he'd beat it at trial – what now appeals?? Fuck him and the horse he rode in on.

With best wishes & respect,
Your friend always – Carl

27 November 2009 to Ray Spadina

Radoslav 'Ray' Spadina was a local and then international drug trafficker. Spadina was snared in a coordinated covert operation in Europe, Japan, Britain and the United Arab Emirates and was charged with conspiring to import 210 kilograms of pseudo-ephedrine from the Congo in September 2008.

Dear Ray,
I just received your letter, dated 11-11-09, and I was rapt to hear from you, you gave me a good laugh. Fucked if I know why it took so long to reach me – someone must of scanned over it somewhere – obviously they didn't know how to operate the photocopying machine – oh well that's life.

As I said your letter gave me a good laugh – I often lay here and think about some of the things we use to get up too, and the laughs we had, it's good thinking about those memories, they were the good times. What about how we use to drive Andy mad – one day he would be on the biggest fitness campaign ever, and he'd train his ass off, the next day he didn't want to do a thing, I guess it depended on what bottle he grabbed out of the fridge. (ha ha)

You were saying that you don't see anyone except for your family, is that you're choice, or slowly slowly have people dropped off? Ray you'll always be someone whom I consider a close friend of mine, we went through a lot together, and just like you know that I would've always been there for you, I know you would've done the same for me – and there's not too many people I put in that bracket.

I know exactly whom you blame for everything, the predicament that I've found myself in – and to some extent I agree with you, as do a lot of others – but what can I do? I often think to myself would everything have happened if I had of made better decisions, or one better one. However, on the other hand, I think what happened was bound to happen. As I didn't see eye to eye with that cocksucker well before what happened happened – and I wouldn't take his shit, and bow down to him, shooting me, and when he started threatening my loved ones, well that was the begin of the end for him, there was no hope that I was ever going to put up with that.

Mate I seen the look on my mum's face after him and his skunky brother[118] tried to threaten my dad in front of her, then bashing my mate TRAV – simply because he was my friend – enough was enough. The only thing is I believe someone should of taken a stance well before I did, or was forced too – but it's no good crying over spilt milk now, after all what happened happened, it's now history.

I can't believe what its come to, Sandra[119] is now renting – hearing that honestly makes my stomach turn, its fucking bullshit, where the fuck are all the people who you've helped out over all those years?? That old to familiar saying, "out of sight, out of mind." Mate believe it or not – when my mum passed away, my dad was also locked up – and not one single person put their hand up to help with the funeral, apart from my friend

118 Carl is referring to the Moran brothers.

119 Ray Spadina's partner.

Trav, Roberta ended up covering all the costs, and thankfully she gave her a good send off. No one cares, it's sad, but it the truth, everyone wants to be around when you're flying, but when it all turns to shit they all want to jump off what they believe is a sinking ship. Jamie who is there with you, always done his best to try and help, and I will forever be grateful of that.

I heard all about it when Horty fucked you up, what can you do. He is fronting Court down here at the moment, a trial. I don't know how it's going – as his at another prison, it been going about 4 weeks already, and I don't even think they're got past the legal arguments. You know I've known Horty for years – but at the end of the day, Tony was the one who I was close to, I have a lot of time for Tony, with all the others it was more or less hello goodbye.

I don't know much about your situation – only what I read in the papers, and I don't take too much notice of that. Have you cleared everything up after that copper circulated the paper work he did? I can only imagine how you were felling, I myself wouldn't have even bother to read it – I'd take no notice – but unfortunately jails are full of fuckhead, desperates who have nothing better to do then involve themselves in other people business, a large percentage of them you would spit on.

So you're facing conspiracy to import 210 kilos of ephedrine, I hear the sentences are huge up there? If they convict you what are you looking at getting?? Only now are they starting to give monster sentences down here for drugs – recently I believe people have been getting minimum terms of 20 down here now for Trafficking Large Commercial Quantity Amphetamines, its a fucking joke – years ago all you'd get is 6 years with 4 years, how times have changed.

I'm the same as you, I don't agree the more statements the better – how the fuck does that make it better, there's more evidence? Like in my case, my Barrister said the more co–accused that turn on you the better. But after reading what they had to say about me, he quickly changed his mind (ha ha) – the more witnesses, the longer the case, which ultimately means more cross examination = more money for the vultures (Legal Team), and at the end of the day, yes they like to win, but to them the moneys more more important than winning.

There's room down here with me for you. I'll tell you all about the Unit that I'm in, and have been for the past 5 ½ years, and look like being for god only knows how much longer. It's what's called a Management/High Security Unit, people with high profiles, or who are trouble makers within the Prison System usually come here once they are arrested, or get into trouble in the system. There's only 3 little units. The regime we're on a more restricted regime. The unit that I'm currently living in, has 6 cells, but at the moment there's only 3 of us who live in here – me and two others, little Tommy, who you'll probably remember from outside, he lived around the corner from Rocky's mums – him and Rocky grew up together. In one little Unit is Tony Mokbel, and two others being Ange and Barry Q. They have the better unit out of the smaller ones, they have a pool table, and the cells in there Unit are the biggest in the whole system, but in time, we'll rotate units.

The visits down here aren't the best though. As you only get one contact visit per month, duration is for 1 hour – you can apply for an additional visit, which is nearly always approved, also you can have two box visits per week, plus 2-child contact visit per month.

The visits Jamie is talking about are congenial Visits, you can't get them until you get to a medium security prison, there sex visits – duration is 6 hours – and you can have them every six weeks, not bad – but a long way off for me.

I'm no longer in Contact with Nicole[120] – and I haven't been now for a few years, you're right thought she was the one for me, I put her through a fair bit though, and she still stuck around. I told her a lot of lies, too many, she told me that she ran into you in QLD, at Versace, and you told her she shouldn't been the one that I married – and I never heard the end of that either – yeah good one! ☺ The coppers gave her a hard time over me too, and one time when she came up here to visit me the media were parked out the front of the jail, and they snapped pictures of her, next day she was on the front page of the papers, was a picture of her, with my mum – saying Carl's new blonde. I'd only been seeing for her the past ten years – smart aren't they, anyway that destroyed her, as you could imagine people at work started looking at her differently, as did some of her family and friends, who weren't quite sure as to what was going on between us. She was good, and I only wish her happiness.

What about that day after the Oaks, after I'd done the business, I got you to ring my phone pretending to be someone else, and that you were coming over – so she had to go – fuck we were bad – but it was fun, and it's makes me laugh when I look back at it now.

With best wishes & respect,
Your friend always – Carl

29 November 2009 to Danny Heaney

Dear Danny,
I just received your letter dated Sunday 22/11/09, and as you'd expect it was my pleasure to hear from you again, as it always is.

---

120 Nicole Mottram.

Nothing much is happening over these neck of the woods, just putting Two Guns through the ringer, but these day that's an everyday occurrence, we wind him up big time. He must shake his head and think to himself how the fuck did I end up here with these two, god only knows how long they keep him here for too, after all he buzzed up[121] to get the fuck out of there (*or so the rumours are*). ☺ The other night out of the blue he got a letter from Goldie,[122] saying he supports him, and he always will – but he also added that he actually heard him buzz up, but maybe he was just after panadol – two guns swears he never buzzed up full stop. You had to be here for the integration that followed what a laugh. Buddy for a good laugh, can you either write it to me, or him directly, letting us know that people throughout the system are still talking about him buzzing up, and then the way they got him out of there – by ramping cells, and pretending they found something in his cell, which they never, it was all a plan, but from who I still don't know. ☺

With best wishes & respect,
Your friend always – Carl

29 November 2009 to Roberta Williams

Dear Roberta,
Hey Bert how's things? All good I hope, as for me I'm ok.

I just finished a visit with you, Rob, and Dhakota, it was good to see you all, but 30 minutes was nowhere near long enough, by the time I got out there, it felt like it was time to come back. You know I love it when I see you, but I'd rather not have a visit then have one for 30 minutes.

121 'Buzzing up' is using a cell intercom to speak to prison staff, usually after lock-up.

122 Aaron Fenton.

First things first, I am a little stressed about you after our visits, when I mentioned about your eye going lazy, and you said what you did to me. I could see you wanted to talk to me, but like me, you like talking when it's just us two there. You have to take good care of yourself Roberta – as I would die if anything ever happened to you, as you how much you mean to me, so there's no need for me to inflate you head and continuously tell you. ☺ I will talk to you more about it when we get our phone calls back (*which I hope is soon*), or when I see you on our monthly contact visit, which if I have my way will be sometime this coming week. You know a funny thing, I know you that well, that you sometimes don't even have to say anything, as your eyes say it all – and today you had that look in your eye, shifty bitch you are. (ha ha)

You were saying that you want to go away somewhere, you should. Roberta, don't worry about what you could do with Dhakota – as there are plenty of people who will have Dhakota, if you wanted to have a break and go away. So don't let her control your life, for fuck sake she's only 8 years old, she's not the boss, although I can see she likes to think that she is – takes after her mother. ☺

Again I tell you you have to watch Dhakota with her weight, for numerous reasons – I don't want her becoming obese, I want her to be healthy, remember heart condition is heredity, actually this week I am going to see the doctor to have a full check up on my arteries, to see if there're are blockages. Let's face reality, I'd have to be a candidate, I'm nearly 40, and my dad had his first open heart bypass operation before he was 40 – 38 I think he was.

Write back to me – you last bitch

MWAH! – Love you Roberta, and just for the record, I always will. ☺

Love & respect always – Carl –xoxox-

2 December 2009 to Roberta Williams

Dear Roberta,

It was so good to get to talk to you today, after 3 months of no calls, over that 3-month period I really did miss you, never thought you'd hear me say that did you now. (ha ha) But I tell you now, after we finished talking, I did a lot of thinking, and you sent my mind into a spin, which I'm not sure is a good or bad thing.

There's a lot of things that I don't really talk to you about, and I think vice versa, as it's just too hurtful to go ever. I just wish that I were out there with you. I know I've made a lot of mistakes in my life – that I for one wish I could reverse – but unfortunately, that's not possible. I know some of the things that I did when I was outside hurt you a lot – and believe me, I've had a lot of time (*years*) to sit here and think about it all, and I kick myself for that.

You're a good person and you certainly never deserved some of the shit that I put you through. You know when I pleaded guilty, and virtually kissed my life goodbye, I did so for the ones I love – you, my mum and dad, and the kids. As I wanted each and every one of you to live the rest of your days in peace, and I knew by me doing what I did, that was the only way it was ever going to happen. In addition, I knew the battle that I was facing was to say the least an uphill one, and I knew the authorities would never give in, until they had me in jail forever – and in the process they intended on wrecking my loved ones lives. Even if it meant throwing them in jail for crimes that they had absolutely no involvement in.

But believe me, it was one of the hardest things I reckon I've ever had to do – stand up there and repeatedly say guilty, knowing full well the consequences, but I did – because I'd caused each of you enough pain in one way or another through my actions, and enough was enough.

That day I knew 100%, that I'd never get to see Dhakota walk down the aisle. I also knew what I had with you was 100% gone. I knew I'd never see my mum or dad alive again as a free man, but I knew I had to do what I did, as I believed that it was the right thing to do, despite my mum crying in court, and begging for me not to do it. I often think to myself, was what I did that day the breaking point of her, I'll never know – and I try to convince myself that it wasn't – because if it was, it was the biggest mistake that I've ever made, you don't know how bad that does my head in.

Then within 18 months, my mum takes her own life – which absolutely crushed me, and a lot more thaen what you could ever imagine.

As you know I was with Stacey – and I'd be lying if I said I never enjoyed her company, because I did. After all I'm only human, and I enjoy female company. When I got with her, I tried not to make the same mistakes that I made with you. Then what happens. Right whack, some would say. I know in my heart I'll never have a proper relationship ever again in my life. After all what girl in their right mind would want me? What can I offer them – nothing! Plus, who'd want to come here week after week to see me? Yeah, they might stick it out for a year or two, like Stacey did, and who could really blame her for not wanting to put up with it anymore – not me!

I just wish that I had my time over again – how I would do things so differently. I now only wish that I had a partner who worshipped me, and I was her everything – but I know in my heart I'll never ever have that again – yeah, I had that one day, and I never knew what I had until I lost it, which is always the case they say.

There are heaps more things that I want to say to you, and talk to you about, but I don't really like saying everything through the mail. I'd much rather talk to you face to face – and I might when I see you – might being the key word, nothing against you, but these days I really find it hard to talk, and open up.

I don't really have much up to add, therefore I guess I will leave it there for now, and I hope to hear from you soon.

Love & respect,
Always and forever - Carl – xx-

3 December 2009 to Roberta Williams

Mr. Carl Williams.
C/- Locked Bag #7, Lara, Vic 3212

Dear Roberta,

I trust this letter finds you in the best of health and spirits, with few troubles, as it leaves me fine.

I spoke to you this morning for a few calls – and it was good talking to you, as it always is, I enjoy my calls with you, I really do look forward to them.

Mail just arrived, none from you again, ☹ – alls I got was one measly card, that's all.

I enjoy it when I get mail – as it makes me feel good, and like I am no forgotten, but these days I don't really get to much of it – and haven't ever since Stace and I split. I must admit it was good when she was in the picture, as she's use to write to me every night without fail. As well as come and see me at least twice a week, it's very hard to find someone who is committed like she was, I doubt it if I ever will – don't get me wrong she did have her faults, but don't we all.

I've written about 10 letters to you, and surprise, surprise, all of them have gone unanswered, what the fuck do I have to do to get a letter from you??

This morning when I was talking to you, I pointed out how you'd lied to me, I'm not going to go over old grounds, what's the point. However, Roberta you know the old saying, you can trust a thief, but you can never trust a liar. I hate it when you tell me lies, as it's not the Roberta I knew. I honestly consider you probably the closest person to me, along with my dad, Brea and Kota. One thing I can't handle is being lied too and treated like a fool – and sometimes I think that's exactly what you do to me. I'm not sure if you do it on purpose or not though – but I would like to think that you don't, reason being I'd like to think that I mean more to you than that, but that's something only you know, as you tell me one thing, and then you do another.

I'm looking forward to seeing you next week, as I've previously told you I enjoy it when you come by yourself, as we can talk openly, and discuss things that we can't when someone is there – you know what I mean.

That's all for now from me – as I have nothing else worth adding, plus I've probably already bored you to death by now – hope so (ha ha).

I hope to hear from you again soon, really soon for that matter. ☺

Love and respect,
Always and forever
Carl Anthony –xoxox-

6 December 2009 to Roberta Williams

Dear Roberta,
I was looking so forward to talking to you today – I actually woke up at 5.00 am, looking at the clock waiting for the hours to pass so I could talk to you, but you stayed in the City, and obviously, you couldn't be fucked making your way back to Essendon to talk to me. I wouldn't thought you like me, would've been hanging out to talk to me – after not having calls for 3 months, and going from how much you say you miss me – not to be though. They say absence makes the heart grow fonder – your heart doesn't seem to work that way though.

I'm looking forward to seeing you this coming Wednesday – actually I can't wait, whatever you do, just make sure you get here. I'll tell you something now but promise me you won't laugh though – I've been counting down the hours to our visit on Wednesday – stop laughing dickhead, it's not that fucking funny – I told you not to laugh. I feel like a complete dick now even telling you that.

If I don't get a reply to this letter, than fuck you, I won't waste my time writing to you ever again, the balls now in your court.

Love and respect,
Always and forever
Carl Anthony –xoxox-

9 December 2009 to Roberta Williams

Hi,
I trust all is as good as it can be for you out there – as for me here I have no complaints.

I thought I would write you a quick letter to send with your card, seems I know how much you love it when you receive mail from me. ☺

Well what can I tell you – its Wednesday night – its 9.15 pm, Christmas is nearly here. Hey what about poor old Tiger Woods, and his Harem, by the sounds of things he had all the girls – nearly as many as I had when I was out there, you deserved that one, especially after the shit you gave me today (ha ha). I hate the media, as they're the ones who are causing all the troubles for Tiger and his family, what about his poor wife, and poor innocent kids – they've done nothing at all wrong, how must his wife be feeling, I know that feeling. I believe the embarrassment his brought upon her is going to be too much for her to stay with him, she can't – last count 11 mistresses have some forward, these whores can not only can they not keep their legs shut – they also can't keep their mouths shut, sluts they are. They obviously knew he was married, before they opened there legs for him, all they were only after was his money, and were looking to be fucked by someone who's a somebody, unbelieve these girls, they obviously have no morals or pride in themselves, they'd suck you off whilst you were driving – cheap sluts.

What about you today, saying Jamie from Carlton was hot – or sexy, whatever!! I know you were only trying to stir me up, and just for the record, it never worked. After all, I weren't with you – I was with someone else – living with them in an apartment in St.Kilda Rd. ☺ If Jamie was so good, than why did you come running back to me, thank god you did anyway, as you gave me the best thing anyone could have giving me – my beautiful little Dhakota. If I got anyone else apart from you pregnant – straight to the abortion clinic – true, I think I'd better shut my mouth before I put my foot in it. ☺

Hey, I was thinking how you're always letting me know that when I was with you I weren't the loyalist of people – correct! However, rewind your memory back to when we first got together, when you were with me, but you were also sleeping with Dean. Like one night when he and his friends were ringing you up all night, calling you all sorts of names, you were on the phone crying to me – then he came over drunk and slept with you – that broke my heart – I was actually talking to you when he got there – you hung on on me, and then you went and slept with Dean. Therefore, my point is, when I actually think about it thoroughly, I honestly don't think you're in a position to say how unfaithful I was.

I don't really have much more to add, therefore I guess I'll leave it there for now, and I hope to hear from you again soon.

ME –XOX-

Ps) Don't forget to get those photo of Dan's graduation done for me, not A4 size, half that size.

10 December 2009 to Breanane Stephens

Dear Brea,
I trust this letter finds you in the best of health and spirits as it leaves me fine.

SHOCK HORROR!!! – I finally received a card for you, which really did put a big smile of my face, and made my night.

I received about 50 cards tonight from people all over Australia, wishing me luck – and amongst them were a few girls – half my luck hey, it's good to know that I still haven't lost my touch, maybe I'm just a born natural. (lol) It goes without saying yours is the first letter which I answered, as you are the most important girl in my life along with Dhakota – and my mum who I miss so much, with all my heart.

I'm wrapped that I'm getting you the same necklace that as I have – I only hope they can copy the design – as it's a very unusual one – it's a Gucci, I like unusually things, take a look at your mum for instance. (lmao)

Next year when you start your new school, you're going to have to make sure you attend their everyday, and concentrate. Also I think you should walk Dhakota to school before you go to school, as that would take a lot of pressure off your mum, plus who wants to wake up hearing her voice first thing in the morning? As much as I love her – not me, that's one thing I don't miss.

You wanted to know how my last Contact visit went with my girl, Roberta. Not as good as the first one went, not as much kissing, but I still had a very enjoyable visit – I'm slowly making progress though – I still managed to get a few kisses, passionate ones too. She always tells me she loves me, and that she will never love anyone like she loves me, but she tries to turn her felling off as the situation is too hard. I know she loves me, and I know I'll always love her. I know when her and I were together I made a lot of mistakes – which I now kick myself for, but unfortunately I can't turn back the clock – if I could believe me I would. I think Rob makes her happy, and I really like Rob, but at the end of the day his not me, and I know her hearts with me – but you know what they say, if you can't have the one you love, then love the one you're with. I think in time she'll be begging to get back with me – will I take her back – what do you think???? (lol) Would you like her and I to get back together????

Please done take to long to write back to me again as I really enjoy your letters.

I don't really have much more to add, therefore I guess I'll leave it there for now, and I hope to hear from you again soon.

Love you and miss you heaps,
Always and forever – Carl –xoxox-

11 December 2009 to Wayne Howlett[123]

Dear Wayne,
I trust this letter finds you and your loved ones in the very best of health and spirits, as it leaves me fine.

You asked me about Mick Gatto's book, mate I don't know him, but I'll gladly tell you what I do know about him.

I've never had anything to do with Mick Gatto in anyway shape or form, his just never been my cup of tea. Every since I was young – most of the older people I knew, and or hung around with all warned me about the so called Carlton Crew. What I was told and I believed to be the truth, was all they do is borrow money and have no intention of ever paying it back – stand over the harmless – work with the Police, by giving and receiving information, that was more than enough for me to give them a wide birth. Later on in my life, unfortunately for me, I did cross paths with him a few times, which I will tell you all about in detail later.

I'd often see Mick at that Horse Races and that boxing. I know Mick has said in his book, that when I was younger he use to see me at the two up, that he ran – and he'd give me money for a taxi home after I'd lost my money – that's a blatant lie. I believe I've only ever been to the two up school once in my life – it weren't a place I'd hang around. I went there one night with a friend of mine – after we'd won a lot of money at the trots, my friend was a big gambler and he was looking for somewhere else to have a bet – Crown Casino weren't around at this time. One of the other guys who was with us took us

---

123 There is no evidence that this letter was ever sent to Wayne. Unusually, it was not written in response to a letter received. It is clearly in draft form and may have been written at a time when Carl was toying with the idea of writing a memoir and he felt a need to record some of his personal recollections in preparation for that exercise.

to some broken down two up place – with drunks, taxi driver, and desperate inside – I guess that would've been Mick two up school. We didn't stay there very long, as my mate couldn't get set for the amounts he wanted to bet. I reckon if we tipped everyone in the joint upside down, we would've been lucky if we had of got a small percentage of the money we walked in with in our pockets. I said to my mate this isn't a place for us, and shortly after we left, that's the one only time that I've been to a two up school – if it was Mick's school – good luck to him – but he never gave me a cab fare home – I don't think he would've had the money too.

As I said, I would often see Mick Gatto at the races, and at the Boxing. When I was younger and we were all at the races – we'd all have a pocket full of money – we were always all cashed up. Mick and his so called crew on the other hand, were always dressed the part, but unfortunately for them they never use to have much cash. Often I'd spot them hanging around other people who were there with me asking them what they backed cheering for it to win – and if it did they would ask to borrow money – which if it was given any they'd never pay it back. I always purposely tried to keep my distance from them, I knew who they all were, and all I would ever say to them, was hello and goodbye – I would always be polite, but I never wanted to know them.

I remember one day I was at the races with Mark Moran, and a few other – Mark spotted Mick and his crew, he laughed and said they've here again – I looked and there was Gatto and his gang – all dressed in black. We'd call them the desperate degenerates, the poor fella's, no one use to like them, or have a good word to say about them. I said to Mark what do you reckon of them? He said Jason talks to them all, but I do not have any time for any of them at all, as all they do is borrow (snip) money from me, and never pay it back. He said, but Mick gets a lot of useful information as to what's going on around town, so I keep him sweet to get it out of him – Mark said his in with all the coppers – that how his survived for so many years.

After the murder of the Munster – Mick Gatto quickly made contact with Andrew – to see what was going on, and to try and play detective and question him to see what him or I knew about the murder, or if we had any involvement in that murder. Andrew came to see me, I was still in bed when he arrived – he said mate did you hear what happened – I said yeah – he said the big blokes wild – I said who cares. He looked at me and laughed, and said you're a funny cunt, he said buddy he asked us to keep away from his mate – I said yeah, and we have after all he wish is our command, Andrew just smiled and said come on get up lets go for a drive – that meant we were going to have a chat. We left and drove to the shopping complex close by. We walked around discussing what had happened, neither us of were too bothered about it. He said the big blokes going to want to see us – I said yeah so – he can come and see us. I'm not sure how long after it was but Andrew came to see me again he said buddy he wants to see the both of us, he wants us to go to Carlton to see him – I said I thought you said he wants to see us – he said that's right. I said well who the fuck is he dictating when we see him – ring him up and tell him I'll see him, but I won't be coming to Carlton – I'll see him in a park in Fitzroy. Andrew rings tell him what I said next minute Andrew goes is the Casino ok – I said yeah that'll be fine. I think Mick thought that the Casino would be a safer place to meet us then in some park in Fitzroy. Before we hoped in the car I grab a firearm and put it down the front of my pants – I thought I'd better take it just in case, We then went for a walk to discuss what we were going to tell him, when/if he tried to question us. We arrived and parked our car in valet parking, and then we went into the first bar in the casino where Andrew had organized to meet him. We had a few drinks before he arrived – then we spotted him – in he waltzed in a big orange top – with a few of his cronies. I said there's a few of them. They came over in and made their way towards us – with Mick was Mario Condello – Old Ron[124] – Steve the Turk Kaya, Faruk Orman. Mick gave Andrew these bullshit kisses – I shook their hands and then we started talking. I told Andrew when Mick comes in if he be smart or out of line give it back to him – he use to call Andrew trick – meaning that his a shifty bloke. Anyway, Mick says hello tricky to Andrew – Andrew replied buddy I'm not the tricky one, you are. Mick looked shocked by Andrews response – as Andrew never use to say one word out of line to Mick. Mick looks at him and says you're the one who hanging around with that dog Tony Mokbel – Andrew said his no dog, but whilst we on the subject of dogs, your mate Lewis Moran is one – I jumped in and said I've got paper work on him if you want to see it, prove that his an informer. Mick quickly changed the subject, as he knew this conversation was going nowhere fast. He asked if we had heard anything about the Munster and what the rumours were on the streets, as to what had happened to him. Andrew said yeah I heard the triads were responsible for his death – when he said that I nearly spat my drink out, as that was the first I'd heard of it, and I knew Andrew was just making that up – and so did Mick. Naturally, Mick took no notice of Andrew said, and now he asked me what I'd heard. I said all I keep hearing is that I am responsible, however that's not true – as I had reason to kill your mate – and I had nothing against him, all I've ever heard was good about him, (although the part all I've ever heard was good about him was untrue). I said I had no involvement in his murder in anyway shape or form – I than went on to say if I were going to

124 Ron Bongetti, close friend and business partner of Mick Gatto.

get any of you blokes, I would've got you – he looked surprised, and said you wouldn't want to miss – I said what makes you think I would miss, I haven't as yet.

Another time in the early 90's, a few of my friends and I were all under investigation for manufacturing Amphetamines. We were having trouble getting or hands on the Methylamine Gas, which is used in the finally process in turning the liquid oil into powder. A mate of mine who was with us said he knew this Italian guy, who could get his hands on all sorts of Chemicals. I asked who he was, and how long he'd known him for – he assured me the bloke was ok, he was knock about Italian who was apparently big in the grass scene. I said ok, this is what we need; bang he rings him up, meets up with him – no problems this bloke could get anything and everything we wanted. He said he also had a few other things there – I a;lready had them but I said get them anyway save me chasing them next time, I said don't mention my name to him. I went and picked up what we ordered, from teh back of my mates place, paid him for it, and I was on my way. Unbeknown to me the Italian guy who was supplying us with these Chemicals had recently been arrested with a heap of grass, with something like 50 kilos, and he turned Police Informer to save his own skin. So we were all being watch – the Police were actually sitting in a house across the road from my mates place watching me as I picked the Chemicals up from there, they were taking picture of me as I was putting the stuff in the boot of my car.

I drove off with the chemicals – and within a few weeks, my friends were arrested whilst they were in the process of manufacturing Amphetamines. I wernt at teh address that was raided and I quickly got wind that theyed been arreseede – I spoke to teh girls father who I was seeing and told him what had happened he suggested taht I keep out of teh way for awile until we se what was going on – so he organized a place for me to stay at in

Sydney – I went up there and was well looked after. I was given, gI seen w, lucky ma[125]

Casino

Andrews's murder

Roberta tipping him off about Faruk – John W. – Nicola

Letters Allan T.

Meeting in Lygon Street

He asked Andrew to kill me when Andrew and I live together

China Town with Andrew

Meeting Andrew, with Jason, to get Victor and I

I don't really have much up to add, therefore I guess I will leave it there for now, and I hope to hear from you again soon.

With best wishes & respect,
Your friend always – Carl

Ps) Please pass on my best to Shaune and to your family

12 December 2009 to Milad Mokbel

Dear Milad,
The other night I received your letter, dated 6-12-09, and it was good to hear from you again, as it always is.

You prefer blondes, I know that, hey Mel's not blonde, so how about weakening a little bit – or as Horty would say, leaning, and handballing her to me. You know if the roles were reversed, I'd do it for you, get back to me on it – hey is Clare a blonde?

My dad said he has spoken to you – I know that he looks forward to your calls, as he enjoys talking with you, he said all

125 This paragraph is reproduced here as it existed in Carl's letter. Presumably it and what followed were typed in haste and never checked by him, or notes.

he does is laughs all throughout the call. I think his going to write a letter to get permission to come up there to visit you, I've never seen him do that before – but he has a lot of time for you.

I was interested to hear what you had to say about Rocky – stepping on peoples toes out there – the blokes a fuckhead, peanut, mate I have no time for him at all.

I just saw that Rod was found guilty, over that murder 25 + years ago, he'll never see daylight again, as his 64 years old now, oh well that's life.

Horty's case is adjourned again – what the??? – Its fucken bullshit – but what can you do. I only hope when it eventually does come on, that he gets a victory – I like Horty.

You have the best mind set towards your sentence, expect the worst but hope for the best, that way you can never be disappointed – it goes without saying that I hope you get something off on your appeal – fingers crossed for you.

Chucky – nothing seems to change in that relationship. It reminds me so much of when I was with Roberta – as her and chucky have similar attitudes. Both can be good, but then again both can be the biggest ball breaker ever – I hope they work everything out at least for the kid's sake – plus she's not a bad person, but at the end of the day – I vote for whatever makes my mate happy.

If you and Renate ever go your own ways – Clare's in – you're fucking mad.

There's no hope on this earth that Renate will let you escape that marriage, she's good Renate – the other night I sent a Christmas card to her and the kids – hope they received it.

Loddon does sound good for you – you'd be loving life up there – plus you're a social butterfly, you can get around and say hello to everyone. When are you eligible to have congenial visits?

I don't really have much more to add, therefore I guess I will leave it there for now, and I hope hear from you again soon.

With best wishes & respect,
Your friend always Carl

Ps) Please give my love and best to your mum, Renate the kids, and Larry and Harry – thanks.

13 December 2009 to Kylie

Hello there,
I trust all is as good as it can be for you out there – as for me here I'm fine.

I just finished my visit with Penny and Dhakota. Brea never came, as she getting older and can't be bothered. She has other things to do, which I completely understand. The time flew, we had a fantastic visit – and I really enjoyed it. Dhakota was so good out there – she never drank coke or anything – she actually had water, and she weren't scoffing down chips and chocolates throughout the visit – all she had was a caramelo Koala. She actually looks like she's lost some weight. I hope she loses the rest of the weight she needs too.

It was so good talking to you today – 3 calls, the time flew, I could've talked to you for a few more.

I wish I was out there and come out with you last night. I would've wrecked you. I would've fucked you all night. I would've given you the time of your life, I'm on a fat now just thinking about what I would've done to you. I wish you were here, I bet you do too. I want to hold you tight kiss, you passionately, play with you, tease you up, make you all wet, then put my cock deep inside you – how's that sound?

You made me laugh when you said after the visit, when you went out to the car and Grace asked you if there was any action – or something along those lines. Then your mum asked you if I slipped the tongue in. I really do look like I'm weak don't I? ☹ I didn't know what I could or couldn't do – the last thing I wanted to get was a slap in the face from you.(lol)

Hey Kylie – I was thinking, today you said that you start your holidays from the 21st or 22nd. You can come and see me before the 27th if you want to, but it's completely up to you.

Lots of hugs and kisses – Me xoxox-

13 December 2009 to Roberta Williams

Dear Roberta,
You got my dirty today when you jumped down my throat for nothing, in regards to your so-called friend Tyson, who you thought was the ant's pants – but in reality is a young goose, which I think you've come to realise. Roberta at the end of the day, I don't give a fuck about him or his friends. You're the one who thinks they are great people, not me. You'd met him for the first time in your life one day – and a week later you were breaking your neck to be in his company, and calling him your best best friend, yet you didn't even know him or know anything about him. I don't even want to talk to you about fuckheads like him. I want to ring your place and have good phone calls, I don't want to call there, and be spoken down to from you like I was today, otherwise I won't even bother ringing there.

Today I was going through the paper looking at (*properties*) houses that sold. I see that in the last 12 months Broady has gone 33% – 10 months ago the average price was $250, 000 – now it $330, 000 – $80,00 in 12 months, not bad.

When I was looking, I also seen that the apartment we use to have in Fitzroy, sold yesterday – it sold for $ 615,000.

Bert I don't know what you have planned, if you and Rob are going to buy your own place – rent a bigger place, or what – but I do know if you're planning on staying at my mum's place – I'm going to have to start to charge you rent. I don't mind renting it out to you cheaper then I would anyone else, but I have to think of myself for a change, and make sure that I'm secure, and I have money for myself whenever I need it. I could be getting $500 – $550 rent there per-week, about $2300 per-month – at the moment, I don't even get one cent for it. I should have my own money from the rental of that place, yet I have nothing. I don't even have any money to buy the kids Christmas presents, or to get Brea something for her B/Day – I have to ask you to get me something for them. If I need anything, I have to ask you for it, and I hate that so bad, you couldn't imagine how bad I hate it – never in my life have I ever had to ask anyone for money, I hate asking anyone for money, it's not me.

I want to rent my mum's place out, and buy another property – then the rent from both places, can pay the mortgage. I never did what I did to sit here broke, and reply on people such as yourself for money or anything I need. I know I'm still going to be here for a long time, but I'm not dead, I will be coming home one day – and I don't want to be getting out to nothing, asking people such as yourself for money, I'm not going to let that happen.

I know Christmas is here, and you currently have other things on your mind, but come January, if you're staying there – you're going to have to start paying rent. Because you can and do pay rent in the City, and you have done so for years, and you have always paid rent everywhere else you've lived, so why shouldn't you pay it there?

I'll wait until you get out of hospital then I'll discuss it with you further – as I'll be getting on to a real estate agent to handle the rental agreement there, as I don't want to be asking you or whoever is there for the rent every month.

I've attached a document for you showing you what the repayment are, when you borrow different amounts of money – at different interest rates.

I hope you understand where I'm coming from, and you don't take what I'm saying the wrong way, I think I'm pretty fair – I'll always help you if I can – and I think you know that.

I don't really have much more to add, therefore I will leave it there for now, and I hope to hear from you again soon.

Love and respect,
Always and forever – Carl –xx-

19 December 2009 to Kylie

Hello there,
Late last night I received a letter from you, and it was good to hear from you again, as it always is.

In regards to me throwing you in the pool, you said in the cold weather don't men get smaller, so you'd prefer me to carry you into the room, where it's nice and big, Don't worry – it's big enough to please you in the water or the room. You'll feel every inch of it, and love it when you eventually do cop it. (lol) You were saying you can hold your breath – I hope you can also breathe through your nose – all I'll say is there are interesting and exciting days lay ahead for the both of us, happy days.

Am I jealous because I haven't seen your porno face – my word I am – I'd love to see that as I'm banging you hard for you to make expressions like that – at least I'm honest, I'm dying to fuck you, you know it and you love it, I know you'd love my cock inside you. I'm on a fat now – you should be here putting it to good use. ☺ But instead I'm going to have to take matters into my own hand, and cum everywhere, whereas it should be inside you – it's as fucking joke.

I didn't tell my dad to tell you that he doesn't know what you and I talk about. I just don't tell him what we talk about. I tell him we talk to one another, we write to each other and I really enjoy your letters. He knows that you came in here to see me – and I told him that the visit went really well, and I enjoyed it.

Do I want you to dream of anything –Yes, ME! You rocking up in a black leather jacket on, and nothing else, but your high heels on, hot red lipstick so you can see exactly where your mouths been – I have an idea where it'd be? Start kissing me from my mouth and working your way down – I'm big on kissing. I'd love you to be looking up at my with your beautiful eyes whilst you were take all my rock hard cock deep inside your mouth, I'd move your hair off your face and let you work your magic. I'd love to hear you moaning as I'm fucking you. The louder you moaned, the harder I'd fuck you, as you bit my neck, and told me to give it to you harder.

What would I prefer – fucking you, or you finishing me off with your tongue? Fucking you – but I'd be blowing all inside you, I'd love to cum right up you.

Mwah

ME -xoxox-

25 December 2009 to Fabian Quaid

Dear Fab,

I received your letter on Wednesday night, dated 20 December, and it was my pleasure to hear from you again, although I would've much preferred to be hearing from you from the outer, not to be though.

Buddy, I'm so sorry to hear about the verdict – when I heard I was absolutely devastated for you.[126] As you said though, it's not over yet – you still have appeals – but I fully agree with you, you'd like to knock them over first go – but going from what you said you should be a good chance of getting up at appeal.

I can relate to what you said about your Judges charge – speaking from experience, the Judge's charge is what the Jury takes the most notice of, they sit up and listen – at my trial Con Heliotis told the Judge that she turned the Prosecution closing address, from boiled lollies into Darrel Lea Chocolates, she did too, she dressed up up for them big-time. Her charged really fucked me over, she gave it to me hard, dry start too, up until then everyone from my Counsel – the Prosecution, to all the media, all thought I'd had it in the bag, I did too, but in my heart I felt something was coming.

I hadn't heard from Esmerelda for awhile – I thought she'd dropped off me. As I sent her a few letters, and a card, all went unanswered – then last night, I got a card, with a letter enclosed from her, telling me that she hasn't forgot me, she's just been busy. She's nice, a sexy bitch, really easy going too – I really

---

126 On 16 December 2009, Fabian Quaid and Dimitrios Papadimitriou were found guilty of conspiring to import 44 kilograms of powdered ecstasy. Quaid and Papadimitriou pleaded not guilty to conspiring with each other and other men to traffic a commercial quantity of MDMA—the drug used to make ecstasy. The haul at the time was the largest for MDMA in Western Australia's history. In March 2010, Quaid was sentenced to seventeen years' jail with a minimum term of ten and a half years.

like her. She said she was recently in Melbourne for work, and if she had of had more time she would've liked to come and visit me – she's more than welcome to visit me anytime. ☺ In the letter which I received from her last night, she was telling me, that she has a daughter who's about to turn 17 – she's a laugh – good value. Wish I were out there to get to know her better. ☺

Nikki – I think I told you she's moved back to QLD – so I haven't seen, or spoken to her for a month or longer, I wrote her a letter – no reply – then last night I received a card from her saying how busy she's been – and how sorry she was for not writing to me. She's going to be spewing when I tell her the result of your trial, as she was really looking forward to meeting you – she told me that if you won at your trial, you could stay with her when you went to QLD, she was pretty keen – I talked you up to her – all the truth though. She's not going anywhere – she reckons most men out there are fuckwits, probably right too.

We don't get any special meals today – just the normal Christmas lunch. I fucking hate Christmas in jail – this is the hardest time of the year for me to do time. I just rang my daughter – she was rapt to hear from me – but it kills me inside not being there with her, and my dad, and times like these bring back so my memories of my mum – it's fucked, but what can you do – but stay strong and battle on.

With best wishes & respect,
Your friend always – Carl

Ps) Please give my best to Toto

25 December 2009 to Jenny Laureano

Dear Jennifer,

I trust this letter reaches you fit and well, as it leaves me fine.

I received your card last night, thank-you very much for that – you said a letter will on its way soon – it'd want to be, your excused for the moment, as I know what it's like with Christmas with the kids.

Christmas day – I fucking hate this time of the year so bad. This is about the only time of the year that I really miss not being outside – and the Spring Racing carnival. This is the hardest time of the year for me to do time inside prison, another week and we're into the new year – thank god for that.

I don't really have much more to add, therefore I will leave it there for now, and I hope to hear from you again soon.

Love and best wishes – Carl –xox-

Ps) Please give my best wishes and love to your mum – thanks

31 December 2009 to Roberta Williams[127]

I don't even know how, or where to start this letter.

Firstly, I'd like to make it clear to you. I'd prefer it is we didn't fight, or argue, with one another – and become enemies – but sometimes in life things don't work as you'd like them too – so if we become enemies, then so be it, all I'll know is if we do, which I think we will, it wasn't me who caused it to become like that.

I've tried my best to help you even though you continuously keep on making a fool me, you move from bloke to bloke, and

127 Words addressed to Roberta, composed on New Year's Eve, and printed on 2 January 2010. This communication was never received by Roberta and therefore it is clear Carl had second thoughts and never sent it.

hang around with some people who wanted to cause both you and I harm – good form, if I do say so myself. You think people out there all love you – that couldn't be further from the truth – a lot of people out there call you some terrible names, which I hate hearing, because the person you've turned into certainly weren't the persons I knew and fell in love with.

I know you well enough to know that you'll do whatever suits you, whenever suits you, despite what anyone says or thinks about you – and in doing so, you don't care who's feelings you hurt in the process, with you, no–one matters, except for number one – that being YOU!

Along with my dad, in my heart I honestly thought you were my best friend in the whole world, and that you'd never do anything to jeopardize the bond I thought we shared – how wrong I was – again!

You're constantly telling me that you wouldn't even have a roof over your head if It weren't for Rob – I thought I was the one responsible for putting the roof over all your heads – my mum's place – and for the past 6–7 months I have received one cent for doing so. Don't get me wrong, before today I had a lot of time for Rob, more time then you'd ever believe, but after what you told me today, that he doesn't even like me, or want to talk to me ever again. If that be the case, what can I say – I've done nothing wrong by him – after all he backdoored me – and reluctantly, I still forgave him for doing that. I think you are poisoning his mind by telling him things about me to get him jealous – but you only tell him half the story, you water it down, and paint yourself out as a saint. I bet you didn't tell him that only a few weeks ago you were making enquires with Barristers on how you could go about getting my sperm, and having a baby to me. Now you've told me you would like to have a baby with him, that'd make it 5 kids to four different fathers – what the.......... Only a few weeks ago you were thinking about trying to get back with me, telling me all different sorts of things – which aren't even worth writing about. I'll gladly admit that I love you, and I always will, but there's no hope in the world that I'd even consider getting back with you, reason being I don't love you in that way, plus I don't and couldn't trust you ever again. You pretend that you don't need a man, but you and I both know the reality is you can't live without one, for the past twenty years you've jumped from man to man – no breaks in between – actions speak louder than words.

I told you a while back, and I couldn't have made it any clearer to you – that all I ever wanted you to do was keep your distance and have no contact with that bloke[128] – full stop! However, for some unknown reason you couldn't do that, why that is only you and him know. I know you've said when you were with him that he made you so feel special – and what you and him shared was amazing – and when you had sex with him it was so passionate – **YUK!**.You've previously told me it was nothing that you've ever experienced before in your life. Come back to earth.

You've told me that you hated the way he tried to control you, make you cover up – and tie you down (*if/when you go back to him, believe me the same things bound to happen again, and you know it, but I think you like being treated like that, your choice not mine*).

All I'll say to you is, I hope he makes you happy, and gives you a bit of stability. Because at the moment you don't know whether you're coming or going, but that'll never change. Both you and I know, that I was the only one who made you feel safe

128 Carl is writing in furious haste here, but it is clear that 'that bloke' is the man he refers to through this correspondence as 'Omar'. He begins this letter talking about Rob Carpenter, whose relationship with Roberta he usually encouraged, but at this point and from here on he is talking about Omar, whom he greatly detested.

and gave you stability, and let me assure you that cunt is nothing like me.

I also made it clear to you, that if you contacted him, got back with him, or had anything to do with in anyway shape or form – what the consequences were. One being losing my friendship, not that, that means anything to you, now you've made your bed, you sleep in it, I hope at the end of the day it was all worth it, because now there's no turning back.

I know you've recently said that you've been lonely, and I can tell from talking to you that you're far from happy. However, going back with that skunk isn't the answer. Last time you were with him – he made you cease all contact with me – he even pulled the phone plug out of the wall so I couldn't even talk to my daughter – I could go on and on, but I see no point. I know you'll never be happy with him – and deep in your heart you agree, but go for it and give it another go – I only hope you realize what you're lost in doing so. I believe that I am the only person who truly cares for you, and you've now lost me.

I know when you get back with him. That he'll never let me see, or talk to Dhakota or Brea – but over the years, I've learnt to realize there's no point in me stressing over things that I have no control over, so if I see them, I see them, and if I don't, what can I do? Except wait until they're both at an age where they can make there're own decisions, it's sad and it hurts, but as you know some say the truth does hurt.

I know Brea and Dhakota hate his guts, and they will never accept him in your life – not that that will bother you.

I didn't at all mind you staying at my mum for awhile – I was actually ok with you staying there for as long as you wanted too, and if you could afford it pay some rent, but if you couldn't I was happy to let you stay there for nothing. When you moved in there, it was only meant to be temporarily, and you wanted to pay the rent money up front (*didn't happen*) – as you said today, you want to move out of there – and we agreed that you'll be out there by Thursday the 14th January (*our wedding anniversary if you didn't know*). In the meantime, I'll have a real estate agent come past and view the premises, to see how much rent I should get for it

Take care, and best of luck to you in whatever you do. But don't come grovelling back to me when he turns your life upside down "AGAIN" – as he did the last time you were with him, I honestly can't believe how smart you can be at times, and other times what a fuck head you can be, oh well you're life – not mine.

CHAPTER 11

Down memory lane, heading towards oblivion

Since writing his long letter to Ray Spadina on 27 November 2009, Carl's mind had begun to wander down memory lane, recollecting the good times from the past, and making him more conscious than ever of how his celebrity and human contacts were likely to taper off over the 30 years that stretched ahead of him.

Over the previous twelve months some of his closest buddies had been sentenced to long jail sentences. He could see how they were slowly being deserted by their loved ones and friends on the outside, and how the decision to retain expensive lawyers to plead their cases often impoverished them.

He was still a celebrity prisoner—as he observed to Kylie: 'I think the Sunday writers have a hard on for me'—but that in itself spelt danger for him. The journos were edging closer and closer to revealing publicly that he was providing information to the police in exchange for money, for a lessening of his sentence and for the payment of Dhakota's education at a posh school. In early 2009 Adam Shand, then working for the *Sunday Herald Sun*, had learnt of Carl's deal with the authorities but after consideration for Carl's safety decided not to publish the story.

When he wrote to Kylie on 3 February that 'I've had a lot on my mind', no doubt the perils ahead were foremost among his concerns. And yet, while both of his cellmates—Matty and 'Two Guns' Tommy—had recently been absent for significant periods of time, Carl saw nothing sinister in that and seems to have been blithely unaware that he was living in mortal danger.

4 January 2010 to Milad Mokbel

Dear Milad,

Thank fuck we're finally into another year – 32 more to go – what the...... hope I have some luck at my appeal – this isn't jail, this is a nut farm. I don't know when my appeal will come up, but sometime this year I guess, I have a court appearance in March, not sure for how long – I hope it's not too long, I wish you were coming with me holding my hand. ☺

Small world isn't it, that woman Rod was just found guilty of murdering,[129] was Renate's godmother. I agree with you he'll never see daylight again – I've heard he'll be sentenced on that sometime next month – so the next case his due to front doesn't really affect him, nothing does from here on in, unless of course he gets up on appeal, time will tell.

Mel – she's always welcome to come and visit me, you know I always talk highly of Mel – from what you've told me about her, she's had a hard life, I hope she comes into see me, her call though, it'll only be a box visit, and no doubt she'll be talking about you most of the visit. As for Roberta, buddy, a wise man once told me, I can't give away what's legally not mine – and thank god she's not, buddy, I love you and your family too much, I wouldn't even thrown an enemy in there. I don't know what the fuck Dean was blueing about – looking back now he should've been paying me, I'm actually thinking about filing a law suit against him for damages, and I reckon I'd get up too. ☺ Nah all jokes aside, she's going ok – she's good, I haven't talked to her for a few days, which makes me like her even more, the less I talk to her, the more I like her – true.

---

129 Dorothy Abbey and her husband Ramon were murdered in Heidelberg West by Rodney Collins and Mark McConville in July 1987, while the couple's three children slept nearby. The Supreme Court found Collins guilty in 2009.

Roulla[130] had a good result – considering – thank god they never jailed her, I bet that's one less stress off Horty's shoulders – hopefully he goes home in April, please pass on my best to him when you talk to him.

Nothing much has been happening here – at the moment there's only Matty and I in here – as they kidnapped our chef – hopefully we'll get him back tomorrow, the wires have been crossed somewhere, just hope we can get to the bottom of it, and quickly, as his in Unit 4, and Rizzo from the company is there with him. I hope that Rizzo don't get hungry and eat him, he'd eat the horse and chase the jockey – he'd eat the date off the calendar, fuck – you wouldn't want to get in the way of him and a bucket of KFC.

I don't really have much more to add, therefore I guess I will leave it there for now, and I hope hear from you again soon.

With best wishes & respect,
Your friend always – Carl

Ps) Please give my love and best to your mum, as well as Renate the kids, and Larry and Harry – thanks.

4 January 2010 to Kylie[131]

Hello there,
I just received your letter, and it was my pleasure to hear from you again, as you know it always is.

You think that I'm good at hiding how I sometimes feel – both my mum and I use to laugh, and say how the both of us could

130 Zaharoula Mokbel, Horty Mokbel's wife.
131 Edited version of a three-page letter.

often manage to smile in the most difficult of situations, everyone thinks just because you're smiling, you're happy, when in fact sometime that's not the case. I often smile when I'm in the worst situations. I'd be guessing you've seen footage of me at Court – walking shackled to the prison van smiling – smiling – of course I wasn't happy. One time I can remember the media saying how cocky I thought I was simply because I was smiling – I guess I've always been cocky – but that smile I manage to always put on my face isn't through cockiness, what would they rather me looking sad, I bet they would too. I wouldn't let them see me like that even if I was – wouldn't let them have it over me, what think they're winning – over my dead body.

Yeah it'd be good if they let me reverse the charges, and gave me unlimited calls – imagine you're phone bill if they did though, we'd be on there all day. Phone in my cell – now that I'd love, wouldn't that make my time fly – imagine our conversations at night, what we be the topic of conversation – I guess.................... (lol)

Why don't I want you dancing on the Podium again, because I'm not out there – happy you heard it! If I were out there no problems, but I swear if you and I were seeing one another, and I seen you dancing on the Podium, and you were teasing me up. The minute you jumped off, I'd drag you off and fuck the guts out of you, that I promise you, and I'd cum all inside you, what would you want me inside you giving it to you, than pull out? I doubt it very much – you might say it now, but you wouldn't if we were in the middle of it – maybe if you've already cum you might – bitch! Answer that and be honest with me. How would you feel hopping back up there with boys all hovering around you – with all my warm blow deep inside you – I can picture your cheeky smile now looking at me, laughing – the one that the boys just wanna fuck – true? It would be fun, wouldn't it?

Now do you think it would've happened years ago if I had on ran into when you were dancing at Heat? I do, I would've made sure it did, I would've fucked your brains out, and had you cum multiple times. (lol)

I really enjoy talking to you, and exchanging letters with you, you make me smile, and make me happy, which means you're doing something right. What do I want? I think if I was to say I wanted a girl, you, or anyone else, to be with me, and me only, to remain loyal to me, to be there for me for the next 30 years, than I'm asking too much of them. As they'd be doing my sentence with me – which I don't think is fair on them. I think if I were to ask that of someone, then I would be being selfish, and honestly I don't think any girl could do it, they might think they could, but in 5–10 years that view might change. Of course, I care about you; I care about you a lot.

MWAH

ME -xoxox-

6 January 2010 to Wayne Howlett

Dear Wayne,

Last night I received your letter, and it was good to hear from you again, as it always is.

Thank God, Christmas has been and gone – I hate spending that time of the year in prison, away from my loved ones. I think all up this was my 10 Christmas that I've spend in prison, another 32 to go – what the.........

You were saying you've spoken to Roberta a little bit lately – I usually ring their everyday – although I can never get hold of anyone to late in the afternoon, as they sleep until lunchtime – no way on earth would she have been doing that if I were out, but I guess I'm not, and how things quickly change. She's been crook lately, after her operation – give her the world and she'd still complain – woman – what do you expect. (ha ha)

Buddy now that you're out, I'm sure you'll get plenty of the girls over there to write to me, aerobics instructors – ok, I'll leave that in your capable hands, maybe I'll get letter with photos enclosed soon. ☺

With best wishes & respect,
Your friend always – Carl

Ps) Please pass on my best to Shaune and to your family – thank-you.

12 January 2010 to Barry Q.

Dear Barry,
I just received your letter, dated 10 January, you took awhile to reply to my last letter – nevertheless it was my pleasure to hear from you again, as it always is.

We got the meals that you all cooked for us on Christmas day – and the sausages were beautiful, what type were they? Let me know when you write back, as I'll order them on the cooking program.

Matty and I are back running out together here, which is heaps better than one out. On New Year's Eve, they took Tommy across to Unit 4. I believe MOU will be seeing us this coming Thursday, and hopefully they can shed some light on what's going on – and bring him back here with us.

I'm slowly slowly getting back into my training, over the past few days it's been too hot to run though – plus I've had a few things on my mind.

Roberta and the kids are currently on holiday in QLD – Dhakota was so excited to go up there. Roberta just got released from Hospital on Saturday. The other week she had some operation on her bladder – got out – then she hemridged – so she was rushed back into hospital – got out again – then one week later she lost a lot of blood – so they rushed her back in there for a few blood transfusions, she was in there for 3 days. Apparently, she's lucky to be here with us – she could've easily died – they told her she's very lucky that she never fell asleep, and never woke up – she lost 1/3 of her blood. Personally, I think instead of going away, she should be resting, but you can't tell her that, as she has a mind of her own, and thinks she's knows what's best, sometimes she's mad, I just hope she's ok.

I don't really have much more to add, therefore I guess I will leave it there for now, and I hope hear from you again soon.

With best wishes & respect,
Your friend always – Carl

13 January 2010 to Roberta Williams[132]

When you and I got together, we kissed at Footscray whilst Dean was in the bedroom sleeping

We all went out together for Lee's[133] B/day, & you were playing with my leg/feet under the table

We'd met at the beach and kiss – and then you would go home to Dean

Dean would sleep at my place, and I would sneak over and fuck you

132 Carl drafted this letter on this date. There is no evidence that he ever sent it to Roberta.

133 Probably Lee Pascu, who had been an associate of Carl and the Moran clan before Carl was wounded by Jason Moran in 1999.

Omar

Everyone says that when you were around him, you were as quite as a mouse

When you went anywhere with him – he use to drive, not you, you were a passenger

He got you to shave your head

Got you to turn Muslim – yet you were right into everything catholic

He said to Horty what would I want with an old hag like her, when I can get young chicks

Questions

- How long were you seeing Jamie from Carlton for – where did you use to see him, where were you living at the time
- Giorgio's in Armadale, have you ever eaten there, years ago someone reckons they spotted you there with Andrew[134]

15 January 2010 to Roberta Williams[135]

Roberta

I told you that I didn't agree with what you said in your book, as to how we first got together or kissed. As it never happened that way – you never came over to my place after being bashed, me comforting you – then we kissed – this is how I remember it, let's see who's memory is the best. I think this is the blind leading the blind. (ha ha)

The first time I ever laid upon you was one day whilst I was at the footy watching Kensington play – I was there with a friend

134 Presumably this is Andrew 'Benji' Veniamin. Carl always believed that his mate Benji had had an affair with Roberta.

135 This was drafted at 6.30 in the morning of this day, but it was almost certainly never sent as Roberta never received it.

(*Vince*), he knew you, you two said hello to one another, and when Vince and I walked away from you, he told me who you were, Sharon's sister. I said she's a good sort; he laughed, and said she's already with someone.

When we first got together, or we first kissed, I should say. You were living with Dean, and I wouldn't say you were in a happy or healthy relationship. I was single and seeing a few different girls. Months before you and I first kissed, we became very close friends. We would often ring one another up, and buy each other clothes, and gifts, if we seen something that we thought the other would like. I believe that I was someone who you knew that you could talk to about anything, it wouldn't go any further, and I felt exactly the same way with you. You and I use to get along really well with one another – we were good friends, I think it would be fair to say that I was more your friend, then I was Dean's.

Either one day you rang me, or I rang you, and asked if the other one if they'd like to go shopping and to get something to eat at Highpoint Shopping Centre, Anyway it doesn't really matter who rang who, as we ended up going there. You came over to my place (*Fitzroy*) and picked me up; I was with Smokey at the time, as he slept at my place the night before. We both went with you in your car, and you drove – as you never were one to be a passenger, as you would always complain that everyone's else's driving made her carsick. From memory we got there had a look around at some shops. I remember you trying on some jeans in a surf shop, they were low cut and sexy ones – and although you would've only been about 27 years old at this time – you never use to dress sexy. You'd dress more like a 40-year-old mother, yet despite having 3 kids, you had a body any girl with no kids would have envied, and died to have. You had a hot body, and the best ass that I'd ever seen (*I'm a ass man, which you know*), everyone use to say what a good ass you had. Anyway, you tried these jeans on, and they looked hot on you, but you thought otherwise – you would've much preferred to buy some old granny jeans. I told you how good they looked on you, and they suited you, as did the sales assistant – I told you to get with the times, and I'll buy you those jeans. You turned around and asked me how your bum looked in them – I said hot – which was the truth, the sales assistant laughed, and asked if I was your bloke – you laughed and said no we're only friends.

You then went on to tell the girl that you have 3 kids – which the girl didn't believe, she thought you were having her on, and was taking the piss out of her.

I said nah it's the truth – the girl was amazed – she said you don't look like you've had one kid, never mind 3 – and you don't have any stretchmarks either. You just laughed, but I could tell you liked what she had to say about you. We left the shop empty handed, your choice, not mine – as you wouldn't let me buy you those jeans.

Once we were out of the shop, we laughed to one another about what the girl said, I said I told you that you have a great body, and they really looked good on you. I wouldn't tell you to get some jeans if I didn't think they looked good on you, or suited you – I wouldn't let you get around like some dickhead. You said thanks Carlos (*that's what you always use to call me*), you said you always say nice things about me – you give me confidence and make me feel good, whereas Dean is forever trying to strip my confidence away from me. I didn't know what to say, I just said I think you have a good figure, and as you know the lady in the shop also said the same, and I'll always say it how it is. *(Just for the record, I think at this time we both had a crush on one another, I dare say you'd agree – because you'd be lying if you didn't).* ☺ I think we had something to eat – and then we left. When we were walking to the car and you said thanks Carlos for coming with me today – and slapped me across the back – that was your way of saying thanks, and showing affection. We got back to my place in Fitzroy; Smokey had to go somewhere so he jumped out the car when we pulled up out the front, and went his own way. You came inside with me. We were sitting on the couch and having a laugh – we started messing around – and we had a moment, and kissed – we both knew we shouldn't have done what we did – but on the same token, it felt so right, and just for the record you were a fantastic kisser. We looked at one another, laughed, and both said we shouldn't be doing this, and then we kissed again, we're bad! We were lying on top of one another on the couch, with our bodies pressed up against each other, then we heard keys at my front door – someone opened my front door – it was Hutchy. Both you and I quickly got up and made out like nothing was going on – I remember when Hutchy walked in he was laughing, and said what are you two up too, he didn't know or see anything, Hutchy was just having a laugh and taking the piss out of us. You stayed for while longer, but we never kissed again – not on that day anyway. Years later, I asked you what would've happened that day if Hutchy never disturbed us? You'd always laugh, and say I'd never do it on the first time you kissed someone – but then you'd add that on that day you did feel in the mood, I did too. As all my blood had rushed to a certain body part – and it weren't my head either, or not the one on my shoulders anyway, which I think at the time you would've been fully aware of.

After that we kept in regular contact with one another, we'd text and ring one another all days ever day, and catch up at every opportunity we got too, there weren't enough hours in the day for us to spend with one another – as we wanted to be in each other's company 24/7. When we were together in each other's company, there was nothing else in the world that mattered.

I remember you telling Dean that you didn't want to be with him anymore – and that you needed some time to clear your head – you said that you wanted to go away by yourself for a holiday to QLD, and you wanted Dean to have the kids whilst you were away. We had organized to meet one another up in QLD; naturally, I was extremely happy about this, as I think you were too. When I arrived up there, I rang you to let her know that I had arrived; you told me what room you were in. I got to the room, knocked on the door, you answer, we hugged and kissed one another, and then we virtually spent the next two days in the room just enjoy one another company to the max, talking and laughing as well as other things. After spending those two days together I believe there was no doubt in either of our minds what we wanted, that being each other.

18 January 2010 to Esmerelda[136]

Hey Esmerelda,
I just received your letter, with pics, dated 13 January, and it was my pleasure to hear from you again, as it always is. I must say you look hot in the pics – but then again when don't you look hot? (lol)

No need to thank me for remembering your B/day, I hope you had a great one, wish I were there with you to celebrate it with you – what a thought. It made me happy when you said that I made you day by remembering when your B/day was, if I can put a smile on your face, I'm all for it – you always put a smile on my face, when I receive your letters – and pics. ☺ I wanted to get you some perfume for your B/day, but I wanted to know what your favourite one was (*let me know when you write back*).

---

136 Edited version of a four-page letter.

I also wanted to send you some flowers, but I never knew if you were seeing anyone, or not, and I didn't want to send them to you in case you were – as some people can get jealous easy, and I dint want to cause any trouble for you. I would've sent them to your work – only I thought that might've freaked you out, nevertheless I was thinking of you – that you can be assured.

Roberta is my EX – I divorced her 3 years ago, but I haven't really been with her for about 6–7 years. She has a partner who she lives with, and I get along ok with him – I talk to her and try to be civil with her, as I try, and like to ring their everyday to talk to my daughter. As I said Roberta is my **EX** – I can be friends with whoever I chose to be friends with – I don't tell her who I'm in contact with – as it's not her business, she certainly not my owner – I'm my own person.

I've had an interesting life you reckon – I guess I'd have to agree with you on that one – never a dull moment. Yeah it is a pity I didn't know you back then, I use to spend a bit of time in Sydney, could've got you a convertible (*your funny*), I probably could've too, depending if you played your cards right of not – I would've, question is would've you have known how to play you cards?!?!?! (lol)

Maila said you where reserved when she rang you for me. I wouldn't usually give your number to anyone – just I wanted to wish you a happy B/day, and I know I can trust Maila 100%. I am very close with Maila and her husband Dennis – Dennis has known me since I was little. I am the godfather of their son (*Dylan*), and I was best man at their weeding. They both know Roberta, but they don't really have much to do with her – truth being known if Roberta weren't my daughters mother, most people I know wouldn't even give her the time of day – but she gets through the breaks because she's my daughters mother, and she knows that. Maila would never ever mention to Roberta that she talks to you, she' knows Roberta but they're not in regular contact with one another. What this, if talking to me will cause dramas, it's just not worth it (*that's not nice*), I would never cause any dramas for you, and I would never put you in a situation or do anything wrong by you, so please don't waste your time stressing over stuff like that.

No current boyfriend – Hhmmmm – interesting!! I agree with you, if you don't have trust, you don't have anything – I'm big on loyalty, and trust, in relationships, and friendships. I don't waste my time even talking to – or saying hello with people that I don't trust, so in that sense I guess we are alike. Yeah your right you can always sort through disagreements, making money, well that's never been a problem to me, sex is always amazing when you have a connection, but without trust/loyalty you have no foundation. I hate it if anyone tries to pull the wool over my eyes, tries to make me look like a fool, or they lie to me – I don't do that to the people I care about – therefore I don't expect them to do it too me.

Glad to hear that you know I still want those other pics, and you promise you'll get them to me eventually – they say all good things come to those who wait, and I guess these days I'm in no position but to wait, sad but true. ☹ I wouldn't show you're letter or pics to people here, no weirdos will see them, you have my word on that.

I don't really have much more to add, therefore I will love you and leave you for tonight, and I hope to hear from you again soon, or maybe even see you in the flesh, could I be so lucky?? ☺

MWAH!

With love, best wishes & respect – Carl –xox-

Ps) Don't forget to tell me what perfume you like – what's your fav?? I can smell it on your letter, smells nice too.

Pss) 4 pages, I hope you return the favour, and you don't keep me waiting, Mwah –XX-

Postscript Joke

A man accidently bumps into a woman and his elbow brushes against her chest. He turns to her and says, "If you heart is as soft as your breast, I know you'll forgive me." She replies, "If your dick is as hard as your elbow, I'm in room 436"

18 January 2010 to Roberta Williams

Hey Roberta,

I'm glad you seemed to enjoy yourself whilst you were away, hopefully you got lots of rest – although knowing you, you wouldn't have. (lol)

So you got along with Nikki well – she's good Nik, I miss her so so much since she's been up there, as I use to enjoy my visits with her, she use to come about twice a month, and she always made me laugh. I remember Andrew was in love with her so bad, he was infatuated with her. He use to drive me mad to get her to meet us out – she'd always come out with us, but she weren't at all interested in Andrew anything more than just a friend. At one stage he even tried to give her those earrings I brought for him, the ones you wear, if she'd go out with him for one date, naturally she just laughed and said I'm not interested, he couldn't handle her rejected him, and I use to think it was funny laugh, but he never found it amusing or seen the funny side of it. (ha ha).

I hope you didn't take what I said to today about my mum's place in the wrong way. I just think it's time that I put myself first. As I have somebody who wants to rent my mum's place straight away off me, for $500–$550 per-week, which is $2166–$2383 per month, which literally means by allowing you to stay there for nothing, or even $1000 per month – I'm robbing myself of up to $1300 per-month, and it's holding me back from making future investments. As I could use that money to buy another place, an investment property for Dhakota and I – or I bank what rent I got from there, and have money there whenever I needed it – instead of asking people for it, like you. Roberta you know better than anyone that I hate asking anyone, for anything, including yourself, I hate feeling like a beggar – I'm a provider, I'm a giver not a taker, and I hate taking anything from anyone. You're with Rob and you have your own life, as do I, or I'm trying to anyway. Don't get me wrong I'll always be there for you, and do anything you ever needed me to do for you – which I think you already know. But you are with Rob, and I believe it's his duty to support you – just like it was mine and not Dean's when I got with you – and I did support you along with the kids, that's one one you can never say I didn't do. I just want to stand on my own two feet, and have some security – because honestly, the only person I know that I can rely on 100% is my dad, as no one else cares – including you, and just saying that really hurts me, but it's the truth. In addition, the reality is his old – his health isn't the best, and unfortunately he won't be here forever. So best, I start sorting things out now for myself, because if something were to happen to him – I'd be fucked, as no one really cares. I'd be left here and forgotten about, left to fend for myself – that's why I want to get things sorted for myself before it gets to that – I hope you understand where I am coming form, which I'm sure you will, and do.

I hope to see you soon; as I'm really looking forward to seeing you.

If you want to write back, feel free to do so, as I enjoy it when I receive mail for you – your call, I won't be holding my breath.

Best wishes,
Love and respect,
Always and forever – Carl –xox-

25 January 2010 to Danny Heaney

Dear Danny,
I just received your letter, dated 19th of January, and it was good to hear from you again, as it always is.

I had to laugh to myself, when you said this planet is fucked, so you might have to get me shuttled off to Mars, and my parole transferred. I know I have to get something off at my Appeal, fingers crossed.

Two guns is back here and he couldn't be happier, he cooled his heel for 3 weeks, running out by himself, over nothing. On Friday, Matty got 10 days LOP's[137] – for two dirty urines[138] over X-mass. On X-Mass day they took him to the hospital, the nurse came down here to the Unit and was asking him all sorts or question – such as where is he – what day, and date is it, ect, ect – anyway he was lucky to get one out of ten right.

---

137 Loss of privileges.

138 Urinalysis indicating the presence of illicit drugs. This demonstrates the ready availability of drugs in prisons. Barwon is the most secure maximum security prison in Victoria, if not Australia. The management unit in which Williams and Johnson were housed is effectively a prison within a prison. It has the most highly advanced surveillance and security systems, including anti-helicopter mesh. And yet Williams' soon-to-be killer failed two drug tests.

The move to Beechworth should be good for you – they say a change is as good as a holiday – I was up there years ago – and it gets hot up there this time of the year.

With best wishes & respect,
Your friend always – Carl

29 January 2010 to Roberta Williams

Hey Roberta,
Hi ya, how's things? I hope you're ok, and everything is going as good as it can be for you out there. As for me here, I'm fine – no complaints.

Last night I received 2 letters from you, as well as a card – all my Christmas's came at once – and I was very pleased to hear from you, as I always am, and let me assure you now. I never had a problem understanding your writing – so your messing writing isn't an excuse for not writing – I'm not copping that one. ☺

Well we have a visit today which I'm looking forward too, as I haven't seen you for about 2 months, and it's safe to say I miss you, never thought you'd hear me saying that did you? – I actually surprised myself. (lol)

MWAH

Love ya Roberta

I hope to hear from you again soon, as I enjoy it when I receive mail from you.

Love and respect,
Always and forever
Carl Anthony –xoxox-

30 January 2010 to Roberta Williams

Hey Roberta,
Thanks for coming up here to see me yesterday, as I had a fantastic visit with you, and I really enjoyed it – the time absolutely flew. I know sometimes it's hard for you to get up here by yourself – but sometimes I need a visit with just you alone, because when it's just us two out there we can both talk more openly, as neither of us are as guarded, you know what I mean.

Fuck, yesterday you looked a lot like you sister Sharon.[139] The last time when you were up here you asked me if I thought you looked like her – and I said no, because I couldn't see it then – but yesterday I could see a lot of her in you. Although personally I still think you're a lot more prettier then she was, I know she wouldn't have agreed with me on that one, and I don't think my opinion would've went down to well with her either (lol). However, you know me, and I'll say always say whatever I think, whenever I like, to whoever – and Sharon knew that too – and I think that was one of things that she use to love about me. Lately I've been thinking a lot about Sharon, and about some of the laughs and fun times you and I had with her, and to tell you the truth I miss her. What about years ago when we use to get all the gossip out of her after she'd had a valium (lol).

You know sometimes I don't say, or do the right things, but at the end of the day you know my heart is in the right place. And I love and care about you a lot more than any words could ever say, so please don't you ever forget that, as you mean the world to me, and it goes without saying, you're friendship does too, I love you Roberta, always have, always will.

---

139 Sharon, Roberta's sister, died tragically of ovarian cancer. Sharon had been a lover of Carl's before he hooked up with Roberta, and Carl always had a soft spot for her. Gregarious and world-wise, Sharon was popular and associated freely with gangland figures. She had a tempestuous relationship with Roberta who once took a shovel to Sharon's BMW after an argument.

I tried to ring you up today – no answer, at first I thought you might have been doing an Analya[140] on me ☺, but my dad rang you, and you stayed in the City. I'll get hold of you tomorrow, hopefully anyway.

My dad was saying Dhakota's lost some weight, Hmmm, I'd like to see this one, as I think her pop is just sticking up for her, because you can't say a negative word to him about his granddaughter, he loves her so much. It was good how he spent time alone with her yesterday, whilst you came to visit me, they went into the town, and were looking around, when you get your licence back, you'll have to take her up too his place more often, or drop her up there.

I don't really have much more to add, therefore I will leave it there for now, and I hope to hear from you again soon.

Love and respect,
Always and forever,
Carlos –xoxox-

2 February 2010 to Barry Q.

Dear Barry,
Hi ya buddy, how's things? I hope you're ok, and everything is going as good as it can be for you. I just received your letter, dated 30th of January, and it was my pleasure to hear from you again, as it always is.

Roberta's health has improved, she has to rest and take it easy though, which is something that she doesn't know how to do. The doctor said it will take about six months for her to get back to normal (normal for her anyway) – as a result of her losing so

140 The girlfriend of Carl's stepson Tye.

much blood she's having trouble with her blood circulation and feelings in her hands and feet, plus she's also getting a lot of migraines. She was up here visiting me last Friday, and it was good to see her, as prior to that visit I hadn't seen her for about 6–7 weeks. When she's good, we get along ok – I have to try and maintain a healthy friendship with her for Dhakota's sake, but sometimes she drives me insane, and I get frustrated with her.

From what I've been told, in March apparently there's going to be some Doco about me on TV. They've been asking a lot of people who I know to go on air and talk about me – thankfully most have refused too. I hate it when bullshit about me is on TV, but unfortunately, I can't control things from in here, although at times I wish that I could. They've also approached Roberta to talk about me on there, and at the moment she's said she won't, but I won't be holding my breath on that one, as she loves nothing more than a bit of media attention – fucked if I know why. What I do know though is if she talks on there, she won't be able to help herself from having a dig at me, she'll say something like when he was out here with all his sluts, ect ect – fuck I've heard it all before, enough is enough – when are they going to leave me alone??? Not anytime soon by the looks of things, maybe when Tony's suppression order is lifted (ha ha).

With best wishes & respect,
Your friend always – Carl

3 February 2010 to Kylie

Hi there,
How's life treating you? As good as can be expected I hope – as for me I'm fine. I just received your letter, and I was very happy to hear from you again, as I always am.

You haven't pissed me off – and I'd tell you if you ever did anything that pissed me off, and if you did, it wouldn't affect our friendship. I don't know why you always think that you've done something that pissed me off. You think the spark has gone, hmmmm...... can't you do anything to relight it? I'm sure I could if I were out there with you (lol)

I guess over the last few weeks I've had a lot on my mind, and I've been a little bit stressed, nothing to worry about though, so maybe it's me, it's most certainly not you that's for sure, because you haven't done anything wrong, not to me anyway.

You said you've sent me a few letters, and I never replied to them, I don't know what's going on there, as I always reply to your letters, I received two letters from you, and I replied to them both, "straight away". You're right though we do normal write to one another a few time a week – I was wondering why I haven't been receiving as much mail from you as I use to, and I thought you must have been busy. I thought, or was hoping that you'd write when you got around to it, and you have, which I'm happy about.☺

You were right I was in the paper again – I think the Sunday writers have a hard on for me, it was just another rehashed story, nothing new, same shit, with lot of pictures.

Dhakota still hasn't got up here to visit me – but I'm sure she'll get up here soon. I'm looking forward to seeing her, as I seen her for while, I didn't get see her last month but she was away most of it, and when she's with the other kids having fun, I let her be. As you know my friend Penny usually brings her up here to see me, and she's works in the Casino, lately she's been flat out running the poker tournaments. I'm sure they both get up here to see me sometime within the next two weeks – they'd want to, or else I'll kick both their butts.

I'm talking to Roberta again, at the moment I am anyway, sometime she just gets me so worked up, she really does push my buttons. She actually came up here last week to visit me, and surprise, surprise, I enjoyed the visit with her, it was the first time I'd seen her for a few months. I'd much rather talk to her civil, then argue with her, as I like to ring there and talk to Dhakota as much as I can.

I don't really have much more to add, therefore I will leave it there for now, and I hope to hear from you again soon.

MWAH

ME -xoxox-

Some girls beg & some borrow,
Some girls lead & some girls follow,
Some will bring joy & some bring sorrow,
But the very best girls suck & swallow

4 February 2010 to Danny Heaney

Hey Danny,
I just received your letter, dated 2nd of February, and it was my pleasure to hear from you again, as it always is.

I told you Tommy was back here – and Matty came back on Monday – so things are now back to normal. Matty did 10 days in LOP's which wasn't too bad. Tommy's cooking again, which means I must again watch my weight, as it's too easy to put on, and hard to get off.

Dhakota's back at school now, and she's in grade 3 this year, she says that she's loving school – which I'm happy about – she likes her new teacher too, this week anyway. She said this year she gets homework too – and the other night she went out with her mum and Rob for a BBQ at someone's place – and she never done her homework. So she said dad can you talk to mum, and tell her that I have to be home everynight so I can do my homework – I said couldn't you have done it where you went for the BBQ – she said yeah I could've, but I don't want to go out on school nights, school comes first dad. I don't know whether she was having me on or not, if she was, she played it well.

Today I had a visit with Sean, his now over here in Unit 4 in LOP's, he got her yesterday, apparently he fell out with the old bloke,[141] and he didn't have very kind words to say about the him either, although I must say he didn't tell me anything that I didn't already know. I think the old bloke has lost it a little bit – his going to get along time after being found guilty on the last one he fronted, and I've heard he hasn't really got any strong grounds for appeal, which he even says himself. He sunk himself though by confessing to his girl during a box visit here in Acacia, which was bugged.

I don't really have much more to add, therefore I guess I will leave it there for now, and I hope hear from you again soon.

With best wishes & respect,
Your friend always – Carl

9 February 2010 to Esmerelda

Dear Esmerelda,
Hi ya, how's things? I hope you're ok, and everything is going as good as it can be for you out there, as for me here, I'm fine – no complaints.

I was talking to Maila today, and she was telling me that you tell your friends they have to spice up there love life, I was

141 Carl customarily calls Rodney Collins 'the old bloke'.

laughing, and then I jokingly said to Maila, tell Mani that I said, whilst she talking about spicing things up, she should spice up my letters a bit. Then when I rang her back in the afternoon, I asked her if she'd heard from you, which I always ask her. She was laughing her head off, I said what's so funny, she said you're going to kill me – I said why? She said because I told Mani what you said, Oh I don't know what I'm going to do with you two, the both of you are mad, anyways now I can't wait to receive your next letter. ☺

Esmerelda, you have to get down here to visit me, as I'm dying to have a visit with you, and see you face to face. Maila was telling me that she said to you, that if you're too shy to come out here and see me by yourself, she'll come with you – than she went on to say she'll wait out the front, she's off her head, I have so much time for her, she loves talking with you, she's really likes you. Regarding a visit though, don't stress, if you're too shy to come in by yourself, just come in and visit me with Maila, but there's no reason to be scared, after all I don't bite. I'm sure if you come down here to Melbourne, Maila will happily pick you up from the airport, and bring you out here to see me – that way you can't get lost, and we'll work accommodation out for you. I'd be more than happy to let you stay here with me, but I don't think these captive keepers will allow that, kill joys they are.

I don't really have much more to add, therefore I guess I will leave it there for now, and hopefully I hear from you again soon – by the way you now owe me three letters.

With love, best wishes & respect – Carl –xox-

Postscript Joke

A blonde is showing off her new tattoo of a giant seashell on her inner thigh. Her friends ask why she got that design and in that location. She tells them "It's really cool. If you put your ear up against it, you can smell the ocean."

16 February 2010 to Kylie

Well hello there,
I hope this letter reaches you travelling the best you can, as for me I'm good.

I just received your letter, and it was good to finally hear from you again, as it always is. It been awhile – but I understand you've been sick, so you're forgiven, and I also realize that the world doesn't revolve around me. ☺

You asked how I have been – I've been ok, nothing to exciting has been happening here, I've just taking it easy day by day.

The 28th at 9.30 is fine – thanks for the details, I was about to get my dad to ring to get them for me – so you saved me doing that.

You mentioned that you went out for a coffee with some bloke, you said he was goofy, but made you laugh – and you said, that's it – no more though – than you went on to say you're kinda mad at me again – for what this time? Because I'm not out there? If you're mad at me, you're mad at me, what can I do? As I have no idea, as to why you're mad at me. If I were out there I could get all that frustration out of your system – it'd be simply for me to do, to put it bluntly, you need a good fuck – and you know as well as I do that I'd be able to give you that. I'd fuck the guts out of you, and give you the time of your life. I'd do things to you that you never thought was possible – leave that to your imagination. ☺

Gym had been postponed – which is understandable given your health of late, but I hope you get stuck into it once you're feeling better.

You asked what am I going to put in – you said it sounds interesting. Well if I could, I'd put my cock deep inside you, long and strong – still sound interesting does it???? Think about it – Hmmmm nice thought isn't it? I'd make you cum that quickly, and I'd blow all inside you – deep too (lol)

Interesting – you don't think I need to keep the weight off – according to you I'm a stud and I know it – thanks for the kinds words – although I don't agree with you.

You said your fingers are crossed, that I get some time off at my appeal – thanks, it should come up soon time later this year. You asked if I could get time off for good behaviour, no that doesn't happen anymore in this state – whatever I get as my minimum term is the time I have to serve before becoming eligible for parole.

I don't really have much more to add, therefore I will leave it there for now, and I hope to hear from you again soon.

ME -xoxox-

18 February 2010 to Sean Sonnet

Dear Sean,
Hey buddy, how's it going over there for you, all good I hope, as for me here I'm fine.

I just received your letter, and it was good to hear from you again, as it always is.

From reading your letter, I take it the old rapist[142] got you kicked out, his good isn't he, he knows that I know what he is, I just never said anything. He was suppose to go for his plea today – but it got adjourned, because he sacked his legal team.

142 Another name Carl uses for Rodney Collins.

His due to start his committal in 2 weeks time – I wonder what his up, obviously his got some plan going on in that warp mind of his, but what it is I have no idea, nor do I give a fuck. I just think it strange sacking your legal team on the day of your Plea – as one would think you would want to get your numbers and then appeal – the sooner the better too – unless of course you're up to skulduggery. ☺ I also heard on the grapevine that his girl in playing around out there – how true it is though I have no idea; it's just what I hear.

Who's this new solicitor you're talking about? I reckon Emma looked good when she came up here, she's nice.

Keep in touch.

With best wishes & respect,
Your friend always – Carl

22 February 2010 to Roberta Williams

Dear Roberta,
Hi ya there Bert, how's things? I hope you're ok, and everything is going as good as it can be for you out there, as for me here, I'm fine – no complaints.

Well nothing much has changed in my rather eventful life, same old same old...... I'm just going through the motions and trying to make the best of it.

God only knows how many letters I've written, which have gone unanswered. Surely it's not too much to ask you to write me a letter here and there, or would you rather talk shit and befriend fuckheads who you don't even know on face book, yeah good one.

I just got a letter from Tye, and I was surprised to hear him say that his still with Analya, but she hasn't been up her to visit him, is someone going to tell him what's going on with her, or do I have to through a letter? This Analya must think you are stupid, I have to hand it to her though, she has balls – as I would've thought she would've been scared to play up on Tye with you out there, no but not her, instead she gets you to mind Mia whilst she gets around out there slutting it up. I guess I'd shut my mouth, but it make me sick, someone better tell him what's going on though it not fair to let him sit there like a goose whilst everyone out there knows what's she's up to and he doesn't, I've been in his position, and let me assure you it's not a nice feeling.

I haven't heard from Nikki lately either – I wrote her two letters – no reply, I don't know what's up her arse, as she usually replies to all my letters straight away.

Just a short one-today to let you know you're in my thoughts.

Keep in touch and I hope hear from you again soon.

With best wishes & respect,
All my love – Carl –xox-

Postscript: A few jokes for you.
Q: What do you call a cupboard full of lesbians?
A: A lick-her cabinet

One night, as a couple lays down for bed, the husband starts rubbing his wife's arm. The wife turns over and says, "I'm sorry hunni, but I've got a gynaecologist appointment tomorrow and I want to stay fresh." The husband feeling rejected turns over, a few minutes later he rolls over and taps his wife again, "do you have a dentist appointment too?"

26 February 2010 to Milad Mokbel

Dear Milad,
Hi ya buddy, I trust all is going as good as can be expected for you, as for me here I'm fine.

I just received your letter dated 16.03.10, and it was my pleasure to hear from you again, as it always is.

I seen in the paper that they sold Renate's house, I didn't know what they got for it though – then the other night when Renate and the kids were over Roberta's, Renate told Roberta what they got for it – 1.6 million, it's a nice place though. I think Roberta was taken Robbie and MJ out for dinner tonight, and maybe having them sleep over. I know she can be a dickhead at times, but she loves your kids, and she'll always do anything she can to make them happy, if you or the kids ever need anything I'm sure she'll help out, she's never forgotten how you were there for her after I got arrested.

I heard Danielle and Roula are hanging around together. If they are partying, that's their business. I wish they could all stay home like Renate does though, but in saying that I wish Roberta could've done the same too, but when we're in here we have no say in what they do out there, and cunts know that they are vulnerable, and they take advantage of that.

You think I'm having a lover quarrel with Karina – I talk to her and have her visit me, as a friend and nothing more. She's been asking to come up here and visit me, but I couldn't fit her in lately, I will in a few weeks time though, she's ok, her hearts in the right place.

Mel – I'm looking forward to her coming to visit me, so use you're influence and make it happen. Now that you're at Loddon, you must have plenty that you can handball onto me for a bit of entertainment. Buddy you know I'd give you anything, the blonde ones friend from Sydney is supposed to be coming down here to visit me soon, she hot too, but what the fuck am I going to do with her, oh I guess I can have a bit of fun and pass some time with her, see how it plays out.

I don't really have much more to add, therefore I guess I will leave it there for now, and I hope hear from you again soon.

With best wishes & respect,
Your friend always – Carl

Ps) Please give my love and best to your mum, as well as Renate the kids, and Larry and Harry – thanks.

28 February 2010 to Beau Goddard

Dear Beau,
I haven't heard from you for a while, so I thought I'd just drop you a few quick lines to say hello.

I was talking to Rob today after he'd visited you, and I asked him if he filled you in on what's going on with me, he said he did. I thought you were fully aware and kept up to speed as to what was going on, as you can appreciate it's just so hard for me to tell you everything through the mail. Buddy as I said to you a while ago, I don't care to much about what people say of think, as I know they won't have much to say to me if/when I run into them, however I do care what a selected few think, and you are in those few. After Rod being found guilty on his last blew, I daresay he'll be lucky if he ever sees daylight again as a free man, given his current age. From what I hear his blaming everyone but himself for his current predicament, but the truth be known it was him and his big mouth that got him convicted, after all, he confessed to his girl about his involvement in the murders during a box visit here in Acacia, which was bugged.

He fronts the Committal hearing on the next one in a few weeks time, which as it now turns out it has no effect of his situation. I think he has lost it a little bit, that's if he ever had it.

My dad was just granted permission to have contact visits with me, so he came up here one day last week with Roberta to see me, it was a good visit, Roberta talks a lot, she'd be able to talk under water with a mouthful of marbles, nevertheless I had an enjoyable visit with both her and my dad. Roberta's actually been coming up here a bit lately – it's good to see that's she's making an effort, when she's good we get along well, I still don't know how rob puts up with her – all I'll say is his a gluten for punishment, oh well as long as his happy.

I don't really have much more to add, therefore I guess I will leave it there for now, and I hope hear from you again soon.

With best wishes & respect,
Your friend always – Carl

1 March 2010 to Esmerelda

Dear Esmerelda,
Well what a pleasant surprise I got tonight, one letter (questionnaire) and a beautiful card from you, thanks I absolutely loved the card, and I filled the questionnaire straight away, so I can post it straight off to you first thing in the morning, I'm prompt – unlike some. ☺

Hey, you have to tell me a few more things about yourself, such as what your favourite brands of clothing are, favourite perfume, as well as what your favourite food is, and what you wear to bed?

I was looking so forward to you coming down here to visit me on the 6th or 7th· this coming weekend. Although I'm not sure if you still plan on coming. ☺ Nevertheless, I still have Maila ready to book and pay for you fair for me, the balls in your court. You have to get your phone connected (landline), so that I can ring you up in the mornings, don't worry about the bill, as I will fix it up for you – I insist, I can just imagine how good my days would be after talking to you first thing in the mornings.

Lots of hugs and kisses, from me to you.

With love, best wishes & respect – Carl –xox-

Postscript Joke
An armed man walks into a sperm bank wearing a balaclava. He waves the gun in the receptionist face and says, "Open the safe now!" The receptionist says, "Excuse me, but do you know this is a sperm bank?" The man replies, "Just opening the fucking Safe!" The receptionist does it and the man says, "OK, now grab a container and drink it!" Scared the receptionist does what he asks. The man then takes off his balaclava to reveal he's her boyfriend, and says, "See it's not that hard"

1 March 2010 to Ray Spadina

Dear Ray,
I just received your letter, and it was my pleasure to hear from you again, as it always is.

I hope everything goes well with your upcoming committal, and you get out sooner, rather than later. I don't want to know anything about your matter, and the only advice I can give you is read over and over your brief, as you'll pick up things your Barrister will no doubt miss or over look.

No one knows your case better then you do, simply as that. So don't leave everything up to counsel to do, because at the end of the day no matter how close you think you are to them, when the curtains are down and the show and acting has finished, they go home to their family, no matter what the result is. It's sad but unfortunately it's the truth.

As for my Appeal – I haven't got a date as yet, it was took out of the listing, and will go back in when we request for it to be put back in, I expect it to be heard sometime this year. I know 100% that I will get some sort of reduction – what though is anyone's guess.

I don't know much about what's going on with Tony or Horty matters, as I only see Tony when I bump into him at the visit centre, and don't really hear from Horty, my dad hears from Milad though, Milad rings my dad usually every weekend, his at Loddon. I know Horty only has one more to front, and if he beats that he'll be out, and I think it'd be due to come on shortly too. As for Tony, he still has about 6 trials to front. I heard he appealed the drug conviction, and his appealed was refused, that's the one he took off on – and was sentenced in his absences to I think about 11–8 years. I think his facing an uphill battle, but I wish him luck – I have a lot of time Tony.

I don't really have much more to add, therefore I guess I will leave it there for now, and I hope hear from you again soon.

With best wishes & respect,
Your friend always – Carl

2 March 2010 to Sean Sonnet

Dear Sean,
I just received your letter, dated 28-2, and it was good to hear from you again, as it always is. Mate I was laughing my head off as I was reading your letter, fuck you're funny when you're not even trying to be. I couldn't stop laughing when you said they didn't like you, but jails not some feel good place, so deal with it, and about how you said you're got your cell set up.

Kath was saying that you should be moved out of LOP's soon, but she didn't know where you are getting moved too. As I've told you countless time before if you want I'll push from this end to get you over here with me, or even if you go to Unit 2 over here. As you said the blokes in there are ok, and if you were to get in there, maybe they'll let me come over there and run out with you for at least one run out every day, that way you can do your training, and once you're finished we can have a laugh – that's be good. Put it to them and see what you can do.

The rapist got rid of you, his a cunt of a thing is he, fucken lying conniving little junkie piece of shit.

I don't know about you having a chance with the lawyer who works with Emma, but I reckon you'd be in with a good chance with Emma, in a different environment.

I don't have much more to add, therefore I guess I will leave it there for now, and I hope to hear from you again in the near future.

With best wishes & respect,
Your friend always – Carl

22 March 2010 to Milad Mokbel

Dear Milad,
Hi ya buddy, how's things, I trust all is going as good as can be expected for you, as for me here I'm fine.

I just received your letter dated 16.03.10, and it was my pleasure to hear from you again, as it always is.

Yeah I see Nicola is ill, how ill though would be anyone's guess, if she told me the sky was blue, I'd have to go and check it, you know my thoughts on her – I don't think I'd be on her Christmas card list, nor do I wanna be. (ha ha) It is true that she does have cancer. I don't know how bad it is though, nor do I know long she's had it for. I know it said in the paper that she won't be taking the stand, only time will tell, personally I think at the end of the day they'll get her up there, maybe not at a committal, but at a basha and trial. I do know there were doctor's that went last week to the committal on her behalf and gave evidence, stating that she's to unfit to take the stand – but she's telling the Court and the Police that she's still willing to give evidence, when she's better. So now what's happening is the committal has been adjourned until the 14th of April – that's when it kicks off again – then it'll be adjourned part heard until sometime in June, when she'll be called to give her evidence. If she doesn't go, then they'll ask to get her statement in, and the recording from the wire she wore, and what's happens then is anyone guess – but I don't think she'll get out of giving evidence to easy, as I said at the end of the day I think she'll be there come trial time.

What's going on with Mel – mate you can at least get her to drop me a line, what I will be doing though is holding you to what you said, when she's in Melbourne, that she'll come in and visit me, deal. ☺

Camshaft,[143] I don't know what went on with him and the old bloke. I had a visit with him when he was over here, and he told me that him and the old bloke fell out, he didn't have very kind words to say about the him either, I'm surprised they got along for so long, as the old bloke would be harder to live with then camshaft.

I don't really have much more to add, therefore I guess I will leave it there for now, and I hope hear from you again soon.

With best wishes & respect,
Your friend always – Carl

---

143 Carl's private name for Sean Sonnet.

26 March 2010 to Kylie

Hello hello,

Just received your letter and it was great to hear from you again, as it always is. You said you're the boss, and I can work under you, if I'm lucky – something tells me I don't think I need luck to accomplish that, it's not called luck babe, and you know it. (lol) You also said you could get me up down anyway you decide, and don't I ever forget that – if you wouldn't mind can you share with me just how you'd intend on doing the above, this'll be interesting.

You liked the picture I sent you – super hot you reckon, raw and hot, glad you liked it, where is it besides your bed? You're well overdue to send me some photo, hopefully you'll send me some with your next letter, hint hint.

According to you we were on a completely different page – when you were talking about you'd have some exercise for us to do together if I were out there. You were talking about lots of walking, and I thought you were talking about fucking and sucking each other's brains out for hours and hours on end, and work up a sweat together, one track mind haven't I – silly me, (dah) Nevertheless, the one I cum up with my sounds like it'd be lots more fun, unless of course you disagree, get back to me on that one – please.

I never said my dad didn't like your idea, and no, I wasn't shocked, nothing much shocks me what you come up with, which is one of the things that I like about you. ☺ You tell me is there any truth behind your joke? If you decide to have kids, hit 35, and have no potential then why wouldn't I donate some of my golden sperm to you, make me feel so special why don't you, if everything else fails, call on Carl, it that how I should take it?

You reckon if I were out there now, the practice to get you pregnant would be fun, and the rest wouldn't matter so much,

I agree it would be fun, lots of it too. As I said if I were I'd be cuming inside you, and if you think otherwise, then you really are delusional, and yes you would be good breading stock.

I don't really have much more to add, therefore I will leave it there for now, and I hope to hear from you again soon.

MWAH

ME -xoxox-

29 March 2010 to Esmerelda

Dear Esmerelda,

I just received your letter, and it was my pleasure to hear from you again, as it always is. I've actually been waiting for your letter, as I didn't hear from you at all last week. ☹

I was disappointed that you never got down here to see me, as I was looking so forward to seeing you, but I understand you have your reasons. It's now twice you've been coming to see me but haven't got here, maybe third time lucky – but honestly, as much as I'd love to see you, I won't be holding my breath that I get too. ☹

I read your letter with great interest, where you said you question my morals and values (*which to be honest hurt a little bit*). I must say I have always been upfront and completely honest with you, and I always will be, if it's not too much to ask for I expect the same in return. For some strange and unknown reason I feel like I've known you forever, I talk openly with you, and answer your questions, where as I wouldn't other peoples. I respect you, and have a lot of time for you. As I've previously said to you, a lot of people will have good things to say about me – and I dare say plenty will have negative things to say, although most people who have negative things to say about me, have never met me, and don't even know anything about me apart from what the media have fed them. I'm the first to say, I'm not saint, never portrayed myself to be one though. Yes, I have done some things in my life that I regret, and wish that I hadn't, but I strongly believe my good far outweighs my bad. I have no problem in telling everything there is to know about me, but I won't be through a letter. If you want to get to know me better, I'd love nothing more than that, which I think you already know.

I think the least you could do is get down here and visit me, or get a landline connect so that I can talk to you. If you come once and don't like me – then you don't have to come again, that's your call not mine, but if we get along well, and you want to come down again, I'll fly you down once a month, or once a fortnight, it's up to you. All I ask is don't judge me until you've met me, and you're in a position to do so – which I think isn't too much to ask.

You should come down here on the weekend of the 10th of April and visit me, I'll pay for you fare. Maila will pick you up from the airport, and you can either stay at her place or I'll book you in somewhere, whatever you're more comfortable with. You can stay one night or a few nights, again it's your call.

With love and respect always, Carl –xox-

5 April 2010 to Esmerelda[144]

Esmerelda,

I can't get it out of my head, how you said you question my my morals and values, because of something someone said to you, poisoning you about me, despite this person not knowing me,

---

144 This letter was never sent.

or knowing anything about me, apart from what they've read or heard, I hate that when people.

I wonder if they told you the following:

That on the day when I was shot, I turned up to meet someone who I thought was a friend, we'd had no prior argument or disagreement to that day, and I got bashed over the head and shot for no good reason, apart from greed on their behalf.

That after I was shot, and was recovering in hospital, that I was threatened with my life and in turn had to sign myself out of hospital, when I weren't in any condition to do so, but I felt I had to get to someone where I felt safe.

That a few days after I'd signed myself out of hospital me, Roberta and Brea (who was about 6 at the time) were going to my dad place. We spotted a car sitting off there, and it was Jason and another bloke – they pulled us up in the street, I told Roberta to take off then Jason shot at us, and he'd seen Brea in the car with us.

My parent were at a place where they'd frequent for 20 years or more. When Jason and Mark Moran came in there and tried to lure my dad out the front to shoot him – they threatened him and my mum, and told my dad to tell me its who gets who first, and when they get me they'll be killing me next time around.

When one night Roberta was out have dinner with friends (I was in prison), and Mark Moran came there and made her and her friends feel uncomfortable. Then when it came time to leave, and she went to her car, he came out and grab her keys out of the ignition – spat in her face, threw the keys in the brushes, and told her they were going to kill me as soon as they seen me.

When my kids were scared to go to school, because Jason Moran's kid went to the same school, and if he seen Roberta dropping the kids off at school, he'd spit in her face in front of everyone, and tell her that they were going to kill me on sight.

That they offered countless people money to kill me, and other's money to lure me to a place so that I could be killed, but fortunately for me, I trusted very few people and this never eventuated.

That they bashed some of my mates and threatened many others, for no reason except because these people were my friends.

5 April 2010 to Karina Cacopardo

Dear Karina,
I trust this letter finds you and the kids in the best of health and spirits, as it leaves me fighting fit.

I just received your letter, and it was my pleasure to hear from you again, as it always is.

Court hasn't started as yet – it was due to start, but then it was adjourned, and apparently my services will be required as of next Wednesday the 14th – looking forward to that – not. I'll be right though – before I know it it'll be over.

I've been trying to ring you everyday, with no success, as your phones been disconnected, and I've missed not talking to you soooooo bad. I was wondering what's going on with you, and hoping that I'd hear from you – if I never heard from you this week, I was intending on trying to get hold, by writing you a letter or something – anything. I would've got you somehow, don't you worry about that – you can't escape me that easy.

Well nothing much has changed in my rather eventful life, same old same old...... just going through the motions and making the best of it. The treadmill is broken down, as has been for more than one week now; so I hope they fix it quickly, as my daily runs keep me sane. (lol)

Dhakota's going well, she come up here last week to see me, and we had a good visit, she's coming up again tomorrow, and

I can't wait to see her – she's growing up so quickly. As you know Brea's in year 11, and she's sick of school, and doesn't want to go anymore, she wants to get a job. Before the holiday started she took a week off, I don't think she'll go back, but I told her she has to do something as I don't want her just sitting around doing nothing, she'll do something though, she's a good kid, and she listens to what I tell her. But now that Brea mightn't be going back to school, little miss Dhakota reckons she's sick of school too, but instead of getting a day or week off, she got a tutor to help her improve with her maths and English. And now she reckons she's confused as to how Brea gets days off because she's sick of school, and she gets a tutor which means more school, but at home. I told her don't you worry about Brea, Brea's in year 11, and you're in grade 3, she said dad why do you take Brea's side? She's funny

I don't really have much more to add, therefore I guess I will leave it there for now, and I hope to hear from you again soon, and see you too.

MWAH

With love and respect always, Carl –xox-

5 April 2010 to Emidio

Dear Emidio,

I trust all is going as good as it possibly can be out there for you and Michelle, as for me here, I'm fine, no use complaining as no one listens anyway.

Hey buddy, I have a favour to ask of you again, sorry, if you can do it it'd be great, but if you can't I fully understand. Well there's this chick who lives in Sydney, who keeps in contact with me, and always does whatever she can for me, she's a good friend of mine, anyway lately she's been a bit down, as she's been having a few personal problems. Therefore, I was wondering, if it's not too much to ask of you, could you please do me a favour and send her a pair of shoes, and a jacket or T-Shirt, something like that from me to brighten up her day. If you have a nice pair of Roberto Carvalli shoes, just casual ones, nothing over the top, in size 5.5, as she's a real shoe lover, if she were to get a pair of them from me for a surprise, I'm sure they'd cheer her up, and probably make her all wet too. (ha ha)

This is her name and address, Esmerelda [surname and address deleted], thanks for that buddy, I owe you plenty, and I'll never forget everything you do for me. I wish the world was full of more people like you, and if it were, it'd be a much better place.

With best wishes and respect,
Your friend always – Carl

8 April 2010 to Danny Heaney

Dear Danny,
I trust this letter finds you in the very best of health and spirits, as it leave me fighting fit.

The oven and stuff still haven't arrived – or if they have, they haven't been installed, and I've been looking forward to starting this self catering, bad. I've been assure that we'll be getting it, but when is anyone's guess, let's just hope we get it before I get out. I laughed my head off when you said about Tommy's curry, because we have the cooking program here, where we get to spend $20 between the 3 of us who are here, and make one meal, every second Saturday. I've been telling Tommy that I don't think his a chef – yeah his done some cooking – but I chef, well I'm not too sure. Therefore, I told him the floors his, he can spend the $20 to cook us up a storm and show us something to make us think otherwise – and his doing a curry dish – true story. (ha ha) I'll keep you posted as to how it comes out – surely he couldn't fuck that anyway.

Roberta's been really supportive lately, she's been great, maybe that's because I haven't got any girl in my life at the moment. I reckon if I could get congenial visits I'd be in with a real shot. (ha ha) She came up here yesterday to see me with Brea and Dhakota, we had a family contact visit, and it was a good one too, I really enjoy it. Brea's just had her braces taken off – and she looks so good, I'm sure she's going to have all the boys chasing her now, if she hasn't already, she's all grown up. Dhakota, well, she's putting on weight, too much I think, she'd want to start watching her weight before it get out of hand. If she puts on any more weight she'll start to lose her looks, I keep telling Roberta to make sure she watches what she eats – and control her eating, but you know sometimes some conversations with Roberta can fall on deaf ears.

I don't really have much more to add, therefore I guess I will leave it there for now, and hopefully I hear back from you again soon.

With best wishes & respect,
Your friend always – Carl

9 April 2010 to Nikki Denman

Dear Nikki,
I trust all is going as good as it possible can be for you out there, as for me here I'm fine.

I just received your letter – with the photo you enclosed for me, thanks for the photos, and it was great to hear from you again, as it's been while, better later then never though. In the future, try not to leave it so long between letters, and you won't feel bad or like you've abandoned me, plus I love and look forward to hearing from you so much, and you know that!

Fab, as you know he was found guilty, and was sentenced to 17 years with a minimum of 10 ½ years, so he'll be out in about 8 years. His a good person, you should make friends with him on facebook, nothing more, just friends – he'd be happy if you did that. People like him and I appreciate support whilst we're in here, more then you'd think too. He introduced me to this chick who he knows, and now we write regularly to one another – she's a good sort too, but we're only friends, and I enjoy hearing from her.

I don't really have much more too add therefore I'll leave it there for now and hope to hear from you again soon.

With best wishes & respect,
All my love – Carl –xox-

10 April 2010 to Esmerelda

Dear Esmerelda,
I trust all is going as good as it can be for you out there, as for me here, I'm fine.

Well to say it was fantastic to get to talk to you today would be an understatement; you really did make my day, so thanks for putting yourself out for me today. We talked for 3 calls, and I could've talked to you for another 30. I had a million things that I wanted to tell you about – but then when we started talking, I lost my train of thought, maybe I just got too excited; stop laughing it's not that funny – plus I'm serious (lol)

I'm rapt that you're getting your phone (*landline*) connect, so that I can talk to you, even if I'll only be able to catch you a few days a week, it'll much better than nothing. I hoping that it'll be connected pretty quickly, fingers crossed.

I watched the horses races today on TV – the Sydney carnival, the races were at Randwick, which is my favourite track. If I were out I would've went there today – and I would've taken you with me, naturally that's if you would've aloud me too. I would've brought you a new outfit and shoes of course (*probably more than one pair too*), as I know how much you love shoes, but I would've have been letting you drink too much there. I'm banned from attending all Race tracks in Melbourne – as well as the Casino – there's no good reason behind that ban though. The police banned a few of us down here; but as usually, I was the first of many. They ended up banning me from attending any licence venue in my area, again for nothing too, at the time they were just making life as hard as they could for me, enough about that anyway.

I hope you like your new job that you're about to start, give it a go anyway, I think you'll succeed at whatever you do – I have confidence in you. I think there's places for you to grow there, and as you said today in the future, if you ever wanted too, you could get a transfer to Melbourne, always an option. I liked the idea today what you were telling me about – you designing clothes. You know what you're doing in that line of work – so have a go at it – make money for yourself instead of others.

You were saying today that you wouldn't mind moving to Melbourne, not forever, but just for a period of time. If you let me know what you wanted to do down here – I'm sure I could find you work, no probs, no matter what you wanted to do.

If you moved down here, I'd help you out with anything you needed and I mean that. I think the move would be good, good for me anyway, because if you lived down here, at least than I'd be a chance of getting a visit from you, *chance,* being the key word. ☺ You could get to met my daughter – and I bet she'd love you too.

I don't really have much more to add, therefore I guess I will leave it there for now, and I hope to hear from you again soon.

With love and respect always, Carl –xox-

12 April 2010 to Kylie

Hi there babe,

Just received your letter, and pics – loved the pics, especially the ones of you with the cap on. I'd be rapt if you could get me a copies of the one with you with the cap on, with just alone in it though, love a girl who can pull that look off, and you do it with ease, you look so hot, gorgeous. You made my cock go hard thinking about what I'd do to you, how much I wish you were here with me. I'd fuck the guts out of you babe. Also I loved the pic of you with your hair back – with your cousin – or that's who it said it was on the back.

If I were out, according to you, you'd be my boss – whatever!!!!! In addition, if I were out, you wouldn't mind if I got hungry wherever I like, as long as I came home to eat, if I know what you mean, I comprehend, no probs, all I'd be eaten would be you and you only anyway, and I'd eat every part of you, that's a promise. I'd have my fingers in your pussy, as I was eating every part of you, and I'd suck all your juice up as soon as they started to flow, babe I'd do things to you that would blow your mind.

I think you're making the right decision by not selling your Sunbury property, as you said it pays itself off, therefore I believe it makes no sense to sell it. Where are you looking at buying a unit or town house – what suburb? Melbourne property prices are going crazy.

Yeah I'd like to think that I am special to you, don't get told that much anymore from you though – not feeling the love, anyway, I hope you know how special you are to me. My dad liked the idea you said – why wouldn't he, his a fan of yours.

Fingers crossed next few years that I get those special visits, so we can practice – you'd like practising would you? With me that is.

You said you're happy to be in the moment with me, and whatever happens happens, but you're not stupid enough to fall for boys shit, if the glove isn't on the love isn't on. I'm not going to get into hypothetical's with you – but let me just say if I were out, there's no hope I'd be wearing a condom with you, no way. I'd be cuming inside you and that's all there is to it. What wouldn't you want my blow inside you, nice and warm, wet and sticky, just as you were about to cum, me pushing my cock inside, deep. You feeling it all wet, the noise of our juices would be making as they're mixing together, splashing around, as our bodies are smashing into one another – nothing better, think about it babe, don't tell me just the thought of it isn't getting you all frisky now. I'd love you to be riding me cock now, taking it all in, as I'm holding your ass. ☺

You apologized for taking your time to reply to my letters, times have changed haven't they, as I remember not so long ago when you use to reply straight way. You said the course you are doing is killing you – plus all the extra stuff you've been getting up too – such as???

I don't really have much more to add, therefore I will leave it there for now, and I hope to hear from you again soon.

Let me know when best suits you for a visit – as I'm hanging to see you

ME -xoxox-

14 April 2010 to Jason Paisley

Dear Jase,
I just received your letter, and it was good to hear from you again, as it always is.

Mate I've heard what that old (rapist) is saying about me, his unreal. I'd love to see you face to face and fill you in on everything. I think after he was found guilty on the last one, mind you it was his own big mouth that got him convicted, he lost the plot, let's face it, this next case is going to have nil effect on him anyway, after he gets about 30 odd and the other one, cunt of a thing he is. I wonder if his also telling everyone, how his given his girl info about unsolved crimes to try to collect the rewards money offer – I think not!

Good to hear that you've now got Bert on your phone, I'm sure she'll give you a laugh. I agree with you, she does cook the best chicken schnitzels ever. Also agree she's still in love with me, she's good though, she's got good heart – she's just a bit mad at times – but usually when she loses it, she's in the right, the only thing is she expresses it the wrong way. She came up here last week for a visit, she brought Brea and Dhakota up here to see me, we had a family contact visit, and it was a good one too, I really enjoy it. She's been really supportive lately, she's been great, maybe that's because I haven't got any girl in my life at the moment (lol). I reckon if I could get congenial visits, she'd be in it no probs. (ha ha) Only problem that I could foresee with that would be, if she got one once, she'd want it all the time (*don't let her know I said that* ☺). Brea's just had her braces taken off – and she looks so good, I'm sure she's going to have all the boys chasing her now, if she hasn't already, she's all grown up now, she's a good kid though, very respectful. Dhakota's starting to put the weight on, too much

I think, she'd want to start watching her weight before it gets out of hand. If she puts on any more weight, she'll start to lose her looks. I said to Roberta in front of Dhakota, if Dhakota puts on any more weight, she won't get any more modelling jobs. Roberta said yes she will, for Jenny Craig – you should've seen the look on Dhakota's face, if looks could kill Roberta would be dead. Dhakota quickly responded with "yeah and you could do modelling for liposuction and Botox, she's quick witted, she's so funny, she put Roberta back in her place – she's not cheeky, but if someone says something about her she'll fire up, which is a good thing.

I don't really have much more to add, therefore I guess I will leave it there for now, and I hope hear from you again soon.

With best wishes & respect,
Your friend always – Carl

18 April 2010 to Karina Cacopardo

Dear Karina,
Well hello there you sexy little bitch; I trust all is as good as it can be out there for you and the kids, as for me here I'm fine.

On Friday night, I received your letter, and it was my absolute pleasure to hear from you again, as it always is, I love it when I receive mail from you.

I've missed not being able to talk to you – and I've also missed not seeing your gorgeous face, more than words could say too. ☺ Hopefully after you've been operated on, you can get the sexy ass of yours up here to see me, I look forward to your visits, I think I'd better ease up now, as I might give you too much of a bighead. (lol)

Court has now been adjourned until the 10th of January, next year, what the...... Oh well now I think I'll try and get my appeal heard in between, then at least I know where I stand.

We still haven't started this self catering cooking program. I'm led to believe all the appliances have arrived, but as yet nothing's been installed, let's hope we start it before I go home, ☺ we should've already had it by now – but as you know the wheels turns very slowly in here, unless of course it's something they want to take off us.

I don't really have much more to add, therefore I guess I will leave it there for now, and I hope to hear from you again soon.

MWAH

With love and respect always, Carl –xox-

This letter was composed and printed out on Carl's computer on 18 April 2010. It was the last letter he composed and presumably he posted it on that day.

THE END
19 April 2010

It's 12.48 p.m. and Carl sits alone with his head resting on his right hand in the day-room of the high-security Acacia Unit. He once described this day-room to Kylie: 'about 15 metres long, and 7 meters wide, it has a little kitchen, washing machine, dryer, treadmill, exercise bike, and we also have a table tennis table'.

Seated at a table in the centre of this sunlit room, he flicks through the pages of the *Herald Sun*. He is the front-page story—which tells Victorian taxpayers that they are footing the bill for his daughter's school fees in exchange for information he has provided to police.

He knew this story was coming. A few days earlier, his father George had asked journalist Adam Shand if he knew anything about its impending publication. The story had been doing the rounds for a couple of months in media circles, but *Herald Sun* journalist Padraic Murphy had obtained a letter written by the Victorian Government Solicitor's Office confirming that police had paid $8000 to a prestigious Melbourne private school for Dhakota's tuition.

George had Carl on the house phone and Shand on his mobile and he put the two receivers together so they could converse. Shand asked Carl whether he was getting on with his cellmates and how this story might affect those relationships. If Carl was worried, he didn't betray it. Everything was 'good as gold' in the unit, he told Shand. George had no concerns about Carl's safety either. Shand didn't feel entirely convinced. If everything was good as gold, then why the need for the phone call?

Now Carl is reading the story which has dominated talkback radio all morning. Of course, he has no idea of the outrage this story is generating outside Barwon. Everything feels as normal in his groundhog-day existence.

He has his back to the open door of his cell, alongside a walkway that leads to other sections of the unit. 'Two Guns' Tommy Ivanovic is seen pottering around in the room, and then Carl's other good mate, Matty Johnson, appears in the background. On any other day Carl and Matty would be about to give Tommy a good ribbing.

After leaving the room for just under a minute, Matty reappears, holding a metre-long metal stem from the seat of the exercise bike. Because he has his back to Matty, Carl is totally unaware that the brutal end to his action-packed life is so imminent.

The super-fit Matty bashes him with the bike part to the

right side of his head with all the violence he can muster and Carl drops to the floor, face first. Matty bashes his head in another seven times. Tommy does not move a muscle to intervene.

As Carl lies motionless, Matty places a white towel over his bloodied body. Leaving the room, he takes the bike stem with him. When he returns, he grabs Carl by the ankles and drags his limp body into his empty, dark cell. Closing the door, he places the towel over a pool of blood where the attack took place. Then he walks away.

Lasting two minutes and 50 seconds, this is the silent footage the jury were shown at Matty Johnson's Supreme Court murder trial a year later, in September 2011. Ultimately the jury found Johnson guilty of murder and rejected his claim that he had acted in self-defence. In sentencing Johnson to life in jail with a non-parole period of 32 years, Justice Lex Lasry said it was clear Johnson had murdered Williams because he was helping police in the case against former drug squad detective Paul Dale. In the wake of Carl's murder, the charges against Dale and the alleged shooter Rodney Collins collapsed. To this day, the case remains unsolved.

In January 2011 Roberta Williams, 41, and her fiancé Robert Carpenter celebrated the birth of their son Giuseppe Sebastian Carpenter. The child was conceived on 18 April, the day before her former husband, convicted murderer Carl Williams, was killed in Barwon Prison.

'I was convinced this baby was a sign from Carl that he was watching over me, because he understood having another baby meant everything to me,' Roberta later told *New Idea* magazine. 'To me, this was his way of saying: "I'm leaving your life, but I'm sending you what you want most so you can begin again and be happy."'

His letters told the story of how he struggled with the crushing 35-year sentence that he had been given. The once gregarious and social young man had been slowly ground down over the six years of his incarceration in Barwon. He had tried to maintain his sanity and self-esteem through a fantasy life with a string of girlfriends from Stacey Vella to Kylie and Esmerelda, but Carl's girls were only ever a distraction from the sterile, dehumanising environment that would have been his home until age 71, assuming his appeals against the length of his sentence failed, which was likely. In reality, the cops could have nailed him for another half-dozen killings had they been so inclined. They were determined that he would never see the light of day, in spite of his decision to cooperate. The longer he spent in Barwon the more Carl regretted his actions in the superheated days of the Gangland War. He went into jail full of bravado and self-justification but by the end he knew that he had been the architect of his family's destruction and ultimately his own.